P9-AZU-402

New Perspectives in Early Childhood Teacher Education

Bringing Practitioners Into the Debate

EDITED BY

Stacie G. Goffin
David E. Day

A PROJECT OF THE NATIONAL ASSOCIATION OF
EARLY CHILDHOOD TEACHER EDUCATORS

Teachers College, Columbia University
New York and London

Published by Teachers College Press, 1234 Amsterdam Avenue, New York, N.Y. 10027

Library of Congress Cataloging-in-Publication Data

New perspectives in early childhood teacher education: bringing
    practitioners into the debate/a project of the National
    Asssociation of Early Childhood Teacher Educators; edited by
    Stacie G. Goffin, David E. Day.
        p.   cm.—(Early childhood education series: 51).
    Includes bibliographical references and index.
    ISBN 0-8077-3381-4
    1. Early childhood teachers—Training of—United States. 2. Early
childhood education—United States.   I. Goffin, Stacie G.   II. Day,
David E., 1931–   .   III. National Association of Early Childhood
Teacher Educators. IV. Series.
LB1732.3.N48 1994
370.71—dc20   94-20991

ISBN: 0-8077-3381-4

Printed on acid-free paper
Manufactured in the United States of America
01 00 99 98 97 96 95 94   8 7 6 5 4 3 2 1

CONTENTS

ACKNOWLEDGMENTS

As the title page notes, this book has been a project of the National Association of Early Childhood Teacher Educators. From the moment the idea of this book was presented to the NAECTE Governing Board at their annual meeting in 1989, they have provided support and encouragement. We are both most appreciative of this support and the ongoing enthusiasm for this project. We are also most apprecia-tive of those individuals who have served as our advisory board. This illustrious group included Barbara Bowman, the Erikson Institute; Sue Bredekamp, the National Association for the Education of Young Children; Christine Chaille, Port-land State University; Bob Granger, the Manpower Demonstration Project; Joan Isenberg, James Mason University; Lillian Katz, the ERIC Clearing House on Ele-mentary and Secondary Education and the University of Illinois; and Margaret Yonemura, State University of New York–Binghamton. These individuals assisted us in conceptualizing the book, in identifying its potential contributors, and in pro-viding critiques of the introductory chapter. Finally, we would like to thank our essayists and commentators. Their work made this project as successful as it is.

Early Childhood Teacher Education in Context

David E. Day and Stacie G. Goffin

The 1980s can be characterized as the decade of unremitting calls for school reform. The early years of the decade saw the publication of a series of studies and reports on the status of American public schools (Boyer, 1983; Goodlad, 1984; National Commission on Excellence, 1983; Sizer, 1984). In every case, the education of American children and youth was criticized for, among other things, the apparent absence of high quality instruction. It is not surprising, therefore, that hard on the publication of these volumes came the cry from policy makers for reform in teacher education.

Until recently, though, this spotlight has shined primarily on the preparation of elementary and secondary teachers in public schools. Consistent with their separate social and political history, teachers of early childhood education were omitted from the early debate.

This is no longer the case, however. Early childhood education is increasingly designated by policy makers and state departments of education as the appropriate beginning for young children's formal, public education. In many states, this acknowledgment refers to prekindergarten education for 4-year-olds identified at risk for school failure. In other states, this transformation is reflected in the identification of kindergarten education as mandatory rather than elective. Rarely, though, do these mandates recognize child care as part of children's early education experiences.

Yet, full-day child care programs that serve the needs of young children and also their employed parents have burgeoned. The pressures to respond to the demands of parents and employers for child care frequently overwhelm the attempts of early childhood educators to advocate an educationally appropriate curriculum, even as they doggedly attempt to upgrade the often minimally appropriate environments in which children spend their daily lives (Whitebook, Howes, & Phillips, 1989; Whitebrook, Phillips, & Howes, 1993). As noted by Kagan (1990) in a recent policy paper for the United States Department of Education, even political rhetoric reflects this nation's historical distinction between the care and education of young children. Policy makers and others speak to their concerns for safe and appropriate child care in terms of "quality," but they speak to the need for better education in terms of a demand for "excellence."

In discussions of the preparation of teachers of young children, therefore, early childhood educators suddenly find themselves reacting to two sets of often contradictory public demands and trying to do so in ways that sustain the profession's commitment to both the care and the education of young children, birth through age 8. This introductory chapter lays out some of the structural, psychological, and political parameters within which these contradictory demands and expectations coexist. The resulting framework provides needed context for the insights and recommendations for early childhood teacher education that are presented by the essayists and commentators in this book.

REFORM AND TEACHER EDUCATION

EXAMINING TEACHER EDUCATION

In most cases, critics of the education of elementary and secondary teachers have advocated one of two remedies. First was the creation of an alternative program for teacher certification that did not require the study of teaching at a college or university. The program initiated in New Jersey for the recruitment of individuals with a baccalaureate degree, an interest in teaching, and an available summer to begin preparing was the quintessential model of this approach. Second was the argument for the abolition of the undergraduate education major for those who would become teachers and the substitution of an academic concentration in one of the traditional arts or sciences. The result of this approach has been an increase in the number of 5-year programs, some of which count 5th-year course work, which is linked with state certification, toward a masters degree. Both of these remedies assume that the problems in our public schools are twofold: teachers are not as educated as they should be and are required to complete what are perceived to be ineffective courses in pedagogy.

One of the many curiosities that arose during this period of criticism was that at the very time policy makers were asserting that the study of pedagogy was irrelevant to the performance of teachers in the classroom, scholars were suggesting that a body of knowledge about pedagogy existed. Another curiosity was that even before the print was dry on those studies outlining the inadequacies of schools and teachers, politicians and educational leaders were urging that the primary responsibility for teacher education be taken out of colleges and universities and placed in the hands of school administrators and teachers. Perhaps it had escaped these critics that those who were to be the on-the-job trainers of prospective teachers had just been excoriated for failing to educate our children effectively.

There is no gainsaying that teacher education remains in need of substantial change. Even before publication of the recent school reform literature, the American Association of Colleges of Teacher Education, one of the oldest of the old-boy networks of teacher educators, published a monograph on the profession of teaching. In this publication, Howsam, Corrigan, Denemark, and Nash (1976) called for profound changes in the preparation of teachers, including major study in the arts and sciences, reduction in the numbers of teacher education departments in colleges and universities as a means of exerting quality control, and greater use of knowledge of teaching effectiveness in courses of pedagogy. Goodlad's (1990) recent national survey of teacher preparation programs echoes these conclusions; in too many teacher education departments, tradition and conventional wisdom dominate the curriculum.

The most important teacher education reform literature of the past decade, The Report of the Carnegie Forum on Education and the Economy (Carnegie Task Force on Teaching as a Profession, 1986) and the two publications of the Holmes Group (1986, 1990), addressed the function of schools as well as the nature of teacher education. The Holmes Group, in particular, has linked school and teacher education reform in its proposal for the creation of professional development schools.

Not since the debates stirred up by the books by Conant (1963) and Koerner (1963) has teacher education in the United States been given the amount of attention it has received during the past 15 years. And there is reason to believe that we may only be experiencing the beginning of such attention. Goodlad (1990) refers to current reform movements in public schools and teacher education as an awakening to the link between teaching, teacher education, the mission of our schools, and the nature of American society. The public may finally appreciate that reform of public education cannot be fully and adequately addressed without, at the same time, examining issues in teacher education.

EARLY CHILDHOOD EDUCATION AND TEACHER REFORM

Until recently, little attention has been given in the various reform agenda to the education of teachers of young children. The Holmes Group, for example, was uncertain about early childhood education and consciously omitted it from its agenda (1986). Their uncertainty, however, was not totally unwarranted.

As noted earlier, early childhood education is struggling to reconcile—both for itself and the general public—its diverse histories and practices. Concurrently, policy makers and others increasingly view early childhood programs in terms of their educational potential; others frame their understanding in terms of child development; and still others think of early childhood programs, especially those extending to full-day, as merely custodial. Thus, public pressure to increase the availability of high quality child care (e.g., Boyer, 1991; Committee for Economic Development, 1991, 1993) coexists with beliefs that anyone can care for young children and that child care personnel should continue to subsidize the cost of child care through their low compensation.

Concern over the combined effect of state mandated curricula, erratic certification standards, and false distinctions between the care and education of children recently led the Association of Teacher Educators (ATE) and the National Association for the Education of Young Children (NAEYC) to issue a joint statement on early childhood teacher education. In an attempt to bring unity to professional development in early childhood education, the statement called for the establishment of specialized early childhood teacher certification standards for teachers working with children from birth through age 8 (ATE & NAEYC, 1991).

Reflective of this diversity of interpretation and purpose, the conceptualization and delivery of early childhood education is notoriously fragmented. This fragmentation, in turn, lies at the crux of issues regarding the structure, content, and delivery of early childhood teacher education. Obviously, whether early childhood education is conceptualized as educational, developmental, or custodial directly influences public and professional expectations regarding early childhood teacher preparation.

The early childhood profession is aware of this quandary and has attempted to take a proactive stance as regards the absence of internal, professional coherence in teacher preparation. For example, the NAEYC initiated discussion with the National Council for Accreditation of Teacher Education (NCATE) and acquired separate portfolio review for early childhood teacher education programs in 4-year institutions. NAEYC has also recently launched the National Institute for Early Childhood Professional Preparation, which has accepted the task of conceptualizing a coherent and articulated system of early childhood professional preparation and development.

However, all is not sanguine in these efforts to create a coherent and coordinated system of professional development in early childhood education. The field continues to be affected by externally imposed policies and regulations that are developed by groups with limited understanding of the scope and purposes of early education.

For example, one of the most frequent questions to arise from the Holmes Group recommendations regards an appropriate academic knowledge base for each teaching level. For decades, early childhood teacher education has been concerned with helping candidates address "the whole child." As a consequence, early childhood teacher educators find it difficult to respond to this demand in the ways colleagues preparing teachers for older children might. Conventional discourse regarding the knowledge bases of effective teaching thwarts early educators' attempts to communicate the meaning and importance of the whole child view.

Adding to the complexity of this discussion are questions regarding licensure and certification requirements for child care and preschool teachers not under the auspices of public schools. These diverse considerations directly affect the availability of consistently high-quality early childhood programs and have thrust issues surrounding early childhood teacher education, with all its complexities, to the forefront.

THE NATURE OF EARLY CHILDHOOD EDUCATION

The complexity of early childhood teacher education is confounded by the developmental attributes of young children as well as the multidimensional nature of the early childhood education system. In particular, the question is to what extent, if any, the diverse auspices of early childhood care and education should affect the professional preparation of early childhood educators.

To some extent, the various auspices are informed by the age of the child. The ages of children served in early childhood education programs range from about 6 weeks to 8 years, from infancy to the completion of third grade. By any measure, early education encompasses an enormous range of development and competence. In other instances, auspices are informed by the purpose of the program, usually based upon the assumption that the care and the education of young children are distinctive spheres. As a result, early childhood education is characterized by at least five different program "types," each of which has evolved with different historical and agency associations:

1. Family day care for children from 6 weeks to kindergarten entry age
2. Group infant and toddler care
3. Preschool or nursery school programs for children from 3 to 5 years old
4. Kindergartens for 5- and 6-year-old children
5. Elementary school grades 1 through 3

Such a range creates considerable difficulty when deliberating matters related to the education of those who would teach in each of these program types. To illustrate, the following section briefly describes the character of each type, with the exception of family child care, which is still developing its training paradigm.

INFANT AND TODDLER EDUCATION

Much like the history of the development of nursery schools, infant and toddler programs have, until recently, existed primarily as research and development enterprises under the auspices of colleges and universities. Also, as was the case with the history of the nursery school movement, these programs have begun to move to the larger community and acquire a broader mandate as more and more women seek care for their young children in order to continue their employment and careers.

With the emergence of infant and toddler care for children of middle-income and professional parents has come the realization that, as a society, we are rather uncertain about how best to design these programs. These design issues reflect structural and regulatory issues such as optimal group size, appropriate staff–child ratios, length of program day, as well as the requisite training for staff. These matters are further complicated by the fact that infant and toddler care can occur in private homes or group centers, on college campuses, and, in some instances, in public schools. As a consequence of location of the program, regulating responsibility may be held by departments of health, human services or education, each with different standards of preparation.

The range of program types has led to confusion regarding a common nomenclature for practitioners, regardless of the age of children being served. Are they teachers, child care providers, child development specialists, or nursery school practitioners? Caldwell (1990, 1991) has advocated creation of a new term, *educarer,* to try and express the unique blend of care and education that characterizes early educators' work with young children. Still, to the extent that the emphasis for infants and toddlers, and even for preschoolers, is placed under the rubric of care rather than education, public expectations regarding formal preparation for practitioners tend to be low.

PRESCHOOL EDUCATION

Issues of Sponsorship

The extent of the tension between care and education is, perhaps, most clearly evident in programs for children ages 3 to 5 years. When 3- , 4- , and 5-year-olds participate in a full-day program, usually because their parents are employed, the program is called child care. Teacher qualifications for child care, low by any standard, are determined by state regulation and vary considerably across the fifty states. Furthermore, licensing regulations tend to focus on, or be limited to, the health and safety of participating children, rather than their education. However, recent attention to the conditions in child care programs has generated interest in increasing the expectations associated with providing care in center-based programs. The qualifications for family day care providers are just beginning to receive serious consideration.

When an early childhood program is part of a public school setting, however, it is usually perceived as educational in the sense of preparing children for success in school. Teachers in these programs, which are frequently conceived as early intervention programs, are often required to be certified by the state though they may not be compensated at the same rate as their similarly qualified colleagues who teach at other levels of early childhood education (Mitchell, Seligson, & Marx, 1989).

When outside the public school system and operating on a half-day basis, early childhood programs are commonly labeled preschool, reflecting the generally accepted belief that such programs help prepare children for their first year in public school, although not always through direct instruction or a focus on academics. Expectations for professional preparation of practitioners in these programs are variable and rarely regulated by departments of education. Preschool programs affiliated with particular philosophies, such as Walden and Montessori, however, usually provide their own teacher education.

There has been considerable discussion as to whether the Child Development Associate certificate (CDA) will become the recognized professional credential for entry into the early childhood profession. Boyer (1991) has proposed that community colleges take the lead in improving the quality of preschool programs,

regardless of their length of day, by offering a new, associate, preschool professional degree. Obviously, either choice, the CDA or a 2-year child development
specialist degree, would serve as a further demarcation between those individuals
practicing inside and those practicing outside the public school system.

The irony of this particular discussion lies in the fact that the same 3- to 5-
year-old may participate in all these programs. Yet if, for example, child care were
recognized as an educational setting, it could become a "legitimate" site for
preschool education and a place for early intervention for children in need of such
support. The frustration, therefore, lies in the complexity these programmatic distinctions add to any deliberation regarding early childhood teacher education.

The Preschool Curriculum

Until the late 1950s, there was general and widespread acceptance of preschool programs as noneducational in the traditional sense; they focused more on support of
the social and emotional development of children. The history of the Bank Street
College of Education is one of several exemplars from this tradition. Then called
nursery schools, preschools existed on the campuses of colleges and universities
as laboratory schools or parent cooperatives and in more affluent neighborhoods
because they were tuition based; they provided two or three half-days per week of
group play for children. At the outset, nursery school teachers were educated
mostly as kindergarten teachers in the relatively new curriculum borne from the
progressive education and child development movements.

The emergence of early intervention programs in the 1960s challenged both
the traditional curriculum and the basis for teacher education. Educators and psychologists, many of whom had no tradition or experience in early education, began
to design preschool programs for special populations of children. These new
preschools were characterized as compensatory education programs for children
in poverty. Preschools were designed to achieve, to different degrees, two essential goals: to provide poor children with culturally broadening and enriching experiences they were presumed not to have and to prepare them for success in school.
These early experimental programs helped set the stage for the creation of Head
Start and similar preschool programs that have continued under the auspices of
state and federal education agencies.

The advent of intervention preschools introduced a number of issues regarding both the curriculum for children aged 3 to 5 and the education of their teachers. A major antecedent to these concerns was the profound shift in beliefs about
the nature of childhood that began to occur in the late 1950s and 1960s. The powerful and influential psychodynamic view of the early years derived primarily from
Freudian psychology was challenged by a cognitive psychology drawn predominantly from Piaget, but which also reflected behavioral psychology.

In brief, the argument centered around whether or not 3- ,4- and 5-year-olds
were emotionally and cognitively capable of substantial intellectual challenge and
whether such intellectual challenge made any difference to their future success as

students. Hunt (1961), drawing heavily from the history of western psychology and using Piaget's epistemology, argued that the young child was consistently engaged with his or her environment in substantial intellectual activity. Much of this debate turned on Hunt's challenge to the conventional belief in the fixed nature of development and intelligence.

Hunt's position has prevailed. However, there continue to be widely different interpretations of the meaning of this transactionist psychology, all of which have profound implications for early childhood teacher education. One stance is represented by Piagetians, who study and interpret Piaget's teachings as the source of their knowledge for early education and teacher education (e.g., Kamii & DeVries, 1977; DeVries & Kohlberg, 1990). At the other end of the spectrum, one finds individuals who have drawn their ideas substantially from the American behavioral tradition (e.g., Bereiter & Engelmann, 1966; Gersten, Darch, & Gleason, 1988).

A teacher education program based on these two positions would likely have the following characteristics:

The Piagetian Curriculum
- The study of child development, primarily from a Piagetian perspective
- Play presented as the central interaction modality for children
- Exploratory or constructive activity promoted through a variety of learning areas and activities
- Teachers taught to organize the children's day around large blocks of child choice activity

The Behavioral or Environmentalist Curriculum
- The acquisition of child assessment techniques, not unlike those emphasized in the education of special education teachers
- Direct instruction techniques. The standard curriculum to be presented to the children would be covered
- An analysis of the curriculum for young children by subject matter or skills to be acquired

Quite clearly, the perspective one brings to the question of the curriculum of preschool education substantially influences the form and content of corollary teacher education programs. And, to add still further to the complexity of this discussion, neither the profession nor the public are close to achieving consensus regarding what is best for children prior to school entry.

KINDERGARTEN AND PRIMARY GRADES

Curriculum Issues

For years there was a clear separation between kindergarten and the primary grades. This separation reflected the fact that kindergarten curriculum was primarily informed by developmental psychology, particularly the maturation theory of Gesell. On the other hand, the primary grades were informed by curriculum theory. Additionally, the kindergarten was a relatively small enterprise and is still not mandatory in most states. Until recently, in the minds of most citizens and teachers, "real" schooling began in first grade; kindergarten was a half-day transition from childhood to the rigors of formal education. Kindergarten emphasized socialization to the roles expected of children in school and provided opportunities for children to "get ready" for reading and writing.

This scenario has now changed. As Walsh (1989) recently concluded, kindergarten has become part of the elementary school and is seen by its administrators as the first year of schooling. Thus, much of the standard first-grade curriculum is now incorporated into the kindergarten. Moreover, partly in response to the needs of employed parents and partly in response to the perceived needs of unschooled low-income children, full-day kindergartens have become almost commonplace.

At the same time, there are efforts to influence the academic focus of the primary grades with a more developmental orientation, which has been triggered by the wide acceptance of NAEYC's position statement on developmentally appropriate practice (DAP) (Bredekamp, 1987). This document has influenced not only the redirection of prekindergarten and kindergarten programs, it has begun to inform the practice of teachers in the primary grades as well. This is due, in part, to the influence of recent publications by the National Association of State Boards of Education (1988; 1991) and the National Association of Elementary School Principals (1990). Each of these three publications advocates developmentally appropriate practice through the primary grades. Thus, the contrast of content for teacher education programs for preschool teachers described previously now permeates the preparation of primary school teachers as well.

This movement toward making DAP a pervasive construct is not without criticism, however. There is growing concern among some early childhood academics about the universal appropriateness of DAP (Kessler, 1991; Lubeck, 1993; Swadener & Kessler, 1991). These critics have brought interpretative, critical, and feminist perspectives to their analyses of early childhood education and argue that the perspective presented by DAP does not address the ways in which social forces prevent poor and minority children from achieving success (Bloch, 1991; Delpit, 1988).

Issues of Certification

Diversity of expectations regarding the preparation of kindergarten and primary teachers is also reflected in state certification requirements. Even though state certification currently is a requirement primarily for public school teachers, the lack of consensus across states regarding certification requirements and the common separation of personnel certifying agencies within states is felt at all developmental levels of the early childhood continuum (Morgan et al., 1993).

McCarthy (1988) completed an analysis of the certification requirements for teachers of young children in the fifty states and the District of Columbia. She described what she found as "variety." There is no common definition of early childhood education as regards certification and standards required, which in turn sustains diversity of curricula offered among the various teacher training institutions. At the time of her study, kindergarten and primary grades were conceptualized only rarely as early childhood (as opposed to elementary) education. Specifically, thirty-two states had early childhood certification by title or ages of the children. Among this group, there were eleven definitions of early childhood education. They were: birth–preK (0–4 years), birth–K (0–5 years), birth–3rd grade (0–8 years), nursery (3–4 years), nursery–K (3–5 years), nursery–2nd grade (3–7 years), nursery–3rd grade (3–8 years), nursery–4th grade (3–9 years), K–3rd grade (5–8 years), K–4th grade (5–9 years), and nursery–6th grade (3–12 years).

And, consistent with earlier discussion, McCarthy's findings confirm that in most states the certification of teachers who work with children under the age of 4 is typically the purview of a state social service agency or health department rather than a department of education. In most cases, as already noted, the requirements for a certificate for work with young children in child care or nursery school are substantially less than those required to meet the standards for teacher certification.

Lack of consensus among the states regarding teacher certification is reflected in terms of which programs within institutions of higher education have responsibility for preparing early childhood teachers. Departments of education have maintained primary responsibility for the education of teachers for programs run under the auspices of public schools. The extent to which these programs address issues from an early childhood education perspective, however, varies tremendously, from one or two classes to entire programs. In addition, concern for the education of handicapped children, as expressed in Public Laws 94-142 and 99-457, has served as a catalyst for schools of education to address teacher preparation for the education of children from 3 years onward who are at risk for school failure.

Teacher preparation with a child development orientation, however, is more likely to occur in departments of home economics—now more often called departments of human ecology—or child study. These programs may or may not have established arrangements with state departments of education to ensure that their graduates receive state certification. And, as mentioned earlier, community colleges increasingly are assuming major responsibility for the education of preschool staff.

Given the mixture of settings, requirements, and sponsors, it is clear that the field of early childhood education cannot be addressed as a monolithic entity. The content and configuration of early childhood teacher education is directly affected by the diversity and fragmentation within the field (Katz & Goffin, 1990).

NEW PERSPECTIVES

Katz and Goffin (1990), in their review of issues for teachers of young children, questioned whether, given the diversity of programs and sponsors in the field of early childhood education, all teachers needed the same amount and kinds of train-ing. They asked whether all teachers should be expected to master a common core of knowledge and skills. And, they pondered, "What is the minimum level of understanding about early childhood education, its purposes, and its clientele, below which no early childhood practitioner should be permitted to fall? Further-more, should the answers to these questions be related to the kind of setting in which practice will occur?" (p. 176).

Additionally, in the recent past a substantial number of relatively new tech-niques for use in teacher education have been developed, including the use of case methods, reflective journals, cooperative learning and learning communities, site-based instruction, and mentoring. The literature on teacher education is replete with examples of the possible effectiveness of these methods. The publication of this volume is yet another indication of the profession's interest in matters related to the education of teachers of young children.

However, the questions posed by Katz and Goffin remain unanswered and the most effective use of techniques like those identified in the paragraph above continue to need elaboration and clarification. It is our belief that understanding of these questions and issues will be facilitated to the extent that we are informed by teachers' voices.

Commonly, analysis of issues in teacher education are subjected to the criti-cal analysis of scholars, teacher educators, and policy makers. Inquiry is typically shaped by the careful analysis of the research and scholarly literature. This is a time-honored tradition and an essential feature of informed inquiry. However, unlike this tradition and other recent publications on early childhood teacher education (e.g., Spodek & Saracho, 1990), we have chosen to enter practitioners' voices into the dialogue as a means of probing the issues and examining the questions. Their voices contribute new perspectives to our deliberations about early childhood teacher education.

We have asked thoughtful practitioners in each level of early childhood edu-cation—infant and toddler care, preschool education, kindergarten education, and the primary grades—to answer one of two questions: (1) What is needed to enter an early childhood classroom as a competent teacher? and (2) What is needed to move beyond an initial level of competence as an early childhood teacher? These questions were designed to acknowledge at least two tiers of competence in the care and education of children: those who are just beginning their careers in early childhood education and those who are experienced educators. The teacher–authors have each prepared an essay responding to their question, drawing from their own years of experience, the populations they have served, the institutions in which they have taught and currently teach, their reflections on the needs of the profession, and their knowledge of the teacher education literature. In a very real sense, we have asked each to tell a part of their teaching story.

The essays responding to these two questions have been read and commented upon by three respondents. The respondents were chosen because they represent a constituency served by early educators, are involved with a group that can influence teacher education, or are scholars of teacher education, child development, or American culture. The commentators have been asked to expand and clarify ideas presented in the essays, suggest issues and concerns that were not addressed, and extend or elaborate the essays in terms of their particular perspectives.

A third question has been asked of early childhood teacher educators: "What is needed to become a competent early childhood teacher educator?" These essayists were selected as a result of their thoughtfulness regarding their endeavors and because they represent different types of college or university teacher education institutions. The selection of essayists from 4-year colleges and universities also is consistent with the focus of the National Association of Early Childhood Teacher Educators (which sponsored this text) on institutions of higher education that prepare early childhood teachers for state certification.

It is our belief that the voices of practitioners could provide us with the depth of insight that others have found in their discussions with teachers (e.g., Ayres, 1989). Furthermore, by asking teachers to tell us what they believe to be essential for success in the classroom, we sought some measure of the validity of conventional teacher education curricula.

In some ways the conventional wisdom has been validated when, for example, the essayists cite the primacy of child development knowledge for successful practice. In other ways, they have challenged conventional wisdom by telling us of knowledge, skills, and dispositions necessary for effective teaching, for example, the need to learn continually about children, their individual communities, and the process of learning.

Thus, our goal to learn from classroom teachers has been achieved. Teachers of infants and toddlers, preschoolers, kindergarten children, and the primary grades have informed us of what was essential for them to succeed as teachers of young children. One can draw many implications from their essays for teacher education, school management, and curriculum development in early education.

The response of the six early childhood teacher educators to the question of what is necessary to be a competent teacher educator is more difficult to characterize. At a minimum, one can suggest that the conventional wisdom was not validated by these essays. Rather, the reader will note a wide range of opinion and belief in these responses. One can only conjecture about the ferment in the profession that these essays will generate.

The discerning reader may on reflection think of additions, elaborations on a theme, alternative explanations, or deeper meanings from their experiences than presented by these essayists. But, rather than considering such possibilities as a weakness in the messages, we contend that these essays should provoke us to examine our knowledge, assumptions, and beliefs.

This approach to issues in early childhood teacher education reflects the diversity extant in the profession. It also reflects our appreciation for the need to begin a dialogue with reflective practitioners for advice and insight. What we learn from the careful reflections of the essayists and their commentators will advance our understanding of the complexity of early childhood teacher education and should make it possible for us to frame the next set of questions.

REFERENCES

Association of Teacher Educators and the National Association for the Education of Young Children. (1991). Early childhood teacher certification guidelines: A position statement. *Young Children, 47*(1), 16–21.

Ayres, W. (1989). *The good preschool teacher.* New York: Teachers College Press.

Bereiter, C., & Engelmann, S. (1966). *Teaching disadvantaged children in the preschool.* Englewood Cliffs, NJ: Prentice–Hall.

Bloch, M. N. (1991). Critical science and the history of child development's influence. *Early Education and Development, 2* ,95–108.

Boyer, E. (1983). *High school.* New York: Harper & Row.

Boyer, E. L. (1991). *Ready to learn: A mandate for the nation.* Princeton, NJ: The Carnegie Foundation for the Advancement of Teaching.

Bredekamp, S. (Ed.). (1987). *Developmentally appropriate practice in early childhood programs serving children birth through age 8.* Washington, DC: National Association for the Education of Young Children.

Caldwell, B. M. (1990). "Educare": A new professional identity. *Dimensions, 16,* 3–6.

Caldwell, B. M. (1991). Educare: New product, new future. *Journal of Developmental and Behavioral Pediatrics, 12,* 199–204.

Carnegie Task Force on Teaching as a Profession. (1986). *A nation prepared: Teachers for the 21st century.* New York: Carnegie Forum on Education and the Economy.

Committee for Economic Development. (1991). *The unfinished agenda: A new vision for child development and education.* New York: Author.

Committee for Economic Development. (1993). *Why child care matters: Preparing young children for a more productive America.* New York: Author.

Conant, J. B. (1963). *The education of American teachers.* New York: McGraw–Hill.

Delpit, L. (1988). The silenced dialogue: Power and pedagogy in educating other people's children. *Harvard Educational Review, 58,* 280–298.

DeVries, R., & Kohlberg, L. (1990). *Constructivist education: Overview and comparison with other programs.* Washington, DC: National Association for the Education of Young Children. (First published, 1987, as *Programs of early education: The constructivist view* by Longman).

Gersten, R., Darch, C., & Gleason, M. (1988). Effectiveness of a direct instruction academic kindergarten for low–income students. *The Elementary School Journal, 89,* 227–240.

Goodlad, J. I. (1984). *A place called school.* New York: McGraw–Hill.

Goodlad, J. I. (1990). *Teachers for our nation's schools.* San Francisco: Jossey–Bass.

Holmes Group. (1986). *Tomorrow's teachers: A report of the Holmes Group.* East Lansing, MI: Author.

Holmes Group. (1990). *Tomorrow's schools: Principles for the design of professional development schools.* East Lansing, MI: Author.

Howsam, R. B., Corrigan, D. C., Denemark, G. W., & Nash, R. J. (1976). *Educating a profession.* Bicentennial Commission on Education for the Professors of Teaching. Washington, DC: American Association of Colleges of Teacher Education.

Hunt, J. McV. (1961). *Intelligence and experience.* New York: The Ronald Press.

Kagan, S. L. (1990). *Excellence in early childhood education: Defining characteristics and next-decade strategies.* Washington, DC: US Department of Education.

Kamii, C., & DeVries, R. (1977). Piaget for early education. In M. C. Day & R. K. Parker (Eds.), *The preschool in action: Exploring early childhood programs* (2nd ed., pp. 363–420). Boston: Allyn & Bacon.

Katz, L. G., & Goffin, S. G. (1990). Issues in the preparation of teachers of young children. In B. Spodek & O. N. Saracho (Eds.), *Early childhood teacher preparation* (pp. 192–208). New York: Teachers College Press.

Kessler, S. A. (1991). Early childhood education as development: critique of the metaphor. *Early Education and Development, 2,* 137–152.

Koerner, J. D. (1963). *The miseducation of teachers.* Boston: Houghton Mifflin.

Lubeck, S. (1993). The politics of developmentally appropriate practice: Exploring issues of culture, class, and curriculum. In B. Mallory & R. New (Eds.), *Diversity and developmentally appropriate practices: Challenges for early childhood education* (pp. 17–43). New York: Teachers College Press.

McCarthy, J. (1988). State certification of early childhood teachers: An analysis of the 50 states and the District of Columbia. Washington, DC: National Association for the Education of Young Children.

Mitchell, A., Seligson, M., & Marx, F. (1989). *Early childhood programs and the public schools: Between promise and practice.* Dover, MA: Auburn House.

Morgan, G., Azer, S., Costley, J., Genser, A., Goodman, I., Lombardi, J., & McGimsey, B. (1993). *Making a career of it: The state of the states report on career development in early care and education.* Boston: Wheelock College.

National Association of Elementary School Principals. (1990). *Early childhood education and the elementary school principal: Standards for quality programs for young children.* Alexandria, VA: Author.

National Association of State Boards of Education. (1988). *Right from the start.* Alexandria, VA: Author.

National Association of State Boards of Education. (1991). *Caring communities.* Alexandria, VA: Author.

National Commission on Excellence in Education. (1983). *A nation at risk.* Washington, DC: Government Printing Office.

Sizer, T. R. (1984). *Horace's compromise: The dilemma of the American high school.* Boston: Houghton Mifflin.

Spodek, B., & Saracho, O. N. (Eds.). (1990). *Early childhood teacher preparation.* New York: Teachers College Press.

Swadener, B. B., & Kessler, S. (Eds.). (1991). Reconceptualizing early childhood education [special issue]. *Early Education and Development, 2,* 2.

Walsh, D. (1989). Changing kindergartens: Why here? Why now? *Early Childhood Research Quarterly, 4,* 377–391.

Whitebook, M., Howes, C., & Phillips, D. (1989). *National Child Care Staffing Study.* Oakland, CA: Child Care Employee Project.

Whitebook, M., Phillips, D., & Howes, C. (1993). *National Child Care Staffing Study revisited: Four years in the life of center-based care.* Oakland, CA: Child Care Employee Project.

PART I

What Is Needed to Enter an Early Childhood Classroom and Be a Competent Teacher?

CHAPTER 1

Facilitating the Distinctive Role of Infant and Toddler Teachers

Deborah J. Rowe, Barbara Early, and Diane Loubier

It is a clear fall morning on the campus of the University of New Hampshire and a few infants are settling into their day at school. One teacher sits in a rocking chair at a semicircular table and oversees three young toddlers eating breakfast. She offers small portions of healthy food in bite-sized pieces. She talks with them about what they are eating and lets them decide what will ultimately end up in their mouths, rather than on the floor. Another teacher is on the floor with a 6-month-old playing and practicing crawling. Just as the 6-month-old begins to fuss, a mother walks in holding a clinging and crying 9-month-old. The mother's face looks almost as distraught as her child's; she mumbles that she is already late for work. The second teacher looks over at the table and catches the first teacher's eye; she calmly carries the fussing 6-month-old over to the table for some cuddling and turns to help the mother and her child separate and begin their respective days.

Next door the toddlers also are settling into their day. A 2 1/2-year-old has just arrived; he marches into the room demanding the toy duck that another child is pulling around. "Mine, mine!" he yells while trying to tug the duck out of the child's hand. Meanwhile the child with the duck starts to cry and opens his mouth as if to bite while the 2 1/2-year-old's mother looks on in exasperation. A teacher retrieves another duck from the shelf and quickly places it in the 2 1/2-year-old's hand. Another child is in the bathroom area sitting on the potty depositing little bits of paper beneath him saying, "I do myself!" The teacher with him smiles at her coworker and confirms to the child that "Yes, you are doing it by yourself."

We are three teachers of infants and toddlers at the Child Study and Development Center (CSDC) at the University of New Hampshire. We each came to this field from very different backgrounds. Diane feels that working with young children has always come very naturally to her; she has always had the "intuitiveness" that is so important in meeting the needs of children. When her own children were very young and she sought child care, Diane found it difficult to find qualified, competent, loving people who took their jobs seriously. She realized that by entering this field, she could contribute to parents' peace of mind because their children's best interests were being met. Through her work in various environments, including for-profit centers and licensed home day care, Diane has fulfilled this personal mission for 15 years.

Debbie began working with children after an unfulfilling experience as an attorney. Initially, she worked with toddlers at a for-profit center. From this experience she learned that she loved working with children, but that she preferred to do so in a more supportive environment. CSDC provided such an environment, and Debbie has worked there with infants for more than two years. During that time, she earned her master's degree in early childhood education (not her bachelor's focus). She loves working with very young people and especially enjoys forming the often intense bonds with their families.

Barbara has been in the field full-time for nine years, working in a variety of settings. These have included a charter project under the Office of Economic Opportunity; a low-morale, low-budget, for-profit center; and six years at a center that embodied the ideals that she had begun to discover 13 years earlier. Barbara came to CSDC with an associate's degree, a love of young children, and a thirst for more knowledge. During the past two years here, while constantly learning, she finds that much of her core knowledge comes from the deep love and awe that she has always felt for the emerging child.

We think the teachers' actions in the opening vignette reflect the knowledge, skills, and dispositions necessary to enter an early childhood classroom and be a competent teacher of infants and toddlers. To clarify this conclusion, we discuss seven areas: respect for the child; respect for the family; a working knowledge of typical and atypical development; loving and responsive care; knowledge of health, safety, and nutrition; personal skills; and interpersonal skills. We identify the importance of each area and outline ways we have successfully nurtured and developed these areas in undergraduate students and beginning teachers. We believe that these areas form a particularly critical focus, especially given the distinct role infant and toddler teachers play in the field of early childhood education.

As a university child development laboratory, CSDC exists for three purposes. First and most fundamentally, it provides high-quality child care and education for approximately 135 children between 6 weeks and 6 years of age, as well as a range of family support services for parents. Second, it offers each year over 500 undergraduate and graduate students, from 16 campus departments, a location with mentors for learning about young children and how to interact with them. Third, it provides a facility and climate for research.

Our rural location and role as a major state university affect our mission. Our university affiliation (in a department of Family Studies, which is situated in a college of Health and Human Services) influences our program philosophy and teaching strategies. CSDC has four encompassing themes: technology, international perspectives, health, and respect. These themes manifest themselves in the design of the environment, drive the curriculum, and inform program policy.

The defining characteristics of our infant–toddler classrooms are the children themselves. During the time children are in these classrooms, incredible change occurs. Infants connect with adults and other children; learn much about their bodies and the world around them through motor behaviors; grow from immobile "cooers" to walking, talking toddlers; and, if they have developed a sense of trust in the world, they begin to separate from the very connections they spent the past year and a half forming.

Toddlers are at a point between egocentrism and ideation of their personalities. This can make their behavior sometimes seem erratic and confusing. But in the midst of this confusing time, there is burgeoning language, new complex motor skills, and beginning social skills.

The worlds of infants and toddlers are very different, but these two developmental phases are significantly different from the world of 3- to 8-year-olds. Issues such as diapering, potty learning, bonding, early eating habits, talking, social play, and biting are specifically emerging in this age group. Infant and toddler teachers must be able to read nonverbal cues and decipher early language, respond lovingly and patiently to behaviors such as short attention spans and tantrums, recognize and validate physical and cognitive milestones, and form a team with children and their parents. First and foremost, an infant or toddler teacher must love, respect, and really want to work with these age groups.

RESPECT FOR THE CHILD

Respect for children is essential in providing sensitive and responsive care and is a special quality in successful infant and toddler teachers. A child who is truly valued has a strong foundation from which to draw when encountering the frustrations and disappointments inherent in the early years. This foundation serves as the basis for positive self-esteem and excitement about the learning process. In the opening vignette, the teacher showed respect for the 2 1/2-year-old's current stage of development and found him another toy duck. She did not demand that he share when he was incapable of understanding the concept. As with so many things, respect is taught best by modeling it (Gonzalez-Mena & Eyer, 1989).

Respect for children stems from a knowledge of child development and from an ability to recognize the developmental stage of individual children. No two infants or toddlers go through the same stages in the same way; by acknowledging this fact, teachers show respect for children's diversity. A teacher with special needs children will know what these children require and how to provide it in a well-balanced, thoughtful program. It is, therefore, important for students and beginning teachers to build a strong foundation in child development.

One of the simplest ways to show respect for children is physically to get on their level, by lying down on the floor with an infant or squatting to meet the gaze of a toddler. It is also important to talk in terms and phrases that are familiar and meaningful. Infants and toddlers are uniquely attuned to the nonverbal messages that adults send. Sensitive teachers use this knowledge to communicate love and acceptance of children. The beginning stages of the relationship between a child and teacher are characterized by listening and learning and talking and trusting. This is when a teacher learns to read the child's cues and gains what can only be described as an intuitive sense based on the trust they have built together.

Building on this new relationship, successful teachers develop strategies and techniques that work with different children, a working definition of individualized care. They share these insights with co-workers and discuss the process of discovery with students and beginning teachers so that they may learn how to translate the infant's subtle behaviors and the toddler's puzzling behaviors. These insights enable a teacher to follow a child's lead and openly explore, through the child's eyes, different activities and experiences that very often lead to those "teachable moments" when learning is fun and effortless.

Teachers also show respect for children by the environments they create. A cozy nest for snuggling, a soft rug in front of a mirror, and safe crawling areas demonstrate knowledge of an infant's needs. Providing appropriately sized furniture and activities at a child's level invite toddlers to explore and affirm their newly emerging sense of independence. A teacher can also show respect by structuring the day's pace and routine so that it meets the child's needs. For the infant, this means following the child's cues: he eats when hungry, sleeps when tired, and plays when motivated. For toddlers, a daily routine serves as a learning tool to help them begin to anticipate the next activity and set rhythms for energy levels. A teacher helps children pace themselves by alternating high energy activities with slower, quieter times.

This routine should always include choices for the older infant and toddler. Given the fierce struggle for autonomy going on within their bodies, these children need choices. A win–win situation for children and teachers can be facilitated by letting children direct their actions within a cooperative classroom atmosphere. This requires flexibility on the part of teachers and is vital in empowering children. It also is another way of showing respect for children's abilities and their right to plan for themselves.

RESPECT FOR THE FAMILY

The infant and toddler teacher is an extension of a child's family. The respect shown to children must also be the guiding factor in a teacher's relationship with families. As we respect the individuality of each child, so, too, must we respect the individuality of each adult. It is critical to respect the diversity (i.e., ethnic, religious, economic, and so forth) expressed in a classroom and be supportive of many different family structures. There may be families who are unfamiliar to teachers, but it is our job, as teachers, to support and respect the traditions of all the children and families in our classrooms.

One way to show families respect is to communicate with them. They want to share in their child's day. They want to know how their child ate and slept, their toileting or diapering habits, and anecdotal information that helps them reconnect after a day apart. We have found that specific meetings help families become familiar with a program, allow them to ask questions, and talk about their child's growth and development. Parent meetings provide an excellent opportunity to share information about issues relating to discipline, nutrition, stress, behavior, or anything else of importance to the families. Parent meetings can be eye-opening for students or teachers new to the field. Reading about family issues is one thing, but listening first-hand to families who are trying their hardest, day after day, to do the best job they can is a much more meaningful lesson in gaining empathy for families and their particular situations.

Respect for families includes respecting the personal nature of their private lives and any confidences they may share with us. Trust is an important element in the relationship we develop with families and will emerge as families realize that we are accepting them as they are, without being judgmental. In all interactions with families, therefore, teachers must remember the importance of confidentiality.

It is sometimes difficult for a teacher to agree with the manner in which parents handle a situation, but it is imperative to support their role and realize that they are our clients and that we work for them (Gonzalez-Mena & Eyer, 1989). Part of our professional responsibility, though, is to provide information and materials to families to help them understand better the stages their children are going through and to present alternative perspectives on issues at hand.

One of the most difficult things we face as teachers are angry parents. It is natural to feel intimidated, but very important not to be defensive. Parental anger is often the product of many stressors coming into play at one time. The responsive teacher lets parents talk through their frustrations or anger and listens for the key to their displeasure. Sometimes all that is needed is a supportive, listening ear. At other times, due to the subject or the circumstance, parents need to be directed to a supervisor. Role-playing is an effective way for students and beginning teachers to practice working through some of the tricky family issues.

We try to remember that we are part of a very meaningful team and that high-quality early childhood education depends to a large extent on the relationships we are able to develop with families. It makes our understanding and appreciation of their child that much greater.

A WORKING KNOWLEDGE OF TYPICAL AND ATYPICAL BEHAVIOR

Perhaps the most commonly studied area in early childhood teacher education is child development. This knowledge helps teachers to observe carefully and to guide activities; prepares them to capitalize on teachable moments, alerting them when development is lagging or speeding ahead; and helps them understand why children do what they do. An understanding of development helps explain why infants find it fascinating to push or drop food and toys off of a table over and over again, and why toddlers struggle and demand to do everything by themselves one minute and then crawl into an adult's lap the very next minute and ask them to do something they are very capable of handling themselves.

While child development knowledge is crucial, we intentionally entitled this section a "working" knowledge of typical and atypical development; we wanted to emphasize that having the skill and disposition to apply this knowledge is of equal importance to having the knowledge itself. Attending a child development class is just the beginning. Explaining behaviors such as biting and tantrums to colleagues and parents forces teachers to process their knowledge of development in new and useful ways. Teachers entering the field need constantly to refresh their knowledge by reading books and articles, attending conferences, and developing their own progress plans. The most important step in ensuring that knowledge of child development is not static is a program of observing the children with whom you work (Wilson, 1986).

We have found that a recorded continuum of anecdotal observations of children is very useful. Daily observations range from recording a child's first step at the center to a description of babbling. Careful observation can lead to simple but critical discoveries, such as realizing that telling infants to share when they are struggling over the same toy is ineffectual. Discoveries such as this inspire us to try new, and undoubtedly more successful, strategies. Day after day, week after week, month after month, year after year, these observations guide us in forming new and deeper understandings of how children grow and develop.

Since we believe observation is such a powerful tool, it forms a large part of the work we do with students and new teachers. They read about doing observations and begin making an observation of any child each time they are in the classroom.

Observation also has a role in assessing children. Detailed observations combined with a team discussion, with guidance, perhaps, from a specialist, help ensure that all children benefit from developmentally appropriate practices. Thus, not only must beginning teachers acquire knowledge of child development and strive to keep it current, they must develop the skill of being able to apply this knowledge. We think observing children and working with a more experienced teacher can nurture this skill.

Teaching children of this age range is very personal and individual. Even typically developing children develop at rates that vary tremendously. A successful teacher will have a disposition that allows information to be drawn from all sources, including the child's family. Getting a handle on development, child by child, can be tedious and time consuming, but the patience this requires is more than worth the effort. This knowledge empowers us to provide the loving and responsive care so important to infants and toddlers.

LOVING AND RESPONSIVE CARE

During the first years of life, infants and toddlers are optimally bonding and forming attachments with the special people in their lives (Gonzalez-Mena & Eyer, 1980). This is a time when children should experience lots of physical and emotional closeness with the adults who care for them. They need physical closeness to build security; this security leads to positive self-esteem and encourages children to explore their environment. For a teacher, this need for physical closeness means being able to share your body with children, to let them hug and hold on to you, to sit on your lap and snuggle. Infants need their teacher's physical touch to feel secure in their new world. Toddlers need their teacher to serve as a secure base so they can assert their newfound autonomy and rebel, knowing there is a safe place to which they can return (Ainsworth, 1979).

It is vital that a person working with infants and toddlers feels comfortable with the physical and emotional closeness that they require, has a genuine love for children, and is able to give generously both physically and emotionally. Young children need to know that, whatever they do and whatever happens, their teacher will always be there for them, with a hug, a gentle voice, or reassuring eye contact. Throughout the day, through all the attempts children make to master new skills, they look to their teachers for reassurance and comfort. Thus, teachers should be able to respond in a sensitive, accepting, and positive way.

Being loving and responsive means being able to read children's cues properly. It includes responding quickly and appropriately to their different ways of communicating, such as crying, facial expressions, body movements, and idiosyncratic vocabularies. These responses help assure children that their needs are being met.

Sensitivity to infant and toddler cues helps the teacher to know when they need to eat, sleep, be rocked, held, changed, or assisted in the bathroom. Teachers need to be aware of when an immobile infant needs to be moved to a different location, put in a different position, or offered a new toy. Beginning walkers may need some redirection when they tire and will benefit from a stationary activity now and then. Toddlers need a teacher with infinite patience to let them put on their own shoes and coats, even though this may take 20 minutes. They also need someone who knows when they are no longer being challenged by a puzzle and are ready to tackle a more difficult one. Infant and toddler needs are many and diverse; and these children depend on their teacher either to meet them or to help them to do so themselves.

Thus, responsive care means much more than meeting a child's basic needs. It means responding to a child's physical, socioemotional, and intellectual needs—in other words, the whole child. We should never underestimate the abilities of the infants and toddlers with whom we work; we need to take care that the environment is not static and that we are not complacent. While we are not advocating "miseducating" infants or toddlers, we do think that infant and toddler education should be approached with a very open mind and an active imagination (Elkind, 1987).

KNOWLEDGE OF HEALTH, SAFETY, AND NUTRITION

Health, safety, and nutrition issues are particularly important when working with children under 3 years of age. Very young children cannot tell an adult that their ear hurts or that they feel feverish. They count on us to recognize their cues. Even when their vocabularies have expanded, these children cannot always locate and identify the source of their discomfort. Further, their immune systems are immature, and an unfortunate side-effect of group care is the frequent spread of infectious disease (Hoekelman, 1991; Shelov & Hanneman, 1991). Thus, teachers must be able to recognize the signs of common childhood illnesses, administer appropriate care, and determine when the child should remain in group care or go home.

As children learn to roll over, sit up, stand up, crawl, walk, run, jump and climb, injuries are bound to occur. Further, as children interact at this age they often express themselves physically rather than verbally and, again, injuries occur. Emotions surrounding childhood illnesses and injuries run strong. Parents are often fearful when their baby first runs a fever, guilt-ridden when colds recur and their pediatrician points to child care, stressed when illness requires missing work, and angry and critical when their child is injured at school. Teachers have to remain sensitive to individual families and balance this sensitivity with doing what is best for all the children and their families.

Teachers play a critical role in creating and maintaining a healthy and safe early childhood environment. To help them do this, they need to be trained in their center's sick policy; this enables them to explain the rationale behind the policy and helps them to make difficult decisions. When a judgment call needs to be made, conferring with other teachers or a supervisor often helps. When working with student teachers or beginning teachers we often discuss these difficult decisions and how we arrived at them so that they can learn from the experience.

Teachers also need to be instructed in and follow careful hygiene procedures, including washing toys, disinfecting diaper-changing or toileting areas after use, and washing the child's and adult's hands after diaper changes or bathroom trips and before and after eating (Aronson, 1991). Airing the classroom several times a day, getting the children outside, and using an air filter and the right humidifier, if necessary, are all helpful.

All staff should be CPR and First Aid certified. If children with special needs are included, particular care needs to be used in assessing any medical needs and ensuring that staff are skilled and comfortable with meeting these needs. Developing a system of monitoring areas with other staff helps to cut down on the frequency of accidents. Student teachers or new teachers need to learn how to assess the needs of a classroom upon entering it. They also need to work on scanning areas of a classroom or playground and developing their peripheral vision.

In addition, competent teachers truly observe the children for whom they are responsible and keep in close contact with their families. They know when a child is prone to ear infections and are alerted when a child pulls on his ear or spikes a temperature. A teacher needs to be familiar with children's rhythms: when and for how long they sleep, how frequently and how much they eat, and what their temperaments are typically like; even familiarity with a child's bowel movements is important. An unusually irritable child or one who is more sluggish than usual may indicate a problem. Learning to read a child's cues with the guidance of a more experienced teacher is the best way to ensure a safe and healthy environment.

Children in group care often spend long hours at a center; a large percentage of their daily nutritional intake is monitored and served by teachers. Thus, for teachers of infants and toddlers a knowledge of breast feeding and breast milk, formula feeding, the transition to solids, and appropriate finger and first foods is imperative. Further, a knowledge of basic nutrition, particular facts about children and foods, for example, what they can choke on (Shelov & Hanneman, 1991), and a healthy attitude about eating are necessary (Gonzalez-Mena & Eyer, 1980).

Meals are a time for bonding, social interaction, experimentation, learning, and, finally, eating. It is typically very messy. Children should not be rushed or forced to eat, and food should not be used as a reward or withheld as a punishment. It is the adult's responsibility to offer the food; it is the child's responsibility to choose to eat it or not (Gonzalez-Mena & Eyer, 1980).

Training teachers on nutrition is not easy. Providing good books and articles on feeding children is a good first step (Morrison, 1988; Shelov & Hanneman, 1991). We found a lecture given by a nutritionist very helpful; a course in nutrition would be even better. Another idea is to gather and organize information about feeding and nutrition from the families' pediatricians. Teachers also need to talk among themselves to ensure that in the area of nutrition, as in many other areas, their own personal feelings do not interfere with providing the best care for the child or the best support for the family.

PERSONAL SKILLS

To teach and work effectively with infants and toddlers, teachers need to possess certain personal qualities and skills. A commitment to children, to their development and well-being, and to forming the bonds that are so important to their healthy development is essential. Young children also need dependability. They look to their teachers for guidance, approval, and security. They need to know that they can count on their teachers to support them and guide them through the activities of their day.

Working with infants and toddlers requires a certain "intuitiveness," an inner sense of what they need at any given moment and the ability to respond to those needs quickly and appropriately. Teachers must have the ability to read children's cues and be attuned to children's special and individual ways of communicating.

When you talk about teaching infants and toddlers, you are talking about lots of motivation and energy. The teacher's motivation is essential in guiding them through the many stages of development and enables the teacher to facilitate the learning process. But there can be no shortage of teacher patience and flexibility.

Because infants and toddlers learn through trial and error, adults need the patience to allow a child to make mistakes and keep trying until the skill is mastered.

It seems that children's energy never quits; so teachers need to know how to pace themselves through the day. We've learned that it's important to know the peak energy times of the day and when to take a break. By communicating with co-workers, we have learned how to work together to balance each other's energy levels.

Teachers need to create a positive atmosphere and convey a positive attitude throughout the day. The ability to deal with stress in a calm and reassuring way is essential. Infants and toddlers pick up on nonverbal cues, and a teacher under stress can turn a classroom into chaos just by reacting to the day negatively.

A sense of humor and a good imagination go hand-in-hand with teaching infants and toddlers. The activities that young children pursue can result in a teacher being an elephant or a cow, rowing an imaginary boat, or "shaking out her sillies" (Raffi, Simpson & Simpson, 1977). To enhance children's imagination, teachers need to let their own imaginations take charge and to be comfortable with whatever activity is required.

In training teachers to acquire these skills and qualities, it is important that they be able to observe infant and toddler classrooms to see how trained teachers respond to the many different situations that arise. Role playing is another method of training that can be used to demonstrate effective ways of dealing with different situations and emotions, and to encourage teachers to expand on their imagination. By receiving feedback from trained professionals and parents, students and beginning teachers learn the meaning of commitment and the important role they play in the development and well-being of young children.

INTERPERSONAL SKILLS

The opening vignette showed some of the ways that interpersonal skills come into play during work with very young children. The two infant teachers decided who would manage the table and who would care for the children on the floor and greet the families as they arrived. With just a look, the two teachers understood each other and arrived at a means of meeting the children's and the frantic mother's needs in a calm and efficient fashion. In the toddler room, one teacher monitored the bathroom area while another was out on the floor with the children.

The area of interpersonal skills is included to acknowledge the social aspect of working with young children. It is often erroneously assumed that in order to work with young children one only needs to know how to relate to them. This is simply not the case. As the field of early childhood education grows, a teacher's role grows with it (Almy, 1975). This growth involves interacting with many adults as well as with children. Parents are involved, but now grandparents or others may be raising children. Colleagues and administrators are involved as well as volunteers, student teachers, teacher's aides, outside therapists and consultants, medical people, and children's agencies.

This results in layers of interpersonal interactions. Teachers need to work well with members of their teams and with the families in their classrooms. This ensures high-quality, loving, and responsive care. They also need to communicate effectively with superiors and the center's administrators. Often teachers know when problems are brewing; their ability to communicate with superiors or administrators allows a situation to be handled in anticipation of a crisis, rather than in reaction to one. Finally, teachers need to interact well with members of the center's community. Teachers' spheres of influence can be broad; by maintaining positive interactions, they are consistently able to be advocates for children and families.

A key aspect of training in this area is the provision of positive role models. But role models alone are not enough. We have found that following a particularly important or difficult interaction amongst colleagues or with a family, it is helpful to take a student or new teacher aside, explain why the situation was handled as it was, and discuss alternative courses of action. This approach is useful in training positive communication skills, an open-minded attitude, flexibility, and maturity.

Another aspect of training in this area mirrors our work with children; that is, we explain the natural consequences of a student's or new teacher's behavior. If one teacher is late for work, we explain that this has resulted in another teacher being alone with six infants and in need of help, and that this is unacceptable. This approach can also be used to show the importance of communication, flexibility and strong organizational skills.

We work hard on communication. We communicate with parents through daily notes, in person during drop-off and pick-up, through telephone calls—sometimes to discuss a problem, sometimes just to say hello—at casual brown-bag lunches, on outings to the park or to the beach, at parent meetings, and at parent conferences. We communicate among staff throughout the day, at staff meetings, informal get-togethers, and over the telephone while at home. People need practice in communicating with each other. Thus, we try to give plenty of opportunities for this to take place. We also try to set up an environment where people feel safe to take some risks and make some mistakes.

Finally, as is the case with children, the issue of ownership is critical. We try to involve all teachers and, to a lesser extent, students in all aspects of the classroom. Giving students and teachers ownership of the classroom in which they work affords them opportunities to work on their communication skills and their ability to approach a situation with an open mind, to be dependable and flexible, to handle a situation with maturity, and to use and develop organizational skills.

CONCLUSION

We three teachers have each come to this profession from very different backgrounds. We agree on what knowledge, skills, and dispositions are necessary to be successful in working with infants and toddlers, but we cannot say that any one approach to education and training is best. We do agree that infants and toddlers are special people and that teachers who work with them must know something about them and be interested in learning more. Formal instruction is valuable, yet nothing is more important than directly working with children and their families, guided by someone who is more experienced and knowledgeable and can show the way. Prospective teachers probably will not find in their textbooks that a child pulling on his ear suggests ear infection. Books definitely can't teach you about individual children.

Prospective teachers need to work with other teachers, listen to children's families, observe the children themselves, and search to see if they have the commitment necessary to enter this field. While the demands are high, the rewards are plentiful. It never grows old to see a child take his first step or hear him put together initial sentences. The intensity of the child–teacher relationship is professionally unparalleled. While these children require us to reach deep down and share ourselves physically and emotionally, they reciprocate with smiles, hugs, and by sharing a never-ending stream of thrilling accomplishments.

ACKNOWLEDGMENT

The authors wish to acknowledge with gratitude the editorial support and valuable counsel of Michael Kalinowski.

REFERENCES

Ainsworth, M. D. S. (1979). Infant–mother attachment. *American Psychologist, 34,* 932–937.

Almy, M. (1975). *The early childhood educator at work.* New York: McGraw–Hill.

Aronson, S. S. (1991). *Health and safety in child care.* New York: Harper Collins.

Elkind, D. (1987). *Miseducation: Preschoolers at risk.* New York: Alfred A. Knopf.

Gonzalez-Mena, J., & Eyer, D. W. (1980). *Infancy and caregiving.* Palo Alto, CA: Mayfield Publishing.

Gonzalez-Mena, J., & Eyer, D. W. (1989). *Infants, toddlers, and caregivers.* Mountain View, CA: Mayfield Publishing.

Hoekelman, R. A. (1991). A pediatrician's view: Day care, day care: Mayday! Mayday! *Pediatric Annals, 20,* 403–404.

Morrison, G. S. (1988). *Education and development of infants, toddlers, and preschoolers.* Glenview, IL: Scott Foresman.

Raffi (music), & Simpson, B., & Simpson, B. (words). (1977). *Shake my sillies out* [song]. Canada: Homeland Publishing.

Shelov, S. P., & Hanneman, R. E. (Eds.). (1991). *Caring for your baby and young child: Birth to age 5.* New York: Bantam.

Wilson, L. C. (1986). *Infants & toddlers: Curriculum and teaching.* Albany, NY: Delmar.

CHAPTER 2

Defining Competence as Readiness to Learn

Jenny F. Kramer

The new school year had recently begun and the allure of the water table drew Douglas's interest and desire to explore and play. On this particular day his teacher joined him at the table, ready to roll up her sleeves and get wet. New to this school setting and in many ways a novice to working with preschool-aged children, she wasn't quite sure what to expect. Something inside, however, told her to watch Douglas; it was her hope that, through his activity, he would indicate how things could proceed.

A selection of water toys was available on a nearby shelf. Douglas selected a measuring cup and a water pump. He placed the measuring cup in the water, filling it partially. Weighted in this way, the cup sat at the bottom of the table. Then Douglas placed the pump nearby and began to draw water up through it. After passing through the pump, the water cascaded down into the cup located below its spout, quickly filling it to capacity.

During this time the teacher was also using a water pump. She experimented in a parallel fashion and even copied Douglas's idea to fill a cup with water. As both their containers neared capacity, the teacher began to anticipate the need to empty her cup if she was to continue the activity. Although her inclination was to empty her measuring cup by pouring the water back into the water table, impulse directed her to wait and watch. Just then Douglas did something that gave his teacher reason to pause and review. After briefly reviewing the situation before him, Douglas lifted the base of his pump out of the water table and placed it in the water-filled measuring cup. He then continued his pumping procedure, drawing the water back out of the cup and returning it to the trough.

As Douglas's teacher, this incident reminded me that not all people look at a problem in the same way and, if given the opportunity, they often find alternate and equally successful and satisfying methods for solving problems. I am grateful that I did not choose to enter Douglas's exploration as an expert.

Clearly, there is always more to learn, and this conclusion forms the core of my response to this essay's leading question: "What is needed to enter an early childhood classroom and be a competent teacher?" I've concluded that teaching is a skill that is never once and for all. Good teaching is a process of experimentation, review, reflection, and reapplication. Good teachers don't view themselves as masters of their art filled with all there is to know about the subject of teaching, but rather, are able to view themselves as learners—constantly looking at choices and questioning what works.

I think new teachers need help to recognize that good teaching does not mean having all the answers, but instead means knowing how to offer experiences that help generate interest and help extend curiosity and the desire to explore. This is the first, and perhaps the most important, attitude for teachers to make their own. Such teachers are not afraid to make mistakes, because it is from mistakes that we all grow.

It might never have occurred to me to solve the water pumping problem in the same way Douglas chose. I have since wondered whether Douglas would have followed through in the same manner if I had emptied my cup of water by pouring out its contents before he had had the opportunity to try his solution. Would he have settled for my answer to the problem or would he have gone on to discover his own solution? I fear that as teachers we too often give children answers prematurely or communicate to them that there is only one correct solution. Just as the young child requires time to grow, so does a teacher.

My feelings and beliefs on this subject have been shaped by my personal and professional experiences and choices. I am thirty years old, white, Jewish, and the product of a middle-income upbringing. Politically, I consider myself left of center. I grew up in the north Bronx, attended public school, and later went on to spend four years at Bennington College in Vermont. I have since received my master's degree from the Bank Street College of Education. I have been employed as a head teacher for the past seven years in independent school settings in New York City, where I taught kindergarten and first and second grade.

Currently, I am working as a head teacher at the Wimpfheimer Nursery School at Vassar College in Poughkeepsie, New York. My classroom is staffed by a head teacher, teacher, and at least two student teachers. Eighteen children are in the class, 10 girls and 8 boys. At the beginning of the school year in late August, children ranged in age between 3.6 and 4.11 years. In addition to my classroom teaching responsibilities, I work closely with student teachers from nearby community colleges and facilitate a weekly conference with students enrolled in the Vassar College practicum course. I sought out this position because I was eager for the opportunity to learn more from and about this age group.

WHAT A GOOD PRESCHOOL TEACHER NEEDS TO KNOW

A good early childhood teacher—or any teacher for that matter—is a special person. Many of us are fortunate to have had at least one teacher who has taught us or touched us in some way. Whatever the reason for their specialness, we tend to remember such teachers with fondness and, perhaps more important, we remember the lessons they have taught us.

What makes good early nursery school teachers? What characteristics do they possess? What knowledge do they have and how do they go about teaching so that the students learn? What do they need to know in order to confidently enter a classroom and teach? I contemplated these questions in terms of teacher qualities or characteristics. These qualities are listed below and are accompanied by brief explications.

1. *Good teachers are able to view themselves as learners.* They possess a willingness and desire to explore and discover and model this process for the students in their care. They do not demand of themselves the answers to all the questions about the subject of teaching; yet they do not avoid a subject because they lack the knowledge. They are committed and willing to find out what they don't know and constantly to look at the choices before them, questioning what works.

2. *Good teachers are willing and able to grow.* Because they do not view knowledge as finite, good teachers seek out opportunities to grow personally and as teachers. Each group they work with has different needs and abilities. The problems and successes they encounter through their work continually warrant new knowledge and skills. Good teachers are ready to meet these challenges, and ideally, are supported in their quest to develop their competencies.

3. *Good teachers are keen observers.* Crucial to teaching is the ability to observe and listen to children. It is through this process that teachers can discover students' skills, interests, and needs. Good teachers are able to use the information they gather to augment the learning environment so that it can both nourish children and grow from them. In this way, teachers are responsive to their students rather than dependent on a preset curriculum. Observing and listening to students are skills that develop through experience. They require judgment as well as understanding of the broader contexts in which students live (Kohl, 1976).

4. *Good teachers know the community in which they teach.* They are aware of and understand that there are socioeconomic, cultural, and political factors that affect the lives of the children and families with whom they work. Competent teachers honor and respect differences within the classroom population. They understand that parents are a valuable resource and are an essential part of the parent–teacher–child learning triad.

5. *Good teachers possess a strong content background in child growth and development.* It is with this knowledge that they are able to look at children and consider their individual growth and development within a basic framework.

6. *Good teachers have something they care to teach.* It is important that teachers learn things they can teach their students. Time and energy must be devoted towards developing and nourishing the artist, musician, naturalist, mechanic, crafts person, cook, poet, dancer, and storyteller in us all.

7. *Good teachers understand how young children learn.* They understand that not all children learn in the same way or at the same pace. They also understand that children need time to play, explore, re-explore, and rehearse their growing body of knowledge and experience. They allow children to learn their own way rather than imposing their style on them. Because they understand that young children need to move to learn, they consciously weave in opportunities for children to experience learning through their bodies. In understanding this fundamental connection between action and learning, a good teacher endeavors to work with children to create an environment that allows for the hands-on exploration of materials. Such an environment provides children with an opportunity to experiment with ideas, make errors, and be active co-constructors of their learning. Perhaps most important, a good teacher believes that each child has infinite potential.

8. *Good teachers need lots of energy.* They have a sense of humor and laugh with children. Need I say any more?

9. *Good teachers ask questions that motivate children.* They are comfortable with leaving conclusions open; their questions are open-ended and investigate their students' thinking. Good teachers are not in a hurry to bring investigation to closure, relishing instead the process of investigation and discovery. They allow children to do most of the talking and encourage them to risk ideas and ask their own questions. They are ready to facilitate the growth and development of concepts by providing materials and experiences through which children may deepen their understanding.

10. *Good teachers are able to take risks.* This quality does not mean putting children at risk but rather speaks to teachers looking beyond the obvious and digging below the surface (Barbour, 1992). Like children, we can often learn best from what doesn't pan out exactly as we might have planned.

11. *Good teachers understand that organization and order are important.* They are careful not to become so compulsive that openness and creativity are compromised. Instead, they involve themselves in the process of developing an environment that is inviting and inspiring and in tune with the needs of young children.

12. *Good teachers are skilled at group management.* Teachers can have wonderful ideas, understand the connection and interdependence between curriculum areas, and be creative and resourceful, but if they are unable to manage their group, all this may be lost. Children benefit from sharing their feelings, but limits are important and necessary. Group management, however, does not mean imposing a set of rules and regulations on children. And when rules don't work, it is important to examine them to see if they continue to make sense. Moreover, sometimes it is necessary to set plans aside and deal with the issues surrounding development of community.

13. *Good teachers possess a willingness to "mess around" and explore.* They do not point and direct children through activities. As models, they are able to present an image of a learner as someone whose curiosity is greater than the desire to keep their clothes free of mess! In many ways, good teachers are willing to return to their roots as learners—actively pursuing experiences through sensory investigation and discovery. In this way, teachers are able to keep in touch with the explorations and learning styles of the children with whom they work.

14. *Good teachers are flexible.* They must be willing to set aside their agendas in favor of what may make better sense at the moment. Planning is important and should not be considered lightly; yet the business of working with children is not always predictable. As a result, flexibility can open exciting possibilities for learning.

15. *Good teachers are filled with a sense of wonder.* They are connected to nature and all its beauty and depth of knowledge. They are curious and willing to share in the young child's discovery of the mysteries of nature.

16. *In order to be a good teacher, one must love teaching.* Good teaching is hard work. It is a profession fraught with pressure and responsibility. To do it well requires an enormous commitment of time, energy, and thought. One must be creative, resourceful, and strive to keep current with developments in the field of education. There are some days—many days—when trying to be a teacher of this caliber will seem nearly humanly impossible! What sustains a good teacher is the passion and the joy experienced in the process of being a teacher.

THE ROLE OF TEACHER EDUCATION

Learning to be a teacher is an ongoing process. Teacher education should lay the groundwork necessary for this process to begin. Teacher candidates and new teachers alike benefit from a well-balanced diet of theory and practical knowledge. Because the way in which teachers are taught will be reflected in their approach to teaching, this task should be accorded the most serious attention.

Experience may be the best teacher. For this reason, practicum experience for preservice teachers is essential. This hands-on approach to learning provides the opportunity to witness and experience child development and teaching practice as it happens. Student teachers reap enormous benefits from working closely with experienced master teachers who serve as models. All the theory in the world will seem empty and disconnected from reality if new teachers are denied the opportunity to experience the practical ramifications of their education in a realistic setting.

Many teacher preparation programs recognize the importance of hands-on learning. Unfortunately, many new teachers are left to sink or swim on their own after graduation, falling victim to the isolation that befalls those who teach in "island" classrooms. It is here that schools—in collaboration with teacher training institutions—can make a difference. By working together to develop and implement professional growth programs in which teachers may continue their development, teacher education programs could continue to support teachers as they enter the field. And through their participation in such a support structure, schools would show their commitment to quality education for both children and teachers. (One example of how the trickle-down theory actually *does* work!)

Teachers should be enabled to visit other classrooms and attend conferences. Opportunities should be made to share their observations, ideas, and concerns. The importance of getting out and getting together can not be overstressed. I heard Bev Bos sing "Together we're better" at a recent Association for the Education of Young Children (AEYC) workshop and, having had the opportunity to work in this way, I understand the message and hope that others can hear it as well.

Teacher education programs should also strive to motivate teacher candidates to be teacher–researchers. Through such involvement, teachers can learn to look closely at the activities of children in classroom environments; they can begin to examine their own teaching practices. Through such examination, teachers can reflect on how materials and approach affect the behavior of and interactions among and between the children in their classrooms.

But to be able to do this, teacher candidates need to be helped to develop observation and recording skills so they can collect data to inform their teaching methods. Teacher candidates should also be helped to become questioners and interpreters of the information they collect. Then, in response to their review of the collected data, teacher candidates must be helped to appreciate what next steps to take in their work with children.

For this outcome to be achieved, teacher education programs should help teachers to understand how children learn. Because children learn through a variety of styles, a teacher must be prepared to provide learning opportunities that make provision for individual needs and approaches to learning. In doing so, a teacher is sensitive to the fact that each child is a unique individual. A teacher's practice endeavors to create an environment that supports individual children in their attempts to succeed. For example, if a child is exhibiting difficulty sitting as part of the circle during a large group meeting, a well-prepared teacher would think: Is this a realistic expectation for this child? Is meeting time too long? If the meeting incorporated some movement games, would this child experience the meeting as an enjoyable and successful experience? Would the child be supported by sitting next to a teacher? Teachers who ask themselves these questions are looking at how the environment affects behavior instead of questioning why a child can't conform. Children who feel good about themselves as learners become more excited and curious about learning.

Teacher preparation programs often err by spending so much time on theory and the history of education that their students are provided insufficient time to learn the things they care to teach (Kohl, 1976). I do not mean by this statement to devalue the importance of studying educational theory and history. Such knowledge provides important background and context for understanding and working with children. However, curriculum courses in arts and crafts, woodworking, music, science, math, and language and literature are an important component of teacher education programs.

Teachers should be encouraged to learn as much as possible from getting their hands on materials and "messing around" freely. For many adults, such exploration may be met with feelings of inadequacy and embarrassment. We must all be reminded that trying to do something that is difficult and new is healthy as well as a reminder of the struggles young children may themselves encounter at school.

Another key component of teacher education programs should include the teaching of group management skills. Learning how to facilitate group discussions and how to pace a day, the value of well-thought-through transitions, and the importance of consistency (especially as it relates to discipline) are all skills that prove useful throughout a teaching career. Learning how to give directions with clarity so that young children can understand and follow through, providing win–win choices that empower children and bolster their feelings of autonomy are strategies to master.

Understanding the connection between the developing needs of children and the organization and arrangement of the classroom to best meet these needs is also vital. Learning the importance of eye contact and exploring the versatility of the voice as a teaching tool should also be stressed. Practice is important to the development of these skills. I believe that the more practical knowledge teachers have and the more comfortable they are in doing these things themselves, the more able they will be to teach their students. Thus, it may be valuable to view (not judge) oneself on video tape or listen to oneself on audio tape to learn more about what does and does not work.

Finally, I believe it is important for teacher education to prepare teachers to work together with parents. Parents must be seen as an important resource and not as rivals. They know best their child's detailed history and the ways he or she reacts to certain people and circumstances (Rudolph & Cohen, 1984). Their observations and information provide valuable insight and augment the teacher's view of the child at school. Children are best served when teachers and parents share and compare their perceptions.

CONCLUSION

I consider myself fortunate to be working at a school that encourages its teachers to grow as educators and learners. The laboratory school setting is one that continually asks its teachers to examine and re-examine teaching practice. By nature, it is an environment that encourages teachers to risk new ideas and study behavior in an effort to inform and further enlighten their teaching. Teachers are encouraged to attend both regional and national conferences and workshops and in many cases are offered some kind of financial support or compensation.

I recognize that not all teachers are supported as I am in their quest to grow in their profession. In searching for employment, the employer's interest and commitment to staff development have been important considerations that figured heavily in my decision. I find learning stimulating and energizing; it is why I became a teacher.

REFERENCES

Barbour, C. (1992). Issues in education: Teacher candidates learn most from children. *Childhood Education, 68,* 195–196.

Kohl, H. R. (1976). *On teaching.* New York: Schocken.

Rudolph, M., & Cohen, D. (1984). *Kindergarten and early schooling* (2nd ed.). New Jersey: Prentice–Hall.

CHAPTER 3

Preparing Early Childhood Educators for Constructivist Teaching

Georgann Olson

The sign on the door reads "Kindergarten, Where Dreams Begin." Pierpont School, which is located in Ventura, California, is uniquely characterized by a playground bordering the Pacific Ocean. The Channel Islands loom majestically, less than 20 miles off shore. Schools of dolphin frequently swim by the playground on their way to new feeding beds. The migration of gray whales signals a change of season much as falling leaves do in other parts of the country.

This school by the sea has been home to my kindergarten class for the past 10 years. My classroom is in a separate building; with its adjacent playground next to the ocean, it is almost an island to the rest of the school. In the winter, snow can be seen occasionally on the mountains in the distance. The beautiful setting and Mediterranean climate are but part of the story, however. The sleepy coastal town, surrounded by agriculture and oil wells, gradually has given way to suburban sprawl and tourism.

This school is an integrated school, with about 80 of its 275 children bused at least five miles from their homes. The school is very small with only eight teachers. The library is housed in the cafeteria, and the computer laboratory, special reading teacher, speech therapist, and psychologist share an empty classroom on alternating schedules.

Of the 17 elementary schools in the school district, Pierpont has the highest percentage of Aid to Families with Dependent Children (AFDC) recipients. Approximately one third of the school's kindergarten children have had no previous school experience. Children in my class live in motels, apartments, campers, beach homes, low-income housing, condominiums, boats, and very expensive waterfront homes.

Fifty-three percent of the children entering kindergarten in California belong to ethnic minorities, which have now become the majority. Poverty is a fact of life for

23% of California's kindergartners, a percentage on the rise as the state of California staggers under the ongoing loss of jobs. Sixty percent of California's children will live in a home headed by a single parent before they reach the age of 18; 54% of the children who live in two-parent families live in homes where both parents work.

And the staggering statistics continue. Of the state's babies born in public hospitals, 15% are drug or alcohol addicted; many suffer from low birth weight and some are HIV positive. Close to one-third of the children have a first language other than English, and 1 of every 6 children is born in a country other than the United States. Thirty-five percent have moved twice in the last three years (California Department of Education, 1992).

The educational implications of these demographics are heightened by California's current political climate. The governor and state legislators are grappling with an $11 billion deficit. Local school districts are responding by enlarging the already crowded classrooms, containing an average of thirty-three 5-year-olds; furthermore, the reliance on average class size means some classrooms balloon to as many as 37 children. California now ranks 50th in class size and teacher–child ratio. As teachers attempt to respond to the incredible task of meeting the educational needs of these children, they also face the very real possibility of salary cuts, loss of benefits, and tighter budgets. Hence, to enter an early childhood classroom in California and be a competent teacher is an enormous challenge. New teachers confront an increasingly diverse student population, huge classes, and insufficient resources.

ENSURING A SUCCESSFUL BEGINNING

I think that there are two interrelated factors that greatly affect the potential success of early childhood teachers. The first is that teachers tend to teach the way they themselves were taught. Consequently, it seems unrealistic to expect beginning teachers, who have experienced little other than direct instruction, to be able to interact with children as facilitators, practice observation and assessment skills, provide provocations, and develop positive communication skills.

Second, beginning teachers rarely have the skills to immediately and independently transform their theoretical understandings into practice. Even though I have worked with early childhood student teachers for over 10 years, I continue to be astonished that, for the majority of first-semester student teachers, their entry into my classroom represents their first working experience with young children. Clearly, teachers must have many opportunities throughout their professional preparation to observe, discuss, and practice the theories and strategies they are learning about in their course work. Furthermore, in too many instances, first-year teachers are "deposited" in their new classrooms with little or no support from a knowledgeable and experienced administrator, university staff member, or mentor teacher.

I have come to believe that teaching young children is both a science and an art. The art seems to manifest itself through a teacher's dispositions. Temperament, character, and personality are all interwoven in the art of teaching. These characteristics seem less amenable to professional development.

The scientific aspect of teaching, however, which emerges from the core knowledge and skills of the profession, can be taught to those wishing to enter the profession. During my 10 years as a kindergarten teacher and student teacher supervisor, I have identified four knowledge areas I think enhance a beginning kindergarten teacher's effectiveness: (1) knowledge of child development and learning theory; (2) knowledge of developmentally appropriate curriculum; (3) knowledge of how to create a healthy, safe, and supportive learning environment; and (4) skills in communication and child observation.

A fifth factor, active decision making, is woven throughout a teacher's work; kindergarten teachers make hundreds of decisions on a daily basis. Teacher's knowledge base in the four areas just identified informs the daily decisions we must make concerning learning and teaching. They are essential to a new teacher's ability to respect cultural and individual diversity, to cultivate cooperative family relationships, and to gain a sense of professionalism.

KNOWLEDGE OF CHILD DEVELOPMENT AND LEARNING THEORY

A teacher entering a kindergarten classroom with knowledge of the theories of child development and learning will have the ability to nurture emotional, social, and moral growth. Contextualizing the various theories of learning and development in an actual classroom setting can deepen a prospective teacher's understanding and appreciation of each child. Beginning teachers, for example, need to be aware that it is "normal" for individual children to display a developmental span of as much as five years across different domains (Caine & Caine, 1991).

Lisa, one of my former kindergarten students, weighed a little over 1 pound when she was born. At 4 years, 9 months, she entered our kindergarten classroom. Thick glasses magnified the size of her eyes. Lisa's classmates accepted her immediately; it was the adults who thought her "not ready" for school.

This was Lisa's first school experience. It was my challenge to provide an environment and curriculum that would allow Lisa to learn and develop at her own pace. Children's physical health and family circumstances influence the rate at which they develop and the particular aspects of development that may be of most importance at any given time (Bronfenbrenner, 1979). In order to support Lisa's development, I needed to learn that in good early primary practice, individually appropriate curriculum interacts with age-appropriate curriculum.

I have come to believe, along with Eleanor Duckworth (1987), that "the having of wonderful ideas is the essence of intellectual development" (p. 1). This means that the focus of teacher education should be on the learner's point of view. Consequently, I think that before teachers begin their professional careers they should have a working understanding of Piaget's theories of cognitive development. My own recent attempts to implement constructivist education have been enhanced by awareness of the work of educators such as DeVries and Kohlberg (1987/1990), Kamii and DeVries (1980), Forman and Kaden (1992), and Loris Malaguzzi (Forman & Kaden, 1992), who envisioned the now famous preschools of Reggio Emilia. The thinking of these educational leaders has convinced me of the importance of Piaget's stages of cognitive development and the value and place of social–cognitive conflicts.

KNOWLEDGE OF DEVELOPMENTALLY APPROPRIATE CURRICULUM

When I use my knowledge of cognitive development to plan curriculum opportunities, I try to keep in mind what David Hawkins (1978) has said of curriculum development: "You don't want to cover a subject; you want to uncover it. Good teaching is an art of indirection. Made absolute, as it so often is, the straight path degenerates—to coloring between the lines, painting by number, doing algebra by rote" (p. 9).

Teachers at all levels of their professional development must expect to learn along with the children in their class. I'm convinced that curriculum evolves from the teacher and learner in interaction with content and with each other (Duckworth, 1987). To accomplish this kind of exchange, beginning teachers must learn in the way the children in their classes learn. Beginning teachers, therefore, must know how to listen to children's cues when making their curriculum decisions. But responding to children's cues is only part of the stage setting. Beginning teachers also must be able to help children relate to classroom phenomena in such a way that the children can invent their own solutions to problems and go on to construct more coherent theories about people, nature, and machines (Forman & Kaden, 1992). Throughout this process, teachers can provide children with opportunities to explore, investigate, and use symbolic representation to communicate their ideas to others.

Teacher education programs, therefore, need to find ways to rethink their role as "knowledge-givers" and reformulate their expectations regarding teacher–child relationships. Since children's interests are often the starting points of curriculum plans, beginning teachers need to be able to recognize relevant sociocultural issues, create meaningful learning contexts, and integrate developmental domains. Teachers need to be prepared to understand how to facilitate children's construction of knowledge by negotiating their physical environment and social interactions.

No discussion of early childhood curriculum would be complete without mention of the vital role of symbolic play. However, even though there is widespread agreement among early childhood educators regarding the contribution of play to a developmentally appropriate curriculum (Nourot & Van Hoorn, 1991), few teachers, whether experienced or inexperienced, seem to know how to defend the inclusion of play in their curriculum. Yet teachers entering kindergarten classrooms must, of necessity, defend the value of play to administrators and parents.

Research has linked children's play to their development of literacy, problem-solving skills, perspective-taking abilities, creativity, and imagination. Creative thinking, with its link to flexible, divergent thinking, is of crucial importance for children facing the twenty-first century (Nourot & Van Hoorn, 1991). Beginning teachers, therefore, should have a clear understanding of the role and value of play, have the skills needed to promote classroom play, and appreciate its use as a vehicle for individual assessment. I have found Vivian Paley's narrative accounts of play (e.g., Paley, 1984) particularly helpful in developing a deeper understanding and respect for the variances among children's play.

Cajal (1937) suggested that a scientist's personal style is laid in the earliest years of life. He "always believed that the games of children are an absolutely essential preparation for life" (p. 29).

In my kindergarten classroom, play now occupies one-third of each day; it is a central component of the curriculum. The dramatic play area may be transformed into a house, post office, store, restaurant, hospital, library, gas station, school, or farm. After observing that children were frustrated by insufficient time to complete their block structures or change roles in the dramatic play center, I lengthened the free play period to about 60 minutes.

As a result, I experience fewer discipline problems because the children now have time to complete their plans and resolve their problems. The extended time period also provides me with a natural time for assessing children's social and emotional skills, as well as their language, creativity, and problem-solving abilities. I also have learned to be a player as well as an observer. But enacting this role means that beginning teachers need to know how to use active learning strategies such as encouraging children's thinking, helping children learn to ask good questions, following children's ideas and interests, seeking out children's intentions, recording children's actions, and, finally, supporting children's abilities to do things for themselves.

PROVIDING A HEALTHY, SAFE, AND SUPPORTIVE LEARNING ENVIRONMENT

Our knowledge of teaching further requires that a beginning teacher build an environment that provides for the health and safety of all children. Designing an environment that provides for creativity and imagination is equally crucial in a kindergarten classroom. It is not enough simply to hope that creativity will happen. According to Malaguzzi, "We must offer children the instruments—the thoughts, the words, the rapport, the solidarity, and the love—that sustain the hope of arrival at a moment of joy" (as cited in Goleman, Kaufman, & Ray, 1992, p. 83).

Children's dispositions towards learning and their feelings about themselves represent the foundation for their learning in the cognitive, social, and physical domains. A teacher entering a kindergarten classroom should be able to set up a learning environment that supports children's feelings of physical comfort, safety, and security. The environment also should reflect the dispositions fostered by the learning environment: self-respect and respect for others, cooperation and responsibility, and a sense of initiative. "An assessment of space in terms of its implications for children's social development and cooperation can add another dimension beyond the structuring of space to favor a sense of belonging, trust, independence, and exploration" (Gandini, 1992, p. 28).

A beginning teacher should understand how the environment helps to predict children's behavior, can be used as a planning tool for teaching and learning, and supports developmentally appropriate assessment. Kindergarten teachers implement a constructivist curriculum through their roles as "the providers of props, materials, time and space in which a child can work" (New, 1991, p. 28). The environment, however, extends far beyond a classroom's physical setting. It also includes access to the outdoors, furniture and its arrangement, structure of time, role possibilities, available materials, and behavioral expectations.

As noted earlier, skills require practice; in many instances, knowledge and skill go hand in hand. A knowledge base of Piaget and Erikson can help the beginning teacher provide a supportive environment, but prospective teachers also need practice in the layout of space, the creation of objectives, the set-up of structures, and the presentation of activities that favor children's choices and discoveries in the process of learning.

Facilitating a constructivist curriculum, however, entails much more than providing a rich environment. Teachers must strive to engage children in the phenomenon or problem at hand (Katz & Chard, 1989) and, according to Duckworth (1987), provide opportunities for children to explain to others what it is that they have observed and understood.

I believe that this intertwining of the curriculum and the environment is a major strategy for providing a quality kindergarten program. In the classic text, *Logic of Action,* Frances Hawkins (1986) reminds us of what I think is an essential principle of learning: "within a climate/environment of play and affection, which offers phenomena of the real world, water, bubbles, balance, colors, and materials to explore their properties, children will take a large part in designing their own learning" (p. xiii).

COMMUNICATION AND OBSERVATION SKILLS

Communication skills include helping children ask good questions (Forman, 1989), a skill discussed earlier in terms of creating a developmentally appropriate curriculum. Communication skills needed by beginning kindergarten teachers also include the art of listening to children. Beginning teachers also need to know how to use nonverbal cues, utilize "I" statements, and verbalize their perceptions of children's feelings and behaviors. Verbal strategies also can be effective in helping children to evaluate and correct their own behavior, thereby internalizing self-control and prosocial values (Watson, 1981). More challenging is helping beginning teachers learn to use these communication and observation skills as a means for developing reciprocal exchanges with children around meaningful learning opportunities.

It is in the role of researcher or "kid watcher" (Goodman, Goodman, & Hood, 1989) that the teacher can observe the behavior of children in various contexts. Through their observations, teachers become a sort of memory bank for children.

My experiences with the programs in Reggio Emilia, Italy, have helped me to appreciate that observation involves not only "looking" at children but also documenting their thinking through the use of photographs and transcriptions of activities, and helping children to be reflective thinkers. Later, these observations can be used to assess children's progress and as a source of information to be shared with parents and support staff. In many cases, these observations point to the direction the curriculum will take. To become skilled in this way as an observer requires time and practice, and beginning teachers should not be expected to have these skills unless their teacher preparation programs have provided for their development.

Finally, it is through close observation that a teacher may notice signs of emotional stress or neglect and abuse. Beginning teachers should be aware of their responsibility in these circumstances and be familiar with the procedures for reporting suspected abuse and neglect to the appropriate authorities. Although never easy, this responsibility must be taken very seriously.

Communication skills are not restricted to interactions with children. Communication with parents in ways that encourage their involvement is absolutely essential to the successful integration of culturally diverse children in American classrooms (New, 1992). This communication often involves helping with parenting skills, explaining the importance of developmentally appropriate programs, reporting assessment results in a clear and supportive manner, and linking with community resources in cases of need. Beginning kindergarten teachers must understand how to respect each child's unique heritage and background and to reflect this understanding in their interactions with family members. Furthermore, this spirit of cooperation and collaboration is needed not only in relationships with parents, but also among teachers.

As meaningful partnerships are built with parents, these relationships can begin to extend into the community. And, when teachers share, cooperate, collaborate, and assist in each others' professional development, a team emerges with the ability to facilitate change.

MY OWN PATH TO CONSTRUCTIVIST TEACHING

These conclusions regarding the competencies needed by kindergarten teachers at the beginning of their careers certainly differ from my own beginning as a classroom teacher. I graduated from Colorado State College with a degree in elementary education. My first job was in a first grade classroom in a rural community in Colorado. The room was filled with rows of student desks. During the first week, boxes of workbooks and ditto sheets arrived. My desk was piled high with books, and I was instructed to "just do what it says in the teachers' manuals."

The next year I moved to a new school that was one of five featured in *Life* magazine. Ultra-modern in style and design, carpeted and windowless, the school provided learning pods, accordion walls, and climate control. Even with all these "innovations," however, the teachers' manuals, workbooks, and boxes of dittos awaited me. The words *child-centered, relevant, meaningful,* and *integrated* were not part of their teaching prescription—or mine.

I began to use extra activities for the children during reading; I called these "activity centers." While one group worked with me, another group went to "centers," and a third group worked at their seats. I found that this strategy helped solve discipline problems and provided opportunities for art, games, free reading, and creative writing. Later, after a move to California, I transferred this same strategy to my third grade classroom. But at this point I viewed these activities more as an organizational scheme than as an issue of ensuring meaningful learning activities for my students.

In this new setting I was expected to teach all the subject matter areas: music, art, science, health, physical education, social studies, spelling, handwriting, math, English, and reading. I felt overwhelmed! I started to search libraries and professional journals for answers and solutions to my concerns about curriculum and children's needs. I discovered an article about thematic teaching and recognized a possible solution to one of my most significant problems, namely, how to cover eleven subjects in a 5-hour school day. During the next eight years I developed integrated thematic units. I not only began once again to have a life outside the school, but the children also seemed more engaged with the curriculum.

Then in 1982, when five schools in my district were closed, I accepted an assignment at Pierpont School as a kindergarten/first grade teacher. Since I had taught first grade for six years, I presumed it appropriate just to give the kindergarten children a watered-down version of first grade. This assumption, furthermore, was mirrored in other kindergartens in the district. I planned to use state adopted texts and follow the district curriculum guides.

The first week at school, however, the children cried and simply refused to do the required standardized tests. They struggled to sit quietly at their desks and complete the assigned seat work. Parents expressed concern when their children did not want to come to school, and I worried whether I could get these children ready for first grade.

In addition, as the year progressed, I was having discipline problems and I was not pleased with my classroom management. Turning once again to libraries and professional journals, I discovered books by David Elkind (1986, 1987) and articles by Samuel Meisels (1986, 1989). Their conclusions sounded an alarm with which I could identify. And the writings of Vivian Paley (1981, 1984, 1986, 1988) and Jean Piaget (1962, 1966) gave me a different picture of early childhood education. I decided to teach differently.

I stored the workbooks and dittos, bought blocks, dramatic play material, toys, paints, and clay. I threw away all of my craft patterns—never again would thirty identical rabbits grace my classroom walls. The activity centers once used for "fill-in" now became my curriculum. In addition, I refused to do standardized testing in my classroom. None of my children were retained because they were "not ready," and the world did not crumble around me when I made these decisions, although at first there was concern by some administrators. It has become district policy not to give standardized tests in kindergarten or first grade, and now retention is viewed as a last alternative. At this point, not a single kindergarten child has been retained during the past six years.

Most recently, after a visit in the summer of 1991 to the early childhood programs in Reggio Emilia, Italy, I have rethought my curriculum once again. My curriculum is now project-based. The projects emerge from children's natural encounters with their environment, shared teacher and child interests, and teacher concerns regarding specific cognitive and/or social concepts.

This personal transformation undergirds my conclusion that the beginning kindergarten teacher needs to develop communication and observation skills and the ability to structure the environment and curriculum in ways that facilitate children's construction of knowledge. These skills, in turn, need to be linked with the investigative attitude of a researcher. These are the more scientific aspects of our craft.

The art of teaching manifests itself in one's dispositions and personality. Malaguzzi wrote, "Without truly radiating and receiving joy, an adult cannot foster an atmosphere where children can invent and create" (as cited in Goleman, Kaufman, & Ray, 1992, p. 83). Hence, the slogan "Nothing Without Joy" has become a maxim for schools in Reggio Emilia, which have been identified as the best early childhood programs in the world. These same words on my bulletin board remind me that teaching is more than a science.

I would add to my list of important dispositions those of trust, flexibility, humor, curiosity, integrity, and sensitivity. The ability to trust oneself and the potential of children allow a beginning teacher to value and accept "not knowing," to feel less need for a preset structure for instruction. I firmly believe that the absence of flexibility and humor in many public school classrooms may help to explain why far too many teachers leave the field after five years.

In addition, I suspect that many of us are feeling overwhelmed with the expectations and demands of our jobs. The social, political, and economic circumstances surrounding the provision of early childhood education in California challenge even the most competent and experienced teachers. This year, for example, one of my two classes includes 36 kindergartners and first graders. I share one classroom half-time with 32 other kindergarten students. I work from 7:45 AM to 10:30 AM in one classroom and then move to a second classroom from 10:30 AM until 2:15 PM My contract expired in June of 1992, and like many of my colleagues, I am now working without a contract.

Beginning teachers, therefore, must be capable of learning with and from others—teachers and children. No four year course in an institution could possibly prepare teachers for all the vicissitudes of public school teaching.

CONCLUSION

Clearly, recent findings in cognitive psychology have influenced my thinking and actions as a classroom teacher. I believe these findings also have profound implications for teacher training. Thinking, problem solving, communication, and judgment skills need to pervade all the subject areas being studied by prospective teachers. As Caine and Caine (1991) note, "All learning is developmental, including the learning of educators" (p. 180). Opportunities for observation, cooperative learning, and reflection need to be incorporated into teacher preparation courses. Most important, prospective early childhood teachers need to have access to the phenomena they are studying—namely children.

Even as freshmen, students should be provided opportunities to ponder both what and how they are learning. Case studies and field experiences need to begin early in their program of study. Theory and practice must be reintegrated. Study should extend beyond conventional textbooks to include the primary writings of authors such as Vivian Paley, Constance Kamii, George Forman, David Hawkins, and Eleanor Duckworth. Students should also be familiar with the publications and resources distributed by professional organizations such as the National Association for the Education of Young Children (NAEYC), the Association for Supervision and Curriculum Development (ASCD), and the Association for Childhood Education International (ACEI).

I think these needed changes are most likely to occur when universities and school districts form partnerships and become resources for each other so there can be a continuous exchange of research, pedagogy, and support. Whereas new teachers, at least through their fifth year, can gain support and guidance from an ongoing linkage with a university, more experienced teachers can benefit from the ongoing exchange of information and collaboration.

College professors, however, need to be aware that they are sending new teachers into overcrowded classrooms lacking in financial support. In states such as California, teachers without a bilingual credential are unlikely to find a teaching position; yet although my classroom is not designated as bilingual, I became Raul's, Julio's, and Ruby's teacher when the bilingual classroom became overcrowded. Another of my students, Ryan, suffers from ectodermal dysplasia. He was born without teeth and sweat glands and I have the responsibility of helping him remain cool. Despite carefully designed lesson plans for the month of November, my first-grade students and I met together only 10 times; mini-courses, parent conferences, in-services, holidays, award assemblies, and ice-cream parties consumed the remaining days of the month. These circumstances force me to be flexible; humor bridges the valley of despair.

Last week, Vivian's second-grade teacher told me that Vivian has started to read. Vivian has moved forward, her self-esteem intact. The sparkle in her eyes reflects my joy and love of teaching. I do not fill up empty vessels; I am a co-constructor who learns along with my children and shares in their wonder. I have chosen teaching because in my classroom I am truly a life-long learner.

REFERENCES

Bronfenbrenner, U. (1979) *The ecology of human development*. Cambridge, MA: Harvard University Press.

Caine, G., & Caine, R. N. (1991). *Making connections: Teaching and the human brain*. Alexandria, VA: Association for Supervision and Curriculum Development.

Cajal, R. Y. S. (1937). *Recollections of my life*. (E. H. Craige & J. Cano, Trans.). Cambridge,

MA: MIT Press.

California Department of Education. (1992). *Elementary grades task force report. It's elementary.* Sacramento, CA: Author.

DeVries, R., & Kohlberg, L. (1990). *Constructivist early education: An overview and comparison with other programs.* Washington, DC: National Association for the Education of Young Children (originally published in 1987 by Longman).

Duckworth, E. (1987). *The having of wonderful ideas and other essays on teaching and learning.* New York: Teachers College Press.

Elkind, D. (1986). *The hurried child.* Reading, MA: Addison–Wesley.

Elkind, D. (1987). *Early childhood education on its own terms.* In S. L. Kagan & E. Zigler (Eds.), *Early schooling: The national debate* (pp. 98–115). New Haven, CT: Yale University Press.

Forman, G. (1989). Helping children ask good questions. In B. Neugebauer (Ed.), *The wonder of it: Exploring how the world works* (pp. 21–24). Redmond, WA: Exchange Press.

Forman, G. (1993). Constructivism. In J. Roopnarine & J. Johnson (Eds.), *Approaches to early childhood education* (2nd ed., pp. 137–155). Columbus, OH: Merrill.

Forman, G., & Kaden, M. (1992). Research on science education for young children. In C. Seefeldt (Ed.), *The early childhood curriculum: A review of current research* (2nd ed., pp. 175–192). New York: Teachers College Press.

Gandini, L. (1992, May). Creativity comes dressed in everyday clothes. *Child Care Information Exchange,* 26–29.

Goleman, D., Kaufman, P., & Ray, M. (1992). *The creative spirit.* New York: Dutton.

Goodman, K., Goodman, Y., & Hood, W. (1989). *The whole language evaluation book,* Portsmouth, NH: Heinemann.

Hawkins, D. (1978). Critical barriers to science learning. *Outlook, 29,* 3–23.

Hawkins, F. (1986). *The logic of action.* Boulder, CO: Colorado Associated University Press.

Kamii, C., & DeVries, R. (1980). *Group games in early education: Implications of Piaget's theory.* Washington, DC: National Association for the Education of Young Children.

Katz, L., & Chard, S. (1989). *Engaging children's minds: The project approach.* Norwood, NJ: Ablex.

Meisels, S. J. (1986). Testing four- and five-year olds: Response to Shepard and Smith. *Educational Leadership, 44,* 90–92.

Meisels, S. J. (1989). High-stakes testing in kindergarten. *Educational Leadership, 46,* 16–22.

New, R. (1991, Winter). Projects and provocations: Preschool curriculum ideas from Reggio Emilia. *Montessori Life, 3*(1), 26–28.

New, R. (1992). The integrated early childhood curriculum: Interpretations based on research and practice. In C. Seefeldt (Ed.), *The early childhood curriculum: A review of current research* (2nd ed., pp. 286–324). New York: Teachers College Press.

Nourot, P., & Van Hoorn, J. (1991). Symbolic play in preschool and primary settings. *Young Children, 46* (6), 40–47.

Paley, V. (1981). *Wally's stories.* Cambridge, MA: Harvard University Press.

Paley, V. (1984). *Boys and girls: Superheroes in the doll corner.* Chicago: University of Chicago Press.

Paley, V. (1986). *Molly is three.* Chicago: University of Chicago Press.

Paley, V. (1988). *Bad guys don't have birthdays.* Chicago: University of Chicago Press.

Piaget, J. (1962). *Play, dreams and imitations in childhood.* New York: Norton.

Piaget, J. (1966). *The origins of intelligence in children.* New York: International University Press.

Watson, B. (1981). Positive discipline. In P. Nourot (Ed.), *Early primary curriculum guide,* State of California. Unpublished document.

CHAPTER 4

"You Might as Well Go on Home"

Janet Albarado

MISS JANET: Listen very carefully because this story is very tricky. Think hard before
you answer.
JOHNNY: Miss Janet, just tell us. You know we'll get you.
MISS JANET: I don't know. It's pretty tricky. *I* just might get *you* this time.
TERRY: No way, José! Just try and trick us.
MISS JANET: Okay, here we go: Rita picked 3 pumpkins, Ben picked 2 pumpkins,
and Crissy picked 1 pumpkin. How many pumpkins did the children pick?
(The children go very still and quiet for a few seconds. Hands begin to shoot
up around the circle amidst sounds of "Ooh!" and "I know!")
MISS JANET: What do you think, Angel?
ANGEL: It's 6.
MISS JANET: Are you sure?
ANGEL: (Grinning) Yeah, it's 6. You *know* it's 6.
MICHAEL: Yeah, you know it's 6.
MISS JANET: I can't even trick you anymore. I could have just stayed at home today
because I can see that you don't even need my help to do such hard equations.
(The children burst into laughter.)

This teasing banter continued as we went through five or six more story problems
with multiple addends. Little did I know that my flippant remark about staying
home would become a constant reminder that deciding to share my control of the
classroom had been exactly the right thing to do.

In this essay, I discuss my transformation from a beginning teacher with the
usual feelings of insecurity regarding classroom management and discipline, to
one who is much more confident in her abilities. My transformation from a

reliance upon basal readers to a whole language approach provides the context for this evolution. I also discuss the influence of my own teacher education program. I conclude with some thoughts about how teacher education programs can more successfully assist prospective teachers enter early childhood classrooms as competent teachers.

BACKGROUND

There has been considerable political rhetoric in Louisiana about putting children first, but the cold, hard fact is that in 1990 and 1991, we ranked 42nd in per pupil expenditures and 41st in teacher compensation.[1] In 1990 and 1991, 12% of the total teaching force—6,217 teachers—was noncertified.[2] To add to this bad situation, a 10% cut in education funding is currently being considered by the state legislature.

I have been a first-grade teacher in the public schools of East Baton Rouge Parish for 15 years. My first teaching assignment was in an all black school where I taught for 6 years. I have been in my present teaching assignment at Claiborne Elementary for 9 years. The school is located in North Baton Rouge and could be described as an inner-city school. We have been identified by Chapter I as one of the schools in greatest need of services; 90% of our students are considered to be at-risk. Our racial composition is 80% black and 20% white. Because of the low incomes of the population being served, children often come to school without even basic school supplies.

THE BEGINNING TEACHER ODYSSEY

I have had the opportunity to work with many beginning teachers over the last several years. Principals from other schools sometimes send new teachers to observe in my room. I have also had contact with new teachers through inservice workshops I have conducted on whole language. During discussions, first-year teachers frequently express concern over discipline and classroom management issues. Due to the excessive amount of time they spend on discipline, they feel that there is no time left to teach. No matter how carefully they plan, they feel that they are not organized well enough because something always seems to go wrong.

In their attempts to rectify the situation, beginning teachers often resort to authoritarian practices, and then they wonder why things still don't seem quite right. They wonder why teaching young children isn't as much fun as they had anticipated. They question why the things they learned in college don't seem to work in their classrooms. They wonder how they could have made straight As in their education courses and still feel so totally unprepared for teaching. I relate very well to all these feelings of frustration because I remember experiencing them when I was a beginning teacher.

When I attempted to improve my classroom management and discipline skills, I sought the advice of other teachers and attended inservice workshops. I tried everything to motivate the children, from smelly stickers to Hershey's Kisses. I worked to create an attractive classroom environment that was a safe and orderly place in which to learn. I spent time planning smooth transitions from one activity to another. I gave special attention to establishing routines for the use of various materials and equipment. I made sure that classroom rules and the consequences for violating them were clear, and I monitored my classroom discipline for consistency. In short, I took control of the situation—and the classroom. I received excellent evaluations and was considered an effective teacher by my peers and principal.

During my first three years of teaching, these efforts paid off and my management and discipline skills improved. Yet, I continued to have problems getting the children to be responsible for themselves and classroom materials. No matter how many heart-to-heart talks we had, I always seemed to be following behind them, trying to get them to clean up after themselves. I wish I had a dime for every lecture I gave about taking good care of books and games. I would think that my message was getting through only to discover yet another broken toy or torn book. It was frustrating and demoralizing. It took several more years, though, before I realized that the children's lack of responsibility was being caused by a much larger problem—a set of bureaucratic policies and norms that gave teachers and children little or no real control over the life in their classrooms.

In addition to my concerns with discipline and classroom management, my first year of teaching was filled with anxiety over the way I was being forced to teach reading. My teachers at Louisiana State University had introduced me to the exciting world of children's literature and its limitless potential for use in the elementary curriculum, especially in the area of reading. I had been eager to try out their ideas.

Hence, it was incredibly deflating to discover that, to the contrary, I was expected to document what seemed like hundreds of reading skills on a special folder for each child. It was impossible to record these skills, complete the required workbook pages, administer the mandatory skills tests, and *still* find time to use children's literature. Whenever I could, I did, but in the beginning of my teaching career the mandated basal reader provided the basis for reading instruction. The children did learn to read and enjoyed listening to stories, but they rarely chose to spend time in our Library Corner. Puzzles and games, rather than reading, were much more popular choices as alternate activities.

This was not the way that I had wanted to teach reading, but as a beginning teacher, I truly believed choice of pedagogy was beyond my control. My professional preparation had taught me one thing, but my school district required something else. I was totally unprepared to deal with such opposing expectations.

This isolated skills–drill approach, with its basal reader skills management system, continued to frustrate the children and me for several years. There was little interaction among the children because they were so busy filling out ditto sheets and workbook pages. They were not even allowed to take readers home to practice and share with their parents. Because the basal reading program treated literacy as though it occurred in a vacuum, it was devoid of any spontaneity and real meaning. Children were bored, and so was I. And to my surprise, so were the three other first-grade teachers at my school.

Eventually we discovered our common discontent, got together, and decided we had to do something differently. We read Goodman (1986) and Holdaway (1979) and discussed how to apply their ideas in our classrooms. We observed other whole language teachers, attended workshops and conferences, and formed a local support group. Some of us enrolled in graduate courses which provided even more support for our efforts to implement a whole language approach in our classrooms.

We shared our insights with colleagues, loaning them our books and journal articles, and then discussing them at grade level meetings. *The Art of Teaching Writing* (Calkins, 1986) was especially helpful to us. Some of what I was learning about whole language was new to me, but much of it was not. I realized that the underlying principles supporting the whole language approach were ones I had learned in my teacher preparation program but had lost sight of as a beginning teacher. Children by nature are curious and eager to learn. If they see the relevance in what they are being asked to do, and it is important to them, they become involved as learners. If beginning teachers would keep this in mind, they wouldn't have to worry about whether or not the children are learning the required skills.

LEARNING AS A SOCIAL PROCESS

Learning is a social process that requires opportunities for social interaction. People passing by the doors of my classroom tend to assume that the children are "only playing." But if they were to stop and listen to what is really going on, they would realize that it is anything but recess time. Play is a first and essential level of learning. I provide varied experiences for children to engage in purposeful play, during which solving problems is viewed as just plain fun.

Early childhood classrooms should be communities of learners that support and encourage risk-taking as part of the creative process. Children need to engage in social interactions and cooperative learning. Errors must be recognized and accepted as a necessary part of learning.

In contrast with my earlier experiences in teaching reading, my young readers now make predictions and hypothesize as they try to make sense from text. As writers, they experiment with what they want to say, approximate conventional orthography, and try out punctuation to convey a meaningful message. As scientists and mathematicians, they think about a problem, brainstorm solutions, try out those possible solutions, and evaluate the results of their inquiry. Beginning teachers need to learn to value what children *can* do, rather than tediously keeping count of all the things they cannot.

PROMOTING SUCCESS

Early childhood classrooms should be a hive of activity, with children communicating and interacting with each other considerately and responsibly. A competent early childhood teacher provides the supportive scaffolding that allows the classroom community to function in this way. When their classroom community serves as a "safety net" against failure, young children feel a sense of security and are willing to take chances. Individual differences and cultural diversity are celebrated as children learn from each other; everyone has something to offer that will benefit the classroom community. There is a real sense of pride and ownership among children who participate in this kind of classroom community.

I'll never forget the year the children absolutely flipped over *King Bidgood's in the Bathtub* (Wood, 1985). After we read the story, the children acted it out in the Drama Center, using masks they had made in the Art Center. The drama activity mushroomed into an elaborate stage production of the book's storyline. Children worked together to write the script and helped each other learn their lines. They worked in small groups to make costumes, scenery, and props. When problems arose with the script during rehearsals, they talked their way through possible solutions and made changes in dialogue and stage directions. They designed invitations and addressed and delivered them to their parents and to every other class at Claiborne.

The production was a huge success. We videotaped it, and then watched it in class the next day. The children beamed with pride as they watched themselves on the television screen. Everyone's contribution had been important. It was wonderful to witness the respect that the children had for each other during the entire production. Management and discipline problems had been nonexistent; I hadn't needed to bribe them with stickers. The activity itself was motivation enough; they had been totally engrossed in planning for their own learning. They had worked together on something that was important to them.

The traditional view of learning takes exciting and dynamic real-world situations and breaks them into minuscule particles. This is certainly the case with management systems for reading and math. In our arrogance as adults, we often assume that this approach makes learning easier for children. Not only is this an insult to the sophistication and intelligence of children, it bears no resemblance to life in the real world. Since children find it difficult to link isolated skills to real life situations, the subject matter becomes stale and boring to them.

Children need lots of opportunities to practice what we want them to learn in a variety of contexts. Social studies, science, math, drama, and art can provide meaningful contexts for authentic reading, writing, listening, and speaking. *The*

King Bidgood production was much better suited to the needs and developmental levels of young children than workbooks or ditto sheets.

During my transformation into a whole language teacher, I made a rather surprising discovery regarding children's apparent lack of responsibility. I knew that the children needed lots of time to practice reading at school and at home. Providing time for reading at school was easy. However, since most of my children didn't have books at home, providing at-home practice presented a problem. This was a real dilemma for me. Most of my children's literature sets were books that I'd purchased through paperback book clubs. How could I let the children take my paperback books home when I'd always had a problem with getting them to take care of our things? But, given my commitment to whole language, I realized I really had no choice. The books had to go home.

I set up routines for checking books in and out of the classroom library. All parents were asked to sign a letter that informed them of our new reading program and asked them to agree to pay for any book that their child lost or damaged. I talked with the children about being responsible for the books and gave each child a plastic bag for carrying books back and forth between school and home. I was really nervous that first night the books went home. If I lost a lot of books, how would I have enough copies to use with my reading groups?

I need not have worried. My tears over damaged books and materials during the previous eight years had not prepared me for the fiercely protective way this group of children handled *their* books. Please take note of the pronoun because it is important. Children viewed the books from the Library Corner as *theirs*. I didn't have to plead with them to take care of the books or to turn the pages carefully. For the very first time, it wasn't a case of my following the children around issuing reminders to be responsible. There were twenty other members of our reading community who were ready and willing to make a "citizen's arrest" when necessary. It wasn't unusual to hear someone say, "Don't you forget *Pierre* (Sendak, 1962) at home tonight 'cause I want it tomorrow night" or "Put *Brown Bear* (Martin, 1967) in your plastic bag, or it'll get wet on the way to the bus." The books came back undamaged and after the first month, I knew it was no fluke. We lost only one book during the first year, and only one book has been lost in the six years since I abandoned basal readers in favor of a whole language approach.

Although I had always thought of the classroom as *ours*, it suddenly became clear to me that the children had viewed it as *mine*. Now, for the first time, the children felt a sense of ownership and, for that reason, irresponsibility was no longer a problem. Beginning teachers need to be aware, though, that children know the difference between real ownership over a classroom and that which is only superficial. Real ownership involves children in every aspect of classroom life. Although it is necessary to set some rules or limits for safety reasons or due to the availability of space or materials, beginning teachers will discover that classroom management and discipline problems decline when children are involved in setting those limits.

CHILDREN'S IDEAS FOR BETTER TEACHING

A constant source of joy and enlightenment for me is how children continue to show me better ways to teach them. I don't think I was ready to learn from the children during my first few years of teaching. I suppose I thought my admission that I didn't know something was an indication of my skills as a teacher. Ironically, finally admitting that I didn't have all the answers served as the catalyst for my professional transformation.

Questioning, analyzing, and reflecting upon my teaching practices led me to various professional development activities to find answers. The most important answer I learned is that you can never have all of the answers because all of the questions haven't been asked. Once I realized this, I became more confident in my abilities as a teacher and less afraid to take risks.

Perhaps the biggest risk for a teacher is sharing the exclusive control that our position of authority gives us over a classroom. For me, sharing my authority was the biggest and most important step of my professional life; it enabled me to emerge as a more competent teacher.

An important and telling characteristic of classrooms is the role children play in making decisions regarding their own learning. My lesson plans now are more of a back-up than a weekly schedule of activities. We may start out with what I have planned, but if children have better suggestions for how to extend a concept, we pursue their ideas instead.

I've learned how important it is to give children opportunities to make choices and decisions and to assume personal responsibility for learning. It's risky, but even when children make a bad decision (at least from our perspective), they're still learning—in this instance, how to make better decisions in the future.

During my first 3 years of teaching, much of what I had learned in my teacher preparation program went by the wayside because I was so wrapped up in trying to survive within a system that I couldn't even begin to understand. My teacher education program did not prepare me for the problems I encountered with classroom management and discipline. I wanted so much to be a good teacher that, in dealing with those problems, I bought into the superficial institutional definition of an effective teacher. I adopted the outward appearance of an orderly room with quiet children and perfect bulletin boards as my own standard for self-evaluation.

The knowledge that I had acquired in my college classes was forgotten during those early years, because it didn't seem relevant to my survival. Entertainers, writers, and good teachers recognize the importance of "knowing their audience." By narrowly focusing on classroom management and discipline, I failed to understand those problems in the context of the classroom's learning climate. I failed to make the connection that would have allowed me to apply my knowledge of child growth and development and developmental learning theories to my classroom management and discipline problems—to find a more appropriate solution than seizing control. Had I made the connection, I would have recognized that the classroom didn't just belong to me; it belonged to the children as well. I would have recognized the need to share control with the children, thereby creating a sense of empowerment and ownership for all of us. I would have recognized that the real issue was an inappropriate curriculum and concentrated my efforts on learning how to work within the system to make the curriculum more developmentally appropriate.

Clearly, I believe that classroom management and discipline must be addressed in teacher education programs. Furthermore, prospective teachers need more than just a couple of isolated lectures on the subject. They also need practical experiences that can make classroom lectures meaningful and relevant to real teaching situations. This means spending more time in schools observing and working with practicing teachers.

All too often, new teachers continuously change their management and discipline techniques only to find that their problems persist. Prospective teachers need to understand that an important difference exists between poor classroom management and discipline procedures and the management and discipline problems that emanate from circumstances other than inadequate skills. This understanding, however, requires that prospective teachers be taught to consider classroom dynamics holistically.

If teacher preparation programs teach classroom management and discipline techniques in isolation, beginning teachers will logically try to address their problems in isolation as well. Issues of classroom management and discipline must be presented as part of a positive learning climate. This perspective will enable beginning teachers to investigate the real causes of their problems.

SUSTAINING CONTACT WITH TEACHER EDUCATORS

Risk taking is difficult and frightening for beginning teachers. At the same time that the ties to their teacher educators are severed, they are confronted with the real world of teaching. If they're lucky, someone in their school building will take them under their wing, but this isn't enough. I think that during their first year, beginning teachers need a continuing link with their teacher preparation programs.

My own experiences as a beginning teacher would have been very different had I maintained continued contact with my college teachers. Carole Cox and Bessie St. Julien would not have allowed me to become mired in mundane classroom practices. They would have supported my creativity and provided a sense of security that would have made it easier to take risks. They would have questioned me and made me question myself, just as they had done during my undergraduate years. Unfortunately, a mechanism to provide this kind of support to beginning teachers is seldom available.

Colleges of education rarely are able to release faculty members from their teaching assignments, and most professors already have additional responsibilities, such as research or supervision of student teachers. Perhaps support groups could be formed for education graduates in their first year of teaching. These groups could meet with education faculty monthly during the school year to discuss ideas, issues, and concerns. This may be an imperfect solution, but it would be a big step in the right direction. Without support for risk taking, beginning teachers, like their young charges, are more likely to lose confidence and take the safe route of blending in with the system, rather than seeking ways to stretch or challenge it.

THE COLLEGE CLASSROOM

Teacher education programs also need to "practice what they preach." The professor who presents the theory behind social interaction and cooperative learning but allows no class time for students to interact with and learn from each other fails to demonstrate how theory can become practice. The lessons of my teacher education program might have been more real for me and more present in my classroom had I seen them more consistently modeled in my methods classes.

University lecture halls must be transformed into classroom communities that, like early childhood classrooms, support risk taking and recognize errors as a valuable part of the learning process. More class time should be given to group projects, open discussions, and sharing. Divergent viewpoints must be encouraged and explored. Education students must be actively engaged in identifying and analyzing problems and brainstorming possible solutions in their college classes so that they will be prepared to do the same in their own classrooms.

Professors have to take some risks, too. They have to be willing to model shared decision making in their classes by allowing prospective teachers to make some choices regarding assignments, required readings, and research projects. Allowing prospective teachers to make these kinds of choices will lead to more opportunities for independent and thoughtful reflection that, in turn, will begin to shape their *own* personal philosophy of teaching.

Prospective teachers also should be required to write their philosophy of teaching before graduating. Writing down one's beliefs about teaching and learning helps anchor them in memory, to be retrieved when confronted with problems in the classroom. As beginning teachers gain experience, they may modify or refine their philosophy, but I believe the basic core of their beliefs will remain to guide their decisions and actions.

Finally, simply lecturing about developmentally appropriate instruction, whole language, or the use of manipulatives to teach math is insufficient. Prospective teachers need to spend lots of time in real classrooms in all types of schools with various student populations so that they can see theories in action on a daily basis. Far too frequently, professors present a teaching method in its ideal form. But it is extremely important that there be a realistic expectation of how the method is likely to be implemented in a classroom setting. Ideals are what we work toward, but beginning teachers are being set up for failure if they are not prepared for the kinds of constraints they will encounter in schools and taught how to work within those constraints or maneuver around them to achieve their ideals.

The notion of professional development schools in teacher education promises to establish long-term relationships between a limited number of schools and colleges of education. Because they will be working with a small number of schools, professors will be able to work closely with the schools' faculties and be more involved in guiding their students. Fifth-year students will be conducting research projects relevant to their teaching situation. This will provide valuable practical experience in identifying a problem and experimenting with possible solutions. This link may build a stronger connection between the theories students learn in their course work and the practical applications of those theories in the real world of early childhood classrooms. I am excited that my school will be working with Louisiana State University in this capacity next year.

CONCLUSION

I began this essay with transcripts that I jotted down following a math lesson in the early part of the 1991–92 school year. The relaxed dialogue between the children and myself is indicative of the personal environment created by an interactive classroom community. Those children believed there wasn't anything they couldn't accomplish if they worked together and tried hard enough. They knew I was on the fringes of the classroom if they needed me, but they never felt dependent upon me to solve a problem. They had learned that everyone has something to contribute and that their chances of success could be enhanced when they relied on each other and worked through a problem together.

My remark about staying at home came back to haunt me in numerous variations. Comments such as, "You can go check on the other teams because me and Carl don't need your help" and "We'll just come get you if we need you" become the norm when teachers learn to share control with their children. Statements such as these exude self-confidence and independence. To begin their careers as competent early childhood educators, beginning teachers need to know how to be unobtrusive in children's active learning. They need to know how to facilitate without interfering. They must be like good coaches who know how to use a time-out effectively, and then relinquish control back to the players so that they can play the game out to its conclusion.

I wish I had realized how important it was to share my authority during my early years of teaching. It would have eliminated much of my frustration and allowed me to discover the true joy of working with first graders much sooner. I know without a doubt that I would have been a better teacher.

It can be quite a humbling experience to discover that you're not as indispensable as you thought you were. You have to know when to get out of the way and let children learn on their own. You know that you are a competent teacher of young children when you have taught yourself right out of business. And the only way you know that you're out of business is when the children tell you.

> *One morning in April I was having a book conference with Julie when I overheard Matt and Larry reading Heckedy Peg (Wood, 1987) together in our Library Corner:*

LARRY: Down the dusty roads and far away, a poor mother once lived with her seven children named Monday, Tuesday, Wednesday, Thursday, Friday, Saturday, and Sunday. Every day before the mother went to *blank,* her children helped with all the chores. (Larry paused and tried to figure out the missing word, making the "m" sound to himself.)
MATT: What's another word for the grocery store?
LARRY: Market!

> *(Larry reread the paragraph, inserted the correct word, and then finished reading the rest of the page. The two boys continued reading the book by taking turns on each page.)*
> *I had finished talking with Julie and was openly eavesdropping when they caught me. I said, "Y'all are reading that hard book so well that I thought some 3rd or 4th graders had crept into our room to read our books." Larry gave me his shy, toothless grin, rolled his eyes and said, "No, it was us. I guess you might as well go on home now." He turned around and they continued reading as if I weren't even there.*

ENDNOTES

[1]Information furnished by the National Education Association.
[2]Information furnished by the Louisiana Department of Education.

REFERENCES

Calkins, L. M. (1986). *The art of teaching writing.* Portsmouth, NH: Heinemann.
Goodman, K. (1986). *What's whole in whole language?* Portsmouth, NH: Heinemann.
Holdaway, D. (1979). *The foundations of literacy.* Portsmouth, NH: Heinemann.
Martin, Jr., B. (1967). *Brown Bear, Brown Bear, What do you see?* New York: Henry Holt.
Sendak, M. (1962). *Pierre.* New York: Scholastic.
Wood, A. (1985). *King Bidgood's in the bathtub.* San Diego: Harcourt Brace Jovanovich.
Wood, A. (1987). *Heckedy Peg.* San Diego: Harcourt Brace Jovanovich.

COMMENTARIES

The Competence of Entry-Level Early Childhood Teachers

TEACHERS AS LEARNERS

Sue Bredekamp

Several possible strategies exist for defining professional competencies (Burns, 1993). One frequently used strategy is to appoint a panel of experts and review the literature to determine what competencies are required. The "experts" usually generate a set of draft competencies that are circulated to practitioners for review and revised accordingly. In the field of early childhood education, this strategy has been used on several occasions, most notably during the 1970s when the competencies for the Child Development Associate (CDA) credential were developed, and again during the 1980s when the National Association for the Education of Young Children (NAEYC) developed guidelines for early childhood teacher education (Bredekamp, 1990; NAEYC, 1985, 1991).

Another option for determining professional competencies is to ask practitioners to identify the knowledge, skills, and abilities needed to perform their jobs. This job analysis strategy usually results in a draft of competencies that are then subjected to broad review by other "experts" and interested parties. This strategy is currently being employed by the National Board for Professional Teaching Standards (1991); its standards committees, composed primarily of teachers, develop competencies for "accomplished teaching" in various specialty fields.

The latter strategy most closely approximates the approach to defining professional competencies employed in this book—asking practicing, competent teachers to address the question of what is needed to be a competent teacher and then obtaining additional commentary on their perspectives. Presumably, each of the two approaches to establishing competencies (panel of experts or job analysis) should result in similar outcomes. If not, the field in question is probably not developed enough to be advancing a certification program in the first place or there is so little consensus that the knowledge base has not been clearly articulated and agreed upon.

In responding to these essays on beginning teacher competence, I first compare the competencies described by these expert practitioners to the existing sets of competencies promulgated by the larger profession, specifically the CDA competencies and NAEYC's Teacher Education Guidelines. I view this as more than an intellectual exercise because, in a sense, it is a validation of the essayists' perspectives and a check on the real world validity of the guidelines, that is, the maturity of our profession. Then, I comment on the internal consistencies and inconsistencies across essays in an attempt to answer the question of whether early childhood education from birth through 8 is, indeed, one field and whether any preparation program can adequately address this broad age span. Finally, I draw conclusions and implications for the professional development activities now underway in the field of early childhood education.

Before addressing these specific issues, it is important to point out that the essays do not actually reflect an accurate perspective of entry-level practitioners because none of these authors is at the entry point of her career. Each author reflects on past experiences, but none could accurately be depicted as a beginning teacher. Katz (1984) describes the stages of teacher development and identifies the initial stage as survival. Although some survival needs are addressed in these essays, for the most part the authors are unable to address the question from the survival perspective; they are simply beyond this point in their own professional development. For example, the unifying theme of all four essays is that beginning teachers must see themselves as learners; however, teachers in the survival stage are most in need of tools to address everyday problems. Beginning teachers do have lots of questions, but their survival depends most on having some answers.

TEACHERS' PERSPECTIVES AND PROFESSIONAL STANDARDS

In an effort to promote a systems approach to early childhood professional development, the NAEYC reviewed the existing sets of guidelines or competencies and identified a common core of knowledge and skills needed by all early childhood professionals (Bredekamp & Willer, 1992). That core has been described in different ways; but stated succinctly, early childhood professionals must have the knowledge and abilities to:

- Demonstrate and apply a basic understanding of child development, including observation and assessment of individual children
- Establish and maintain an environment that ensures children's safety and their healthy development
- Plan and implement developmentally appropriate curricula
- Establish supportive relationships with children and implement appropriate guidance and group management

- Establish positive and productive relationships with families
- Support the uniqueness of each child, recognizing that children are best understood in the context of their family, culture, and society
- Demonstrate basic understanding of the early childhood profession and make a commitment to professionalism

These same general competency areas appear in all sets of early childhood teacher education standards with greater breadth and depth of knowledge and abilities included in higher levels (ATE & NAEYC, 1991; NAEYC, 1985, 1991; Phillips, 1991). Three of the essays in this section—the infant and toddler, preschool, and kindergarten teachers—list competencies that are highly consistent with the above list. Competencies cited in more than one essay are: knowledge of child development and learning, knowledge of appropriate curriculum, creating a healthy and safe learning environment, observational skills, group management, and relationships with families. It is not surprising that these teachers represent the age-range, birth through age 5, that is traditionally associated with early childhood.

The primary-grade essayist addresses much of this core in her discussion—especially discipline and group management, a developmental approach to literacy, and promoting social interaction in the classroom. However, she basically laments that the expectations of her initial work site did not match this foundation in early childhood education. Her transition as a teacher to a more constructivist approach to learning and a more democratic classroom reflects her increasing understanding of the early childhood knowledge base.

For the most part, the expert practitioners' perspectives on needed competencies of entry-level teachers are consistent with the profession's standards. In their essays, however, these practitioners go well beyond traditional standards in defining the dispositions that teachers need. The NAEYC, however, has been reluctant to set standards that describe personal characteristics, as opposed to knowledge and skills, because, as Olson points out, "these characteristics seem less amenable to professional development." Nevertheless, it is clear from all these essayists that dispositions are essential contributors, if not determinants, of successful teaching. A proposed set of performance-based licensure standards reflects this trend by including standards for knowledge, performances, and dispositions (Council of Chief State School Officers, 1992). Some of the dispositions promoted by these essayists include willingness to explore, flexibility, risk taking, sense of wonder, and love of teaching. According to all four essayists, the most important disposition for teachers is the disposition to go on learning. The theme of teacher as learner permeates the descriptions of entry-level teaching. The challenge for teacher education remains to foster this disposition while also providing beginning teachers with the skills and confidence they need to survive in sometimes adverse circumstances. Each of these teachers obviously demonstrates the disposition to go on learning, but more questions arise. Where did this disposition come from? Is it teachable?

EARLY CHILDHOOD EDUCATION FROM BIRTH THROUGH AGE 8

The NAEYC defines early childhood as birth through age 8 and promotes teacher certification standards and preparation programs (ATE & NAEYC, 1991; NAEYC, 1991) that cover the full age range. Because most programs have not been designed for this broad scope, the concern is often raised that it is an impossible task. The NAEYC has continued to support the broad definition of birth through 8, however, in recognition of the developmental continuum reflected in this period of the life span and as an important strategy to ensure appropriate practices for infants and toddlers as well as children in the primary grades. The NAEYC promotes acquisition of a core of knowledge covering the full age span and recognizes that specializations are probably likely within the age span (infants and toddlers, pre-primary, and primary).

Despite the challenges posed by the differences in development and educational settings across this age span, the consistencies in needed competencies across these four essays serves as support for a unified program and credential. The first-grade teacher's difficult transition to work was at least partly the result of a system that views elementary education as a philosophically different enterprise from early childhood education, as reflected in her preparation program. The challenge is not only to restructure teacher education programs to reflect the broad scope of birth through age 8, but also to change school and community structures to better respect the development and learning continuum.

LESSONS FOR THE PROFESSION

The early childhood profession is engaged in initiatives designed to promote an articulated, coordinated professional development system at the national, state, and local level (Bredekamp, 1991). Existing standards are being reviewed and significant revision is anticipated, reflecting not only new knowledge but new political trends as well. These teachers and essayists provide at least two vital perspectives relevant to that activity. First, the knowledge base of early childhood education informs practice in important and consistent ways across the age span of early childhood. A developmental, interactive, constructivist, and individually appropriate perspective appears to prevail. Second, certain dispositions are not only related to this perspective but essential to its implementation, with the primary disposition being toward ongoing learning. Standard revision, program development, policy setting, and any other efforts designed to improve the professional development of early childhood teachers should strive toward the essential goal of promoting the continuous learning of teachers.

REFERENCES

Association of Teacher Educators & the National Association for the Education of Young Children. (1991). Early childhood teacher certification. *Young Children, 47*(1), 16–27.

Bredekamp, S. (1990). Setting and maintaining professional standards. In B. Spodek & O. Saracho (Eds.), *Early childhood teacher preparation. Yearbook in early childhood education* (Vol. 1, pp. 138–152). New York: Teachers College Press.

Bredekamp, S. (1991). A vision for early childhood professional development. *Young Children, 47*(1), 35–37.

Bredekamp, S., & Willer, B. (1992). Of ladders and lattices, cores and cones: Conceptualizing an early childhood professional development system. *Young Children, 48*(3), 47–50.

Burns, M. (1993). Professional certification programs. Alexandria, VA: Integrated Options, Inc.

Council of Chief State School Officers (1992). Model standards for beginning teacher licensing and development: A resource for state dialogue (draft for comment). Washington, DC: Author.

Katz, L. (1984). The education of pre-primary teachers. In L. Katz (Ed.), *Current topics in early childhood education,* (Vol. V, pp. 209–227). Norwood, NJ: Ablex.

National Association for the Education of Young Children. (1985). *Guidelines for early childhood education programs in associate degree-granting institutions.* Washington, DC: Author.

National Association for the Education of Young Children. (1991). *Early childhood teacher education guidelines: Basic and advanced.* Washington, DC: Author.

National Board for Professional Teaching Standards. (1991). *Toward high and rigorous standards for the teaching profession: Initial policies and perspectives of the National Board for Professional Teaching Standards,* 3rd ed. Washington, DC: Author.

Phillips, C. B. (Ed.) (1991). *Essentials for Child Development Associates working with young children.* Washington, DC: Council for Early Childhood Professional Recognition.

New, with Something More to Learn

COMMENTS ON THE SKILLS NECESSARY FOR ENTRY INTO AN EARLY CHILDHOOD CLASSROOM AS A COMPETENT TEACHER

Jerlean Daniel

The field of early care and education in the United States has long been misunderstood and undervalued. Even though the role of the early care and education teacher requires a complicated set of skills (regardless of the setting), early childhood professionals have struggled under the burdensome task of explaining to our colleagues, employers, and the general public that we are partners in the educational process. As a result, the ability to recruit and retain qualified staff has been in a state of suspended crisis for almost 10 years.

The critical differences between what is expected of the average elementary school teacher and the lead teacher in an early care and education program are twofold. First, the early care and education teacher has daily contact with parents. While this may be true for some elementary teachers, it is also true that, generally speaking, parents' concerns are more intense the younger the child. The essay by Rowe, Early, and Loubier substantiates this view.

Second, the early care and education teacher is usually the leader of a team of adults on a daily basis. For this reason, during 18 years as a child care center director, it was my practice not to hire lead teachers—even if they held baccalaureate degrees—if they lacked work experience. I tended to prefer individuals with associate degrees plus experience over inexperienced but formally trained initiates with 4-year degrees. At issue is the fact that graduates with 4-year degrees are rarely provided sufficient supervisory training.

In general, I chose to hire individuals who had: (1) an understanding of child development and how young children learn; (2) a disposition toward proactive participation in the translation of theory into practice; (3) a substantive sense of group dynamics; (4) an appreciation for the complexities of the child–parent–teacher triad; (5) comprehension of the basics of teamwork; and (6) familiarity with current terminology and issues of the early care and education field. Unexpectedly, the essays by these four practitioners have affirmed my thinking—both about the knowledge base needed by early care and education teachers and the value of experience prior to assuming the responsibilities of a lead teacher. They also illuminate new understandings for our consideration.

These competent teachers articulate well what they do and why with regard to their work. Although every novice has something to learn about the specifics of the first job, the odyssey to competency of these teachers is particularly telling.

MAKE IT REAL

These practitioners vividly point to the need for more reality based training of early care and education teachers. Each author highlights the vulnerability of new teachers to a range of inappropriate practices and expectations, many of which reflect society's general misunderstanding regarding the needs of children. Albarado, in particular, eloquently describes the seductive nature of the traditional view of adult control as effective teaching. This traditional view, however, is diametrically opposed to the fundamental elements of a socially interactive learning environment in which children are free to initiate activities and teachers are free to take risks as members of a "community of learners" (Jones, 1993).

Yet it is impossible to share with novices everything known about the everyday work of their chosen field. Thus, early childhood teacher educators need to provide a knowledge base consisting of, at least in part, theories of child development and learning, philosophy and curriculum formation, and foundations of education. This knowledge forms a base from which a novice can generate viable solutions to problems that may arise.

In addition, these authors imply that a part of one's knowledge base should include the political science or sociology of the teaching profession. Poverty, racial bias, poor health care, and, more recently, drug addiction are now part of many learning environments. Prospective teachers need to be prepared for the political pressures and multiple value systems that are currently a part of educational environments.

The essays give us glimpses of some of these realities. Olson chronicles the statistics of children who speak different languages. Kramer details the need to love teaching in order to withstand the pressures; Albarado recalls having no choice regarding the pedagogy in her classroom; and Rowe, Early, and Loubier highlight the skills needed to interact with diverse families.

Rowe and her colleagues also describe the intense psychosocial and physical nature of careers with our youngest children. Their comments reinforce the implications of our failure to have a uniform system of teacher preparation that ensures children learn from teachers trained to work with a specific age group.

EXPERIENTIAL-BASED LEARNING

The essayists' call for reality based learning is a request that is made shocking both by its simplicity and its absence in so many teacher education programs. Teachers need appropriate models who teach using the techniques necessary for competent practice.

Modeling empowers novices by offering them opportunities to practice what has been learned intellectually. Lab schools were frequently mentioned as sites where modeling can occur. Although there are advantages to controlled laboratory school settings, there are also disadvantages. Reality demands that student teachers practice in more generic public settings. The resolution of this issue may be to have the first student teaching experience in a laboratory school and the second in a community based setting.

Opportunities to be participants in a community of learners will enable novices to bring an internalized, more integrated methods base to their first teaching assignment. Prospective teachers, however, also need time to analyze and reflect upon their experiences.

OBSERVATION IS ESSENTIAL

A socially interactive learning environment, according to these practitioners, requires that teachers have keen observation skills. Professional observation requires that observers make efficient use of their knowledge base, related fields, and experiences with specific children or groups of children. Effective skills are honed over time, but according to current work on portfolio use, observational notes are important tools for ongoing assessment and planning.

THE NEED FOR SUPPORT

The National Child Care Staffing Study (Whitebook, Howes, & Phillips, 1989) concluded that connections to professional associations make a positive difference to the quality of teaching. These essayists emphasize the same conclusion. They repeatedly stress the novice's need for continued support from the university community. Three of the writers document that it took them several years to achieve arguably good practice. With support from a professional community of learners, however, this time span can be reduced.

This need for support, however, is not limited to classroom practitioners. I have recently assumed a position as a teacher educator, and have been assigned the task of teaching the administration and supervision class to child development and child care seniors. The question I now raise for myself is "If I were once again a program director, would I hire my own graduates?" My challenge, of course, is to construct the course so that the answer is yes. These essays, however, have reinforced my appreciation for the fact that I, as a teacher educator, cannot accomplish this task independently.

I concur with Kramer's conclusions that teachers do not have all the answers, but neither do teacher educators. My students and I need support, too, especially from thoughtful, caring practitioners such as these essayists.

REFERENCES

Jones, E. (Ed.). (1993). *Growing teachers: Partnerships in staff development.* Washington, DC: National Association for the Education of Young Children.

Whitebook, M., Howes, C., & Phillips, D. (1989) *Who cares: Child care teachers and the quality of child care in America.* Executive summary of the National Child Care Staffing Study. Oakland, CA: Child Care Employee Project.

Listening to Teachers to Improve the Profession

Thomas Schultz

The four essays in this section offer convincing evidence that practicing teachers can contribute to the academic and political debate about the preparation of early childhood professionals. These 6 women who work with children every day have rich ideas and strong convictions about what it takes to do their jobs well. In the past, professors, officials in state departments of education, and legislators have had the primary responsibility for decisions about teacher education, licensure and certification, and professional development. And it has been their ideas that have dominated debates about what makes a good teacher, how to design training programs, and how to assess candidates for the profession. This set of essays suggests the merit of listening more to what teachers have to say on these questions. This volume represents part of a larger campaign to upgrade the status of practicing teachers—a campaign in which one minor tactic is granting teachers the dominant share of pages in a book published by a prestigious academic press.

These essayists bring a new tone and new ideas to discussion of accomplished teaching and the challenges of professional development. In contrast to more academic authors who pepper their writing with footnotes, these essayists are inclined to tell us stories from their work in classrooms to illustrate their arguments. This inclination for using narrative examples gives their writing special credibility and power.

Thus, giving "air time" to teachers is more than a sentimental or symbolic activity. It offers potential to change the nature of our conversation about important issues. I'll remember for a long time what Douglas did with the water pump while Jenny Kramer watched, what happened when Janet Albarado let her students take paperback books home for the first time, and what Georgann Olson's student Vivian looked like when she started kindergarten.

The essayists also bring a special flavor to thinking about teaching by their stress on the personal attributes of successful teachers. Rowe and colleagues mention a commitment to children, dependability, intuitiveness, motivation and energy, a positive attitude, a sense of humor, and imagination; Kramer lists ability to grow, energy, a sense of humor, ability to take risks, a willingness to "mess around," flexibility, a sense of wonder, and a love of teaching; Olson adds joy, trust, flexibility, humor, curiosity, integrity, and sensitivity; and Albarado emphasizes the ability to share authority with students and risk taking. These qualities also dominate over questions of methodology and content expertise in my own experiences as a parent. I have found the teachers whom my children, my wife, and I value most highly are memorable for their personality, style, energy level, and emotional commitment rather than for where they fall on a continuum of developmentally appropriate to inappropriate techniques. These qualities also resonate strongly in journalistic portraits of great teaching, such as accounts of Jaime Escalante, or Tracy Kidder's (1989) powerful narrative about Christine Zajac's classroom in Holyoke, Massachusetts.

However, these phrases rarely turn up when academic and policy experts talk and write about teaching. Emphasizing these qualities creates complications for organized efforts to improve the status and effectiveness of teachers. They seem subjective, difficult to assess, and hard to foster in preparation programs. They seem to attach to individuals as matters of temperament or life experience rather than as installable modules of knowledge and technical skill. They raise worries of defining teaching as a cult of personality or as a test of emotional commitment akin to parenting rather than a craft deeply informed by technical knowledge and expressed in executive decision making and clinical judgment. However, in my view, our dialogue about improving teaching needs to follow the lead of these authors and struggle with the complications of including these more "subjective" aspects of great teaching in our policy decisions and preparation programs. Beyond these general points of appreciation, I was struck by one substantive problem in this set of essays, as well as several strategic complications in seeking to use these ideas to drive large-scale improvements in early childhood teaching.

PROFESSIONALISM AND THE PARENT CONNECTION

Early childhood education provides a bridge for children between the intimate environment of their homes and the larger world of formal schooling. The relationships between early childhood teachers and parents are crucial because young children are highly dependent on their families and because supportive, active parents can help children continue to learn and grow in classroom settings. In that light, it was disturbing to note the declining attention paid to the issue of parent involvement across the four essays. Rowe and colleagues, who work with infants and toddlers, devote about three pages of their text to the importance of respecting parents and to the priority of effective communication with the home. Kramer, who works with preschool-aged children, expends two paragraphs on knowing the community and urging teacher preparation programs to include attention to parent involvement. However, by the time we reach early childhood teachers at the kindergarten and primary grade levels, Olson grants us only one paragraph on the importance of communication with parents, and Albarado mentions that she required parents to sign letters agreeing to pay for any books which their child lost or damaged as part of an at-home reading program.

Unfortunately, this pattern of declining attention to working with parents as children grow up is a reality in many communities. One explanation for this problem is structural differences between programs for children younger than 5 years and the public schools. Preschool care and education programs are most often sponsored by community-based organizations where parents are the customers who pay for the services and staff salaries and sometimes serve as members of governing boards for agencies. Programs often have parents bring their children to and from the classroom, providing a stream of daily opportunities for communication and interaction. Many centers, such as parent cooperatives and those operated by Head Start, depend on parent volunteers in classrooms to supplement the work of teachers. By contrast, teachers of kindergarten and primary-grade children work in schools where attendance is mandatory and funding is provided by local, state, and federal tax revenues, thus eroding the influence of parents as consumers. Policies, budgets, and personnel decisions are made by local boards of education and central office administrators rather than at the school site where parent input could be solicited. Teachers of young children in public schools also contend with mandated curricula, testing requirements, and other polices that intrude on their discretion and compete for their attention, leaving less time and energy for working with parents. And the culture of many public schools relegates parent volunteers to fund raising and helping in the library or the office rather than as an active presence in classrooms.

However, I also worry that our efforts to upgrade the status, morale, knowledge and skills of teachers may inadvertently work to erode support for parent involvement. As teachers learn more about the intricacies of child observation—great ideas from Vygotsky or Paley and the glories of Reggio Emilia—it is easy to begin to feel superior to "untrained" parents. There is a seductive fascination to discussing our growing knowledge of how young children build understanding and skills in mathematics, writing, and other subjects and in appreciating the multiple roles, varied strategies, and complex decisions exhibited by highly accomplished teachers. However, as we work to enhance the profession of teaching we need to keep parents in the picture. For example, a strong consensus favoring "developmentally appropriate practice" permeates these essays. However, it is important to recognize that many parents may not understand or agree with these values and practices. Part of the ongoing work of the early childhood community is to learn how to explain and illustrate these ideas to parents in very different types of communities, and to listen, learn, and respond to parents' views and beliefs on these issues. Janet Albarado speaks eloquently about the need to share authority with her students and to build a classroom community in which children have true ownership. My caution is that teachers remember to include parents in this process.

DILEMMAS OF STRATEGY:
IMPROVING A "TRIFURCATED" PROFESSION

Working in an organization that represents state boards of education, I tend to be attuned to the problem of translating good ideas into action on a broad scale. These essays offer thoughtful and inspiring ideas about the qualities of effective early childhood teachers. This material has implications for a wide range of policies and institutions, from the certification of people entering early childhood teaching to the design of teacher preparation programs to strategies for ongoing professional development efforts. The essayists offer many recommendations to improve teacher education, ranging from more field experiences with young children, shifting away from a dominance of lecture methods for instruction, extending connections between teacher education faculty and students during the first years of work experience, and creating new partnerships between higher education and early childhood programs. These ideas are an ambitious menu for changing core aspects of higher education programs. However, advocacy to upgrade the early childhood profession must also contend with two unique and interlocked challenges: setting standards for a highly stratified work force and influencing three separate policy systems that govern early childhood programs and institutions.

IMPROVING A STRATIFIED PROFESSION

Teachers of young children (birth to age 8) work in public schools, Head Start programs, and a wide array of independent preschool and child care operations. Kindergarten and primary grade teachers invariably have bachelor of arts (BA) degrees, although their training varies widely in terms of the quantity and quality of courses and experiences specific to early childhood development. By contrast, the dominant credential among Head Start teachers is that of the Child Development Associate (CDA), a national certificate system considered to be equivalent to 1 year of higher education course work. In the arena of child care, many staff enter the field with no prior training or experience and the use of the CDA credential is less common than in Head Start programs. These different profiles of credentials also reflect different levels of compensation, fringe benefits, and patterns of staff turnover, with both child care and Head Start programs reporting serious difficulties in retaining staff.

The problem is how to create a set of standards and a training and development system for a trifurcated profession. Advocates for young children want to see every child educated by knowledgeable and capable teachers, regardless of the location of the program. However, it is hard to move towards consistency when teachers in different types of programs have such different levels of training and education. Can we translate Kramer's 16 characteristics of effective teachers, Olson's 5 areas of knowledge and skills, and Rowe and colleagues' 7 competencies into equivalent BA-level preparation programs for the public schools, a CDA strategy for Head Start, and a largely inservice training strategy for teachers who work in child care?

INFLUENCING MULTIPLE POLICY SYSTEMS

Staff seeking employment in public schools are governed by teacher certification standards established by 50 state departments of education. Qualifications for teaching staff in Head Start programs are set at the national level through performance standards that govern all programs. In the child care sector, staff qualifications are established through licensing standards for individual centers, generally promulgated by state offices of social services.

There are problems with present policies in each system. While state teacher certification systems require training at the BA level, they vary in their recognition of early childhood as a distinctive area for training and certification. For example, almost one-third of the states do not have a teacher certificate covering children younger than kindergarten age (Morgan et al., 1993). In terms of Head Start, the current standards mandate that the lead teacher in every classroom must have earned the CDA credential by 1994. Challenges for Head Start include addressing incentives and support for training beyond the CDA level and gearing up to recruit and train new staff in view of plans for rapid and substantial expansion of Head Start services. And problems abound in the child care policy sector. First, a recent report from the Children's Defense Fund estimates that 43% of all children in out-of-home child care are served in programs that are exempt from any standards (Adams, 1990). Second, 36 of the 50 states require no prior training for teachers in child care centers (Morgan et al., 1993). Third, resources for staff training and compensation are inadequate; so there are few incentives for staff to seek additional education and limited offerings of training geared to the needs and schedules of teachers who are already working with young children and families.

Each of these policy systems also has particular features that influence responses to advocacy. For example, decisions on the education and certification of early childhood teachers in public schools are influenced by other reform movements directed towards the entire elementary and secondary teaching work force. Furthermore, proposals to create a separate early childhood credential for pre-kindergarten through primary-grade practice may collide with efforts of middle-school advocates to create separate training programs for teachers of 6th- to 8th-grade students. Similarly, Head Start is a unique policy system because the federal government manages the allocation of nearly $60 million in training and technical assistance services for program staff and managers. If Head Start changes policy on staff qualifications or training, the federal government must be willing and able to pay for and manage direct implementation of improvements. Finally, efforts to influence standards and training for child care face special difficulties because of limited resources and political resistance to government regulation of this function.

This overview of the policy landscape suggests that the voices of teachers need to be amplified and orchestrated if their insights about effective practice are to benefit their colleagues and all of America's young children.

REFERENCES

Adams, G. (1990). *Who knows how safe?* Washington, DC: The Children's Defense Fund.
Kidder, T. (1989). *Among schoolchildren.* Boston: Houghton Mifflin.
Morgan, G., Azer, S., Costley, J., Genser, A., Goodman, I., Lombardi, J., & McGimsey, B. (1993). *Making a career of it: The state of the states report on career development in early care and education.* Boston: Wheelock College.

PART II

What Is Needed to Move Beyond an Initial Level of Competence as an Early Childhood Teacher?

CHAPTER 5

Moving Beyond an Initial Level of Competence as an Infant Teacher

Claire E. Hamilton

The purpose of this essay is to explore how an infant early childhood teacher moves beyond an initial level of competence. Infant teachers generally have responsibility for children under 3 years; in some programs that may mean caring for infants as young as 6 weeks and, in others, to as old as 2 ½ to 3 years.

More change occurs in infancy than in any other developmental period. Consequently, teachers of these very young children face a unique set of challenges, although the issues they face in developing their competence may be more similar to than different from those faced by teachers of older children.

While it is possible to write about the competencies of teachers at various levels of teaching responsibilities, ranging from aides to head teachers, I am going to focus on the role of head teacher, which, for the purposes of this essay, is defined as someone who has overall responsibility for a given classroom. Infant teachers, as all early childhood teachers, may have a wide range of formal educational backgrounds, ranging from child development courses at the high-school level, vocational training, and certification programs such as the Child Development Associate (CDA) credential, to associate and university degrees. Competent teaching, of course, can occur at any of these levels of formal education; specialized training at the college level, however, appears to be associated with more appropriate infant–teacher interactions (Whitebrook, Howes, & Phillips, 1989).

WHERE DO WE START?

In writing this essay, I draw on my experiences as an infant and toddler teacher. I graduated from a 4-year university with a degree in early childhood education. My formal education included the fundamentals of preschool and early elementary

75

education, elective courses in psychology and human development, and the general education requirements of a 4-year university. In addition, I also had extensive practicum experience and supervised student teaching in a campus nursery school, half-day infant and toddler programs, and a half-day university preschool.

There was a strong emphasis on courses in early education and child development in my teacher preparation program, but less direct formal instruction in the specific educational practices applicable to infants and toddlers. There was, however, a high level of direct supervised experience with children. The bulk of my practicum experiences, though, occurred in part-time, heavily staffed "model" programs. The question then arises, what happens when a beginning teacher with those skills hits the "real" world of child care?

WHAT IS COMPETENT INFANT AND TODDLER TEACHING?

There are many aspects of teaching infants and toddlers that are directly tied to the developmental capabilities of these very young children. Infants are totally dependent upon adults for their care. They have limited mobility; they are unable to tell us with words exactly how or what they are feeling or need; and they have not yet mastered even basic self-help skills, such as feeding themselves.

As infants grow, they acquire the skills needed to sit up, to creep and crawl, and finally to run. They gradually incorporate words and language and even symbolic thought into their interactions. They move from a world that is largely centered on their own bodies and meeting their direct physical needs into a world of objects, adults, and peers. As teachers, we need to provide for the individual physical and emotional needs of each child in our care. How we meet these needs in large part determines the nature of the relationship we form with each baby (Ainsworth, Blehar, Waters, & Wall, 1978; Honig, 1985). The formation of secure, trusting relationships with adults is probably the primary developmental task of infancy (Sroufe & Waters, 1977).

Infants and young toddlers are particularly vulnerable from a health and safety perspective and need special protection (Kendrick, Kaufman, & Messenger, 1991). Their teachers must have a broad knowledge and concern for those areas as well as general knowledge of child development. For example, the *Guidelines for Developmentally Appropriate Practices* (DAP) (Bredekamp, 1987) includes a specific section for both infants and toddlers on health, safety, and nutrition—a section omitted in discussion of practices for older children.

In any group situation, the range of children's abilities may be as wide as the range of individual children over the course of the year. While our program must provide individualized care, this care is provided within the context of a group of children. Again, if we look at DAP, we see that appropriate practices for infants are related to the provision of individualized care. There is no discussion of curriculum or how the care of a group may differ from the care of individual children. Thus, our role as infant and toddler teachers is less well defined than the roles of preschool or elementary teachers.

Finally, and no less important, the link between family and child care may be especially critical in the very early years. Infants and toddlers are not able to directly express their needs verbally; so communication between teachers and parents about a child's day and how the child is developing is critical.

In general, the areas of competence that infant and toddler teachers must achieve are those shared by all teachers in early childhood education: direct interaction with children, the details of running a program,(the nuts and bolts) supervising and training staff, working with parents, interacting with other professionals, organizing the day and the year of our program, formulating program goals, and defining our own professional growth. These skills probably are fundamental to all early childhood teachers. However, the way in which teacher competency in these areas is assessed, and the scope of the specific areas of concern, are defined by the particular age group.

INFANT–TEACHER INTERACTION

Infant teachers also share with other teachers a need to respond positively and sensitively to children in their care, model language effectively, help children interact with peers, and discipline in ways that teach rather than punish. Yet, the ways that infant and toddler teachers do this differs from other teachers because of the developmental needs of young infants and toddlers. Infants and toddlers are not very good at telling us what is bothering them or what they need. Consequently, we must observe their nonverbal cues and learn to anticipate when an infant or toddler is beginning to get tired, hungry, or simply bored.

Furthermore, our interactions with infants and toddlers are much more physical than those with older children. Infants need lots of cuddling and carrying; toddlers need special times on teachers' laps, and hugs when they're distressed. DAP provides sound guidelines for these behaviors, and I believe that head teachers have developed skills for interacting positively with children. What may not have developed is a way to balance our own responsibilities for managing the whole classroom with a continued need to model and engage in individual, positive interactions with children.

Much of what we do as infant teachers is routine: physical caregiving tasks that are never ending. As new teachers, we may certainly understand that routine caregiving tasks should be special times for an infant and her caregiver. However, the reality of maintaining these interactions in the face of changing 15 to 20 dirty diapers each day, constantly wiping noses, and spoon feeding yet another bowl of mashed banana, may prove initially overwhelming. Concern for engaging in such positive interactions may become muted as we assume the responsibility for making sure that *all* diapers are changed and *all* noses are wiped, that overall the classroom is kept clean and organized, and that proper record keeping is maintained. We may, for a time, lose sight of the importance of our individual interactions with children when we are faced with the responsibility for the classroom as a whole.

The day-to-day interaction with children is what first draws many of us to working with infants and toddlers, but as we become experienced teachers with increased responsibilities, we tend to spend less time directly interacting with children and more time managing and supervising the group. In these circumstances, we need to step back from our routine and make sure that we who are the most experienced teachers spend time with individual children. Our primary function as head teachers is to provide individualized care and attention. Infants and toddlers need that special time; in addition, our interactions with children may serve as the model for other adults in the classroom.

STAFF SUPERVISION

As we begin to move beyond an initial level of competence, many of us become increasingly aware of and responsible for other adults working in the program. Ensuring that all the infants and toddlers in our care experience good care occurs not only through our direct interactions with children, but through our supervising the interactions of others and managing the classroom.

In these circumstances, we need to serve as models for appropriate behavior; we need to be clear in our expectations of what we consider to be appropriate behavior, and we need to provide explanations as to why particular behaviors are acceptable and others are not. We draw on our own understanding of infant development and our program goals to communicate the importance of various practices to other teachers.

We must be aware, though, of the diversity in teaching experience, educational background, and level of commitment among the adults in our classroom. Some adults may be high-school volunteers, others may be student teachers preparing for a career in early childhood education, others may be experienced teachers, and still others may be parents. In helping adults gain not only an understanding of acceptable practices, but also an understanding of why such practices are important, head teachers with supervisory responsibility have to adjust the level of information they present to the particular adults with whom they work.

We need to learn, however, that different teaching styles may be equally effective. One of my early mistakes as a supervisor was an attempt to mold all adults into my style of teaching. It was only through experience, plus advice from my fellow teachers, that I began to understand that there are many ways to be a competent teacher.

One of the teachers in my toddler program had experience as a Montessori teacher, for example. Her approach to curriculum and her interactional style with children was quite different from mine. Her focus seemed more on materials and children's use of materials. Initially, I was resistant to many of her ideas for activities and to her style of teaching, but after working together for a year, I not only appreciated her style, I found that I had much to learn from it.

We may wish that all of the adults we work with were perfect teachers, but few are, including ourselves. In supervising teachers, I found that the classroom operated more smoothly when I was able to appreciate the capabilities of teachers and find ways for them to do what they did best. One of my constant battles occurred over playground supervision. I found myself always counting heads and being exasperated with those teachers who always seemed to be off with 1 or 2 children, oblivious to the other 9 or 10 children. It took a long while for me to realize that I could balance children's needs for one-to-one time with a teacher and my need for group supervision by simply ensuring that at least one "head counter" was on the playground.

WORKING WITH PARENTS

Parents of infants and toddlers, perhaps more so than parents of any other age group, are presented with conflicts about enrolling their very young children in center-based care. They cannot ask their children how things are going. Their only direct link with their children's child care experience is the information they receive from the teachers. In addition to this uncertainty about their child's daily experience, parents are confronted with the ongoing controversy about infant care. This controversy has been a major focus of developmental psychology for the past 5 years (Belsky, 1988; Clarke-Stewart, 1988). While most psychologists have moved away from the extreme question of "Is child care bad for infants?" to the more moderate question of "How does the quality of child care influence infants' development?" the popular press continues to focus on the possibly negative outcomes for infants enrolled in child care (Wingert & Kantrowitz, 1990).

Parents with children in infant and toddler classrooms may themselves be questioning the wisdom of leaving their 6-week-old infant with strangers. As a result, even when parents become comfortable with the center and their child's teachers, they may still continually have to explain to relatives and friends how they can "leave" their infants in a child care center. Helping parents deal with these issues is a primary teacher responsibility. Competence in this domain lies in establishing, implementing, and evaluating mechanisms for meeting parent needs and in assessing our own attitudes towards parents.

As beginning teachers, we are probably aware of the need for parent communication. It is a cornerstone of DAP. It frequently is addressed in articles in *Young Children* and it is likely to have been a topic in our training. Given that we are aware of the importance of parent communication, I think a common beginning strategy is to find one way that seems to work and apply it to all situations. Moving beyond an initial level of competence, however, means developing new strategies and flexibility in how they are implemented.

Parent–staff communication is a two-way street. We need to get information from parents, on both a daily and long-term basis, and we need to share information with parents. We do this within the constraints of our own program and schedule. We may rarely see parents at pick-up and drop-off times because we are scheduled to work during midday hours. Even if we are present, arrivals and departures may be so busy and hectic for teachers, parents, and children that talking with parents is not feasible. In addition, scheduling parent–teacher conferences during school hours may be difficult for parents and scheduling times after-hours may conflict with our own personal lives.

When I first began teaching I dealt with parent–staff communication by setting up a daily record-keeping system. When parents dropped off their children, they provided some basic information on how the child slept the previous night, whether the child had eaten in the morning, and generally how the child was doing. During the day, staff recorded how much and when the children ate, diapering information, and, hopefully, when there was time, some little anecdote about the child's day.

This system is not unusual, and, in fact, is well documented in books and articles describing infant and toddler care (Leavitt & Eheart, 1985; O'Brien, Porterfield, Herbert-Jackson, & Risley, 1979), but it does not necessarily meet the individual needs of parents. This became more apparent to me as I worked with parents of different language and cultural backgrounds, as well as with parents of varied literacy skills. This insight does not mean that I would throw out written record-keeping systems; it only means that we need to be aware of how the systems we establish actually meet the needs of all the parents in our program—not just our expectations or our needs.

The second area of competence in dealing with parents is attitudinal. The early childhood education literature is filled with the notion that parents and teachers are partners in children's development. Research suggests that family characteristics may be a more important determinant of children's development than their actual child care experience (for a review, see Howes & Hamilton, 1993). Part of our growth as teachers, therefore, involves examining how we feel about being partners with parents and working to establish program goals that are consistent with our attitudes.

For instance, the CDA credential process uses parents as evaluators. Yet, the use of nonprofessional parent evaluators has been challenged (Berk & Berson, 1981). If we feel that parents are partners in their children's child care, how do we draw the boundaries between ourselves, professional caregivers, and parents, who are the foremost figures in their children's lives?

Competence does not mean having one set answer to this or any other issue, but it does mean considering all that the issue entails. Do we feel that parents should evaluate us and, if we do, how should this occur? Do we feel that parents should have input into curriculum matters? If so, again, how should this occur? If we feel that our mission is to share information with parents and to gain information from them about their concerns and knowledge of their own children, how do we do it? In thinking about how we address parent–teacher interactions, we need to consider not only the mechanics of how we do it but the consistency of our beliefs and practices.

NUTS AND BOLTS

Nuts and bolts refers to basic practical knowledge that new teachers may not fully grasp. The first day that I began teaching, I walked into a child care center that was in total disarray. In approximately 2 weeks, a brand new toddler program would start. The first question my director asked, as he waved a saw in the air, was "What should be the height of chairs for toddlers?"

This was child care, and, as usual, money was short; so toddler chairs were being fashioned by sawing off the legs of surplus preschool chairs, an inelegant but certainly affordable and practical solution. I, who had a degree in early childhood education, 2 years of supervised teaching, and specialized courses in infant and child development, did not have the slightest idea how to answer his question.

This is practical knowledge and gaining a firm grasp of it can take appreciable amounts of time. Competent teachers have all sorts of bits of information at their fingertips that they have learned through experience. This practical knowledge base is wide ranging but essential. We gain this knowledge through experimentation and by learning from other teachers. It includes the details of which equipment works best, which tippy cups result in fewest spills, what kinds of stuffed animals are likely to wash well and not lose their eyes, and which baby gates are actually toddler-proof but not adult-proof. It also includes where to get materials and information: Are Fisher Price people cheaper at Toys R Us or in the educational toy catalogue? Is there a toy lending library? What's the best source for recycled paper? How do I find out which plants on the playground are poisonous? This is not the sort of knowledge that I encountered in college nor was a grasp of these details one of my responsibilities as a student teacher. But to move beyond initial competence, we need to acquire such knowledge so we have time and energy for other aspects of teaching.

ORGANIZING THE DAY AND YEAR

The overall management of a child care classroom may be mundane. When I began my teaching career, I assumed that it would take relatively little thought or attention. All I needed to do was make a schedule. For the first year or so of teaching, however, the details can consume enormous amounts of time. The many guides to organizing the day for infants and toddlers (e.g., Leavitt & Eheart, 1985; O'Brien, Porterfield, Herbert-Jackson, & Risley, 1979) provide clear examples of what a day may look like and how we can manage the classroom and establish systems to ensure that chairs and tables are washed before and after every mealtime, toys are regularly picked up and washed after use, and diapering and toileting is accomplished at regular intervals.

In working with infants and toddlers, much of what we do is caretaking, much of which has to be done at high levels of cleanliness. Who keeps track of all the toys mouthed by infants? How do these toys get washed? Who checks to make sure we have enough diapers on hand for the next day? What about wipes? These are the basic ongoing activities that must be organized and routinized. However, at the same time that we struggle to organize the day and the staff to meet caretaking needs, we also need to structure the day around individual children in our programs.

We know from DAP that infants need individualized schedules for napping, diapering, eating, play times, and rest times. We know that toddlers need a mix of group time and individual time and a flexible schedule that meets their individual needs. We also know from experience that toddlers enjoy doing the same thing day in and day out and that these routines help them and us through transitions. In addition, the staff schedule affects our day, as do parent arrival and departure times (especially if there are a lot of half-time children), and the operating schedule of the center.

All of these concerns have an effect on how we schedule our day. Before I started teaching, my student teaching experiences had been in university laboratory schools. None of these programs were full day; some of them were not even full week. They also tended to have an abundance of staff people, which meant that individualized care could be done in a somewhat ad hoc fashion. The availability of sufficient staff made us less dependent on staff schedules.

The demands of a full-time program with more limited staff require a different approach. Experienced infant and toddler teachers are comfortable taking an approach that allows them to set a rhythm, rather than a rigid schedule for the day. Structuring a program like this can be challenging, though, because young infants, in particular, still lack consistent biological schedules. And while it may be expected, for instance, that older toddlers will nap after lunch, provisions still need to be made for the not unusual need for morning naps. Beginning teachers tend to change reactively according to what occurs during the day or may stick so rigidly to a schedule that individual children's needs are not met. Experienced or more competent teachers, on the other hand, are usually better able to plan for change and to incorporate the unexpected into a schedule, qualities which may be the hallmark of a good program.

THE YEAR AND BEYOND

Planning and scheduling go beyond the daily rhythms of the classroom, however, and extend to the entire year and beyond. For example, changes in seasons influence our basic routines. Winter often means long periods of being indoors, and when it warms up enough for outdoor play, the time for dressing and undressing can exceed the time actually spent outside. Summer may also mean changes in outdoor playtimes, and usually implies more unpredictable schedules as parents and staff take vacations. Summer may also mean, as it did in my program, a change in the characteristics of the staff because of youth hiring programs.

Beginnings and ends of the year also are periods of transitions as children, and perhaps teachers as well, change classrooms. Consideration needs to be given to how the needs of children will change over the year and how the entry of new children will be handled. Teachers learn to plan not only for the day but for the long term, and teacher experience over the long term is, in many ways, the only way that this can be accomplished. Competency is this long-term planning means anticipating these transitions and accounting for them. Beginning teachers may look around their classroom and realize that "things aren't quite right"; experienced teachers, on the other hand, begin to plan for change.

Part of this ability relies on scheduling skills, but a larger part of teacher growth in this regard depends on developing a notion of program goals. What is it we want to happen in our classroom? Not just during this art activity or at meal times, not just today, and not only next week, but what are the overall goals driving our program?

DEVELOPING PROGRAM GOALS

Program goals are complex and are driven in large part by our work site. Program goals are developed through integrating our theoretical knowledge of child development and learning with practical knowledge.

Infants and toddlers often are made short shrift of in discussions of curriculum or educational goals. Yet, as teachers, we need to come to some understanding and rationale for what we are doing besides simply meeting the developmental needs of children. Meeting the developmental needs of children may be a goal, but it doesn't tell us how to accomplish it, evaluate its accomplishment, or how teachers fit in. Defining our goals as teachers and the goals of our program is the only way that we can have a coherent program. Goals structure the meaning of our program and how we communicate that meaning to others, including parents, staff, or other professionals.

There are general goals for early childhood education, but there are differing philosophies of education and educational theory. Part of our developing competence relates to our integration and evaluation of these theories, based not only on our own continued practical experience but also on our continued examination of theory. The presence of coherent program goals moves us beyond reacting toward thoughtful planning for ourselves and the children in our care. Teachers who have transcended an initial level of competence should have clearly articulated goals for themselves and their program and be able to implement those goals into daily classroom practices.

WORKING WITH OTHER PROFESSIONALS

Finally, I think that teachers who have moved beyond an initial level of competence are those who have learned to work with other teachers in their classroom and center, other professionals, and their community. Learning from other teachers and from people who work with children and families at different levels and in organizations, such as social services agencies, child care resource and referral offices, or political advocacy groups can help us develop ideas about teaching and provide alternative ways of approaching similar problems and issues.

Often, this is reflected in our decisions to join professional organizations, such as the National Association for the Education of Young Children, attend regional or national conferences, or work with local agencies and boards. The level or formality of our professional contacts is less important than their frequent occurrence. Often, it was the Friday afternoon social hour that provided me a forum for sharing and developing ideas with other teachers. Interactions with other professionals can help us formulate our conception of professional growth and development.

DEFINING OUR OWN PROFESSIONAL GROWTH

While some professions have a clearly structured career or professional ladder, this is not the case in early childhood care and education. Not all assistant teachers want to be head teachers; not all teachers want to be directors or administrators; not all teachers want to work as early childhood advocates or parent educators or teacher trainers. Teachers may also choose to leave classroom teaching altogether and address issues of teaching from a research or instructional perspective as college professors. All of these avenues are possible and developing teachers need to define career goals.

It is difficult, though, to define career goals for ourselves if we want to remain classroom teachers. When I was a classroom teacher, I chose to extend my focus by becoming involved with community issues related to child care. I served as a consultant for a local Montessori school through which I learned much about the Montessori philosophy and the difficulties of budgeting a center. I worked with other local and state child care workers on issues of pay equity. I taught workshops for parents and family day care providers through the local child care resource and referral agency. I talked with other teachers and learned what they were doing and what worked for them. I spoke with parents and gained a better understanding of some of their concerns. I worked with non-child care people and struggled to communicate the needs and concerns of child care teachers. There are many aspects to teaching that we can pursue in our own development, but unlike many other careers, child care teachers need to define a professional path for themselves. For me, a career in early childhood education does not mean adopting a hierarchical career path structure. Rather, it means evaluating the possibilities we want to pursue.

HOW DO WE GET THERE?

How do teachers grow in competence? In many ways, the answer resides in time and experience; we need time to learn skills and explore different ways of doing things. We need an opportunity to assume the responsibilities that accompany the role of head teacher, and we need to be able to make mistakes. Time and experience is insufficient, though, because we also need to evaluate what we are doing, and why we are doing it. I think the greatest asset in teaching is not the particular skills or level of formal education but an attitude that education is for the children in our care *and* ourselves. While experience may provide us with the tricks of the trade and basic know-how, recognition that we, too, are learners encourages us to question what we are doing, evaluate it, and be open to changes.

My reflective approach to teaching came, in large part, from my supervised undergraduate teaching experiences. My supervisors emphasized self-evaluation; I developed an attitude that competent teachers needed to learn as much from their teaching as children needed to learn from their teachers. I feel that this aspect of my formal preparation was essential to my growth as an early childhood educator.

Working with infants and toddlers can be stressful. It can drive a person crazy to spend a rainy day with 10 fretful and crying infants but if we take the time to reflect on what we are doing, we can once again appreciate why we became infant teachers in the first place.

I chose to work with infants and toddlers because I think this age group is the most exciting. Everything is new to an infant, and each infant approaches the world just a little bit differently. I became an infant teacher because of the satisfaction I receive from watching infants learn about their environment and the challenge I experience in finding ways to support their exploration.

I also appreciated the diversity of roles embedded in my teaching. Infant teachers truly care for the whole child. We are involved with physical caregiving and a multitude of health issues; we provide opportunities for learning through structuring the environment; and we maintain close contacts with parents.

The longer I worked in child care with infants, the more interested I became in exploring issues about what makes good group care and how infants in child care develop relationships with their peers and teachers. When I looked at what was being written about these issues, I had a strong sense that the questions being asked were not those being asked by teachers; the research seemed removed from the real world of child care. I entered graduate school so I could develop the skills to examine critically the issues that came out of my experiences as a teacher. I now have entered the research arena, and I am trying to bring together what I learned as an infant teacher with the theoretical knowledge I have acquired in my graduate studies. I hope that some day my research will contribute to the field of infant child care.

REFERENCES

Ainsworth, M., Blehar, M., Waters, E., & Wall, S. (1978). *Patterns of attachment.* Hillsdale, NJ: Lawrence Erlbaum Associates.

Belsky, J. (1988). The "effects" of infant day care reconsidered. *Early Childhood Research Quarterly, 3*(3), 235–272.

Berk, L. E., & Berson, M. P. (1981). A review of the Child Development Associate Credential. *Child Care Quarterly,* 10, 9–42.

Bredekamp, S. (Ed.) (1987). *Developmentally appropriate practice in early childhood programs serving children from birth through age 8.* Washington, DC: National Association for the Education of Young Children.

Clarke-Stewart, K. A. (1988). "The 'effects' of infant day care reconsidered" reconsidered. *Early Childhood Research Quarterly, 3*(3), 293–318.

Honig, A. S. (1985). High quality infant/toddler care: Issues and dilemmas. *Young Children, 41*(1), 40–46.

Howes, C., & Hamilton, C. E. (1993). Child care for young children. In B. Spodek (Ed.), *Handbook of research on the education of young children.* New York: Macmillan.

Kendrick, A. S., Kaufman, R., & Messenger, K. P. (Eds.) (1991). *Healthy young children? A manual for programs (2nd ed.).* Washington, DC: National Association for the Education of Young Children.

Leavitt, R. L., & Eheart, B. K. (1985). *Toddler day care: A guide to responsive caregiving.* Lexington, MA: Lexington.

O'Brien, M., Porterfield, J., Herbert-Jackson, E., & Risley, T. R. (1979). *The toddler center? A practical guide to day care for one- and two-year-olds.* Baltimore, MD: University Park Press.

Sroufe, L. A., & Waters, E. (1977). Attachment as an organizational construct. *Child Development,* 48, 1184–1199.

Whitebrook, M., Howes, C., & Phillips, D. (1989). *Who cares? Child care teachers and the quality of care in America.* Final Report of the National Child Care Staffing Study. Child Care Employee Project, Oakland California.

Wingert, P., & Kantrowitz, B. (1990, Winter/Spring). The day care generation. *Newsweek,* 86–92.

CHAPTER **6**

Preparing Early Childhood Teachers for Careers in Learning

Marion VanArsdell

This question I've been invited to address— "What is needed to move beyond an initial level of competence as an early childhood educator?"—seems to me like a riddle from *Alice in Wonderland*. I have been asked to share ideas regarding essential understandings needed to become a skillful, creative, and accomplished teacher of young children based on my 15 years' experience as the teaching director of a child care center, a Head Start director, and now the teacher of an integrated preschool within a public school system. I am tempted to answer "time and many children," but, of course, it's not that simple.

The question needs to be answered in two stages. First, I need to identify what is critical to learn during our teacher education, to prepare us as teachers of young children. Second, I need to define the experiences and supports that enable us to continue to grow as teachers.

BUILDING THE FOUNDATION: PREPARING EARLY CHILDHOOD TEACHERS

UNDERSTANDING CHILD DEVELOPMENT

Because our formal preparation as teachers must provide us with a foundation solid enough to support years of growth and changes in our careers, I believe it needs to begin with a comprehensive grounding in child development. Looking back at my graduate studies in early childhood education, I now realize it emphasized methods courses at the expense of more indepth study of how young children learn.

My student teaching assignment, which was at the end of the program, was in a large, open-classroom kindergarten in an inner-city magnet school. The classroom was bright and sunny, with clean carpet covering the floor. There were interest centers throughout the classroom; shelves contained inviting materials, and children had numerous opportunities to make choices. I remember that my supervising teacher dressed quite elegantly, often coming to school in floor length wool skirts with matching sweaters. It was in many ways a very appealing and "state of the art" kindergarten classroom. However, something fundamental was missing; the clean carpet and teacher's attire should have alerted me. If I had been taught how young children learn, I would have realized that children who are actively engaged in learning will endanger clean carpets and elegant outfits!

Our first task as teachers—or future teachers—of young children is to understand the developmental tasks that will consume their time and energy during the preschool years. I am convinced that a solid understanding of child development is the critical component of teacher preparation because it can inform all our decisions regarding how to design and implement a program that supports children's growth and development. It is not enough to know *what* to do with young children; we need also to understand *why* we do what we do. Developing my understandings in this area has anchored my own commitment to continued learning.

As early childhood teachers, we need to rely on a dynamic understanding of the psychological issues of early childhood. Nothing is more central to our teaching, because, time and again, we will see children playing out the dramas of early social–emotional development. It happens every day as young children leave their parents to stay in this new place and become increasingly separate, independent, and autonomous; or it happens in the dramatic play area where children's fears and struggles to feel powerful are acted out with a variety of plots and a changing cast of characters.

In our preschool, for example, the children often play a game that centers on the theme of the "lost baby." The child who plays the role of the baby is led or wheeled somewhere in the room away from the house area. Left there, the baby cries until a parent, big brother or sister, or "cop" responds, rescues the baby and brings him or her safely back to the house. The children play this scenario over and over again, varying the specifics but holding to the central theme, an incredibly powerful one for young children who daily are being left at school for the first time and must trust that someone always will come back for them.

For young children who are always being guided by parents and teachers along the path of becoming more "civilized," there is a great deal of emotional energy that goes into their play. Our formal preparation as teachers needs to equip us with an understanding of social–emotional development that is dynamic enough to help us keep up with the dramas being played out around us every day. And similar conclusions apply to the importance of teacher knowledge of children's development in the areas of language, cognition, and the mastery of gross and fine motor skills.

My initial grounding in child development provides the foundation on which my evolving understanding of children has been built. My classrooms have furnished many examples of the developmental sequences I learned about in my formal education. Increasingly, I have been able to see the reality of things that began only as theory.

My understanding of child development has served as a map for setting my direction as a teacher. And I continue to learn new routes from the children with whom I work.

DEFINING OUR ROLE AS EARLY CHILDHOOD TEACHERS

When a solid understanding of child development serves as one's base, the role of teachers of young children is defined somewhat differently from that of colleagues who teach older children. We do not have a body of knowledge that we master, organize, and then systematically "teach" each year to children. Instead, we continually work to master and revise our understanding of child development in order to create a learning environment that supports, invites, and even prods children as they work to master the developmental tasks of early childhood.

If course work in early childhood teacher preparation programs emphasizes knowledge of child development, then student practicums should focus on developing the teacher's role with young children. By working with experienced early childhood teachers, prospective teachers learn to value their roles as facilitators who are respectful of children's contributions to their own learning.

With more experience, I've come to understand the dynamic role of facilitation. My formal education in child development helped me begin to understand this role, but my daily experiences with young children solidified it. When children are "on a roll," our work is to support their sense of exploration and drive for mastery. I intellectually understood this role from my reading and course work, but it only became real for me when I saw it in action—hence, the importance of prospective teachers working with seasoned teachers.

Adults learn through modeling. Opportunities to be a student teacher have been among my most valuable learning experiences. When I contemplate my own career, I realize that my teaching is a composite of values, skills, approaches, attitudes, and styles that have been gleaned from working with a number of other teachers—first as a student, later as a colleague, or director. By working with skillful and creative teachers, prospective early childhood teachers have the chance to observe a diversity of individual styles.

An educator from Italy, describing early childhood education in one of their cities, referred to the teacher's role as one of "provocateur." I find that to be an exciting image to inform our work with children because there often is a mysterious and undercover quality to our work. Hours of thought and preparation setting up our classrooms and designing activities that challenge children may be invisible to children and to adult observers, but I think the undercover nature of our work is part of our success as mature teachers.

A parent recently shared with me her son's revealing view of my classroom role. In preparing to bring a special poster to school, she had helped him to fold it carefully and put it in his backpack. "When you're done," she had said, "Ask Ms.

VanArsdell to help you fold it up and put it away again." "Oh, I wouldn't ask her," he said. "She just plays with us and reads the stories; Mrs. Brown (the assistant teacher) does all the work." On one level, this child's view of my role referred to the fact that a disproportionate share of the classroom's maintenance fell to my assistant while I read the story and led group music time. But I hope it also spoke to the way a more seasoned teacher becomes part of children's play and enters into their learning in unobtrusive ways.

UNDERSTANDING THE IMPORTANCE OF ENVIRONMENT

The longer I teach, the clearer it becomes to me that environment is the basis of the early childhood curriculum. Our behind-the-scenes work in preparing the classroom environment is like setting the bait. If we understand the skills children in our group are working to master, we can provide an environment that offers them a variety of challenges and enables us to support their learning in nonintrusive, facilitative ways.

Consequently, I am forever designing and redesigning areas of the classroom. Ingenuity and creativity have often filled in the gaps created by limited resources. My choice of activity areas or centers in a classroom directly reflects my goals for young children. Each center provides specific opportunities to practice skills in several areas—whether language, fine-motor, visual–motor-integration, or cognitive skills. And, regardless of specific focus, children simultaneously are building social skills through interactions with their peers.

PREPARING TEACHERS FOR INCLUSIVE PROGRAMS

My current focus as a preschool teacher is in providing services for children with special needs in an integrated environment. Therefore, I am particularly interested in how teachers of young children can be prepared to identify and work with children who are not typical learners. As many states move toward models for serving young children with special needs in the mainstream of early childhood settings, some teachers express concern about how they can meet the needs of these children in their regular classrooms, especially without the advantage of special education training.

I think the mystery of serving children with special needs is diminished when the education of early childhood teachers is solidly grounded in a comprehensive understanding of child development. This knowledge base prepares teachers to understand the diversity of ways in which children learn and the variations in rates of learning, and these understandings can be applied to designing programs that serve children with special needs as well as their typical peers. Because of my grounding in knowledge of child development, I *expect* every early childhood setting to include children who are working at very different levels; consequently, I more easily accommodate to the individual learning styles of children with special needs.

Teaching in an integrated preschool setting means my classes also include many typical learners. I am in awe of how naturally and incidentally these children are able to learn from their environment. In contrast, children with special needs are often challenged by their attempts to master motor skills, acquire language, build social relationships, or learn basic readiness skills. Because teachers tend to feel challenged by these children, they need to feel prepared and supported in working with them.

I've come to the conclusion that all teachers, as a part of their teacher preparation, need to develop skills in identifying and working with children with special needs. This is especially true for early childhood teachers, because many children's special learning needs will be overlooked until an astute preschool teacher begins to notice that the way a particular child processes information, moves in space, or struggles to master new information is somehow different. Reflective of this thinking, several states are merging their certifications at the early childhood level. In Massachusetts, for example, there will be a single certification for teachers of young children—typical learners and children with special needs.

If our goal is inclusive education, the importance of all teachers having a greater understanding of special needs is self-evident. At the same time, I would strongly support the need for continuing to have teachers who specialize in working with children with special needs. By merging teacher certifications, we risk minimizing the special challenges that some children face and that their parents, teachers, and therapists share as they support them.

Children with special needs often display differences in their physical, neurological, emotional, or learning characteristics that make it very challenging for them to master skills that come more easily to others. I think more specialized training in neuropsychology, language acquisition, and social–emotional and motor development is needed in order for teachers to be able to identify such children's specific learning styles and potential learning obstacles, and to modify the learning environment for them.

To serve young children with special needs effectively, teachers also need to work as a member of a team of professionals. Teachers who work with children with special needs frequently work with psychologists, speech and language pathologists, occupational and physical therapists, and social workers. Often, the teacher is expected to coordinate service delivery as teams work to provide an integrated approach to providing therapies within the early childhood setting. I think we do both children and teachers a disservice when we minimize the need for some teachers to have more specialized training to help children with special needs make maximum progress.

EXTENDING OUR COMPETENCE AS TEACHERS

LEARNING FROM CHILDREN

In order to continue building our skills and competence as teachers, it is essential that we are willing and able to learn from children. For me, one of the most exciting things about being a teacher is that my classroom is a constant laboratory—in the best sense of the word. When I am able to take the time to carefully observe children in my classroom, they teach me a great deal. That new learning and information, in turn, informs my growing competence and confidence as a teacher.

Consequently, I work to prepare an environment that invites children's exploration and discovery, though I also have to keep learning not to limit the exploration by my own rush to draw a conclusion. I remember watching a small group of children move a grocery scale from the workbench, where it had been set with a basket of small colored blocks, into the house area. They proceeded to balance various items taken from the house area, comparing the reaction on the scale's round dial as they created precarious piles of various props. Soon, they were discovering the relative weight of play dishes as compared to old telephones. Some were able to read the numerals on the scale and had some sense of relative weights in numerical terms. Others were simply experiencing the different way the scale moved depending on the weight of objects.

As the teacher, this interaction provided me an opportunity to stand back and watch the ways children work together to create a learning experience—one that was much more meaningful than the plan I had prepared. Piaget (1983) has cautioned that "each time one prematurely teaches a child something he could have discovered for himself, that child is kept from inventing it and consequently from understanding it completely" (p. 113). In order to learn from the children I teach, I've had to learn to slow myself down so that I can watch and listen to them carefully.

During a recent vacation, I was on a ferry and happened to sit near a group of 7 or 8 young children. They were sitting on the floor of the deck looking out through the railing, while the adults who accompanied them visited a short distance away. As we passed a small island, the children excitedly began to discuss it. They noticed that it was surrounded by water, that it had trees on it and a large rock. Eventually, they decided that you could walk around this island. But, they said, you would need a boat to get there, and because the island was so small, you would need a small boat to go there. At that point, one of the adults looked up, noticed the island, and said to the children, "Look, there's an island." I couldn't help but wonder how often I, as a teacher, resemble that adult, oblivious to children's interests and capacity to think.

A critical skill for maturing teachers, therefore, is the ability to listen and take direction from children's conversations, concerns, and ideas. Then, I think, teachers have an important responsibility to share information and questions that are relevant and encourage critical thinking. I also have learned the importance of listening for clues for how children are thinking and cues for when critical thinking is best encouraged by remaining silent.

One year, during circle time, an interesting discussion developed about a child in our preschool class who had multiple disabilities. One of the children asked whether this boy would be able to walk when he grew older. "No," I explained, "he will still use a wheelchair to move, but when he's bigger he will have a larger wheelchair." The children apparently were unwilling to accept my explanation because the discussion continued. They drew from their own experiences and recalled younger siblings or friends who had learned to walk as they grew older. Once more, I explained the reasons why their classmate would continue to need a wheelchair, but they still weren't ready to accept my explanation as the final word. This was a time for me, as a teacher, to know when to stop talking and to listen instead.

Now the reasoning behind my earlier statement that time and many children provides the most direct answer to this essay's focal question can be clarified. Time and many children provide classroom teachers with the rich experiences that can help us internalize what we have learned in our formal, professional preparation as teachers. My understanding of child development now has many children's names and faces attached to it. I am able to rely on experiences with children in my former classes to help guide my work with individual children. I have a growing repertoire of curriculum ideas and behavioral management strategies and, as a result, I now feel more confident of my ability to handle challenging situations.

SUPPORTING PROFESSIONAL DEVELOPMENT

Children and time alone, however, are not sufficient to move early childhood teachers beyond an initial level of competence. We also need other kinds of experiences to promote our professional development. From my own experiences, opportunities to learn from other colleagues working in the field has been one of the most important supports to my growth as a teacher. These interactions seem to happen most easily in settings such as a large child care center, a university laboratory school, or a public school with several early childhood classrooms. In these types of settings, teachers have more opportunity to share ideas informally and to learn from working in close proximity to colleagues.

Unfortunately, many early childhood teachers are isolated. Many of my colleagues work in small child care centers or in the only preschool classroom within a public elementary school. Our early childhood community recently has tried to address this problem by providing evening workshops for early childhood teachers and parents, supported by funding available through a state grant. Participants have represented family child care, group child care, and public school preschool programs, and their responses have been enthusiastic. These workshops have added to our professional knowledge base but, more important, they also have brought together early childhood educators who work in a variety of settings. This network of professionals working in different ways to support young children and families is becoming an important asset to the growing professionalism of all involved.

For our professional development to continue, however, we need the financial and contractual support of our school systems and child care centers. To remain current in the field, we also need financial support for course work, workshops, and conferences. I've come to appreciate that the extent to which such support is available to teachers reveals a great deal about the way teachers' professional roles are understood and valued by the employing school system or agency.

Furthermore, in the current fiscal crisis in many states and cities, support for professional development has been one of the first areas to suffer budget cuts. This year, my school system is one of many in Massachusetts that has had to reduce expenditures. Teachers no longer can request reimbursement for conference and workshop tuition unless special grants are available. If a teacher chooses to attend a conference or workshop at personal expense, money has been allocated to pay for a substitute teacher for one day. This new policy delivers a powerful message about the perceived value of professional development. It also is an invisible loss to the school system—for now. Taxpayers will not see the loss, but teachers, and eventually children, will feel it if alternative funding cannot be found to support our continued professional growth.

IMPLICATIONS FOR TEACHER EDUCATION

So, what does all of this suggest for planning programs that educate the next generation of early childhood teachers? We often talk about "child-centered" programs when describing excellence in early childhood education. If we want to prepare teachers who will be able to meet the changing needs of the children they will teach over the course of their careers, then I think teacher education programs should also be "child-centered," in the sense that a comprehensive understanding of child development must be the core of the curriculum. With this emphasis on a developmental approach to early education, the inclusion of children with varying learning styles and rates can become a natural part of teacher education and program implementation.

With this academic foundation, I think prospective early childhood teachers then need opportunities to work closely with mentor teachers who can model the role of facilitator. Prospective teachers will be able to watch and learn from their mentors' interactions with children and from their design of environments that support exploration. This part of teacher education needs to be "hands on"—with ears and eyes wide open. And if we are fortunate, prospective teachers also will have the experience of working with a practitioner who can help them understand how to continue learning about teaching every day from the children they "teach."

Our formal education also needs to prepare prospective early childhood teachers for a commitment to continued professional growth that spans the years of their careers. New teachers need to understand that the granting of a teaching certificate does not certify the end of our learning how to teach. Hopefully, as classroom teachers, we continue to be touched by a certain restlessness each September that causes us to seek a better way to do something in our curriculum or in our classroom.

Each year, for example, I find myself trying to invent a better system for recording individual child progress within the context of a busy preschool classroom. I have developed a variety of charts that I carefully set up on clipboards. I have taped skill charts on walls and on the tops of shelves in key areas. I have borrowed the idea of placing small pads of Post-it notes all over the classroom so I can quickly record an observation and later add it to a child's file. Then, in June, when I clean up the classroom for the end of the year, I am forced to confront the inadequacies of whatever system I have used as I uncover half-finished observation notes.

No system can change the fact that preschool classrooms are very busy places in which nothing ever slows down long enough to write down all the things that happen every day. So I do the best I can and trust that my memory and sense of each child's progress will help fill in the gaps. But it is important to our continuing growth as teachers that we continually strive to be even better at what we are doing.

In my striving for excellence, I rely on the foundation built during my formal preparation as a teacher. I also know that my teaching continues to be influenced by the creative and dynamic teachers who were, and are, my mentors. And I have the opportunity every day to observe children and learn from them.

I recently read an article describing a teacher selection process being developed to screen candidates for teaching positions. One of the article's authors commented on the characteristics of candidates who proceeded to be very successful teachers. He said that those who went on to become the best teachers saw themselves less as managers of learning and more as witnesses to learning. His conclusion is consistent with my experiences as an early childhood teacher.

My role as a witness to learning was recently confirmed. While setting up the classroom, I noticed that the grass seed planted in the aquarium for crickets had begun to grow. Later, when a small group of children gathered around the aquarium to check on the crickets, I squatted down next to them and commented, "Something new is happening in there today." The youngest 3-year-old looked carefully for a minute, and then announced excitedly, "Grass is happening!" As teachers of young children, learning is always happening around us. Some of it we have actively facilitated by the classroom environment and activities we have planned. But some of it just "happens," and, if we are watching carefully, we will have the privilege of being witnesses to learning.

REFERENCE

Piaget, J. (l983). Piaget's theory. In W. Kessen (Ed.), *History, theory, and methods: The handbook of child psychology* (Vol. 1, p. 113–118). New York: Wiley.

CHAPTER 7

Deepening Teacher Competence Through Skills of Observation

Anne Martin

"I think his head is alive," said my neighboring teacher, pointing to a tow-headed 5-year-old absorbed in play. It took me a minute to realize that she was referring not to the teeming thoughts and fantasies in his mind, but to the head lice that were prevalent in our school at that time. Even after I understood, I had a hard time letting go of my more metaphorical interpretation. The image of live heads, actively concentrating on blocks, paints, water, sand, dolls, puzzles, books, and games, remained with me long after the lice epidemic had passed. You need only enter a kindergarten room to feel the waves of intense energy that surge towards you and pull you in. The one thing above all that draws me to teaching young children is their astonishing liveliness, an endless eagerness to do, to learn, to know, and to understand.

The children's extraordinary energy is the starting point for me as a teacher. My job—a never ending challenge—is figuring out how to provide scope for the children's eagerness and make productive use of their vitality. In this essay, I attempt to communicate something of my own experience and thinking about kindergarten teaching, based on a long career in the classroom as well as much reading, discussion, and reflection.

Since my own training and inclination is towards description rather than prescription, my purpose is to depict classroom reality as I see it, leaving much of the interpretation to the reader. Towards this end, I draw on this material to suggest some implications for deepening the competencies of teachers, mainly by practicing and applying the skills of observation, description, and documentation, and by making connections with colleagues. If we intend to take seriously the importance of observation, perhaps a good way to start a discussion about kindergarten is to look at the children themselves.

THE CHILDREN AND THE CLASSROOM

Five-year-olds are not like anyone else—a breed apart, I sometimes think. Fluctuating erratically between babyhood and childhood, they are full of what may seem to us like contradictions but to them are perfectly reasonable. They mostly love adult attention and often hang on teachers affectionately one minute, only to be stubbornly asserting their absolute independence the next. They may spend a long time painting a beautiful picture and then finish by deliberately covering it with muddy brown or black. They may smile and say puppets aren't real, but they have prolonged, serious discussions with them. They may be more intrigued with old manual typewriters than new word processors.

On one hand, they are attached to strictly consistent daily routines, making a point of correcting any deviations; on the other, they welcome frequent digressions and disruptions from their friends, the wrigglier and sillier the better. Listening to others and sitting still are often hard for them, but they generally love to talk themselves, and they expect people to listen. Five-year-olds exuberantly give expression to their ideas, which hover somewhere between wild magical fantasy and sharp realism, switching modes casually without missing a beat. Much of the time in the block or house areas, they profess not to be children at all but Ninja Turtles, princesses, cats and dogs, or teenaged older sisters living on their own, their parents having conveniently departed or expired. Paley (1981) provides a delightful and well-documented discussion of five-year-olds' thinking.

Because fantasy and exploration are so characteristic of kindergarten children, teachers can make use of these strong interests to foster learning. The first steps into literacy can be part of daily kindergarten life, with each child finding congenial ways to appropriate print. The kindergarten day, even a short half-day session like mine, offers plenty of opportunity for children to become aware of print, to learn to love books and widen their acquaintance with children's literature, to grow in their ability to express themselves verbally and to explore the possibility of communicating through writing.

Block buildings often require labels or signs (especially the important SAVE sign); the house corner needs message pads at the toy telephone, old phone books, shopping list paper, and drawing paper for drama scenery; board and number games can lead to score keeping; and pictures and paintings may be captioned. Bulletin boards and walls provide space for hanging poems and class dictations written on large chart paper, lists of children's names, descriptions of bulletin board displays or graphs, a lost tooth chart, a boys and girls chart, identifying captions for current science projects, etc. Useful print can be everywhere throughout the room. That does not include labels such as "door," "window," or "table," which seem didactic and superfluous to me. Labels should add to our knowledge and not point out the obvious just for the sake of teaching reading.

In my room, I usually have books all around: butterfly books near the caterpillar cage, seed books by our seed collection, small easy reading books, story books, factual books, "home-made" books (both by the whole class and by individuals), story books and tapes next to the tape player, song books, "big books" that we first read together as a class and are then available for children to read by themselves— as much of a variety as I can gather. We are fortunate to have a good school library where I spend many hours searching for just the right books for an individual child, for a whole class project, for a new subject of study, or for enjoyment.

Reading together, talking, questioning, discussing, and observing are an important focus in the classroom. Writing is necessarily an adjunct, as we record observations, stories, poems, plans, class "news," lists, reminders, etc. At first I mostly take dictation, asking children to help me with (or notice) beginning sounds. But at the same time I encourage children to try their own invented spelling, and each effort, no matter how far from standard orthography, is accepted and highly praised.

As the children "read" big books together as a class, listen to story books every day, write their names and those of friends, and take further steps into independent reading and writing, they begin to think of themselves as potential readers and writers. By the end of the year, some children are reading fluently and writing stories independently in decipherable invented spelling. Many children are reading a little and writing some words; others are writing only their own names and making tentative forays into the recognition of familiar words. Just about all the children recognize favorite books, listen to stories attentively, tell stories themselves, or show awareness of letters and numerals. In short, they have made a good start towards literacy.

Young children have their own ways of learning. They need scope for active exploration of a variety of open-ended materials, social contact with other children and adults, and plenty of opportunities to think and talk about their experiences. Few children of kindergarten age learn best from sit-down paper-and-pencil lessons. The current trend toward moving formal whole class instruction in reading and writing into the kindergarten, including daily drill and workbooks, is, therefore, neither appropriate nor productive. The adoption of such unsuitable curriculum triggers other destructive practices. School systems push back their admission cut-off dates in order to eliminate younger children, while multiplying "pre-K" or "transition classes" to accommodate the children shut out of kindergarten. And parents are holding back their perfectly normal kindergarten-aged children for an extra year because they are anxious for their children to excel or are afraid the children may fail if they seem less "ready" than their classmates.

The possibility of children "failing" kindergarten was practically unheard of not so long ago, when kindergarten was designed to be a gentle and delightful introduction to school life. It seems to me a mistake (and a form of unfair discrimination) to narrow admission to kindergarten on any basis. A wide range of ages, backgrounds, and abilities in a kindergarten group need not be an impediment to learning "skills" of any sort. On the contrary, it widens the pool of experience, attitudes, and personalities that help to spark children's ideas. A kindergarten program can be adapted to the needs of the children, whatever their various levels of "readiness." We need to resist fixed ideas of what we expect of entering children, or rigid preconceived curricula which automatically exclude children.

One reason I moved back to teaching kindergarten after working with other grades is that in kindergarten the immediate effects of teaching are more open and visible than they can be with older children. Since kindergartners generally have not yet learned to don protective veils or show social tact, it is usually obvious how they are feeling at any particular moment. They tend to let you know unequivocally when they are angry, sad, bored, tired, interested, curious, happy, or resistant, and it is then up to the teacher to respond. Usually there is not enough time at the moment to think; so our responses have to be quick, based on previous experience, knowledge, intuition, the mood of the moment, and the circumstances. Sometimes the response is just right—it works!—and sometimes it seems that it was counterproductive. Afterwards, there is time for more reflection, perhaps revision of a plan or attitude, perhaps a resolve to try something different or to hold firm to some basic beliefs. Fortunately, there is always another day, and one day's mistakes can usually be corrected. Young children tend to be forgiving, resilient, and open to a teacher's genuine desire to make connections with them.

THE JOB AND SETTING

Teaching has always seemed to me a job of immense complexity and mystery. A classroom rapidly develops an atmosphere of its own, independent of the teacher's will, engendered by the various persons (including the teacher) who play their parts and interact in a quick succession of scenes. All classrooms are settings for drama, complete with action, conflict, main and subsidiary characters, silent roles and speaking parts, alternating from day to day and minute by minute in a confusing richness of plot. There are good years when the group of children seems to gel and establishes a calm, creative, productive rhythm of its own, and there are difficult years when a clash of too many strong personalities brings anger, dissension, and a disruptive atmosphere, in spite of everything you try.

With all the skills and perspective of years of experience, veteran teachers still find themselves challenged, puzzled, and often troubled by the responses of particular children or groups. Teaching doesn't get easier over the years. The pressures and demands of a teaching job continue to be intense and unrelenting. No matter how long you have taught, the work day never really ends, even after school hours or on weekends. The daily concerns of the classroom nag at us and won't let us go. Teaching inevitably runs over its allotted time into a teacher's thoughts at home and dreams at night—something that is extremely hard to explain to those who sneer about a job with short hours and long vacations. While vacations are a necessary relaxing time to replenish our inner resources, most teachers still keep their teaching closely in mind, sometimes with summer courses or workshops, but also with informal planning for the next year. My trips to the beach, to the mountains, to foreign countries (or only to my backyard!) usually involve collecting nature finds and other materials to introduce into the classroom.

The complexity of teaching comes not only from the people who interact with each other but also the space in which they do so. In my case, the teaching environment is a particularly perplexing one. My kindergarten classroom is not a "room" at all, but a designated area in an open-space primary wing, which was added to our remodeled old building at the tail end of the "open classroom" period in American education. Apparently rather literal-minded, the administrators decided (against the wishes of the teachers) to dispense with walls and produce large vistas of open space reaching across the whole floor (containing about 200 children) and upward into irregular, sharply angled ceilings. Nothing was built in—no bookshelves, no counters, no storage space—and the class areas were supplied with bulky free-standing furniture that looks clumsy, reduces floor space, and is inadequate for display, storage, or organization of materials.

The red carpet and colorful decor lend a surface brightness to the building that impresses visitors with its cheerfulness, but this is deceptive. The clashing colors are disturbing; the stairs (some of them hollow so that they echo footsteps) and railings offer constant temptation to run and jump; the incessant movement and noise are distracting; the overflow from inadequate coat closets spills onto the floor in winter and impedes ordinary passage. The building does look "modern," but the basic needs of classrooms and children were not seriously considered.

It is true that there are a few advantages to the open building, such as the ease of contact with other teachers (no doors to go through!) or former students who wave happily or come and tell some important news as I pass by their areas many times a day. But there is no question in the minds of teachers who work daily in an open-space building that the physical environment is a continual source of unnecessary strain and frustration. Within a few years of struggle in the new wing, the obvious difficulties of maintaining focus in a class space without any visual barriers led to the quick construction of ticky-tacky wallboard barriers. This helped at least to define areas, reduce distraction, and provide much-needed bulletin-board space (which also had been neglected in the original plans). However, the auditory distractions continue. There is no way for teachers to feel comfortable about ordinary noises, such as spontaneous singing or drama, without guilt at disturbing surrounding classes, or to have silence when you need it without the intrusion of the sounds of the neighboring classes' activities. In short, there is no control over the classroom environment and thus there are restrictions to the program that would not apply in ordinary school buildings.

Even in more conventional buildings, the physical environment of a kindergarten classroom has a strong impact on the educational program, and each year it needs some rethinking and perhaps reorganization. Sometimes it takes several years of working in a space to see what works and what doesn't, and often it takes an outside person (perhaps a thoughtful colleague) to suggest some changes that can then be tried out with the children. Their reactions can be illuminating or startling. One year, I moved a block shelf after school in order to expand the block building area. When I asked the children the next day what had changed in the room, they thought carefully for a minute and then said, "Oh, you moved the window!"

Sometimes the children do their own space rearranging. As our house corner occasionally changes into a store, a spaceship, a hospital, or some other setting, a small group of children usually decides on a new arrangement and sets it up, with only a minimal amount of adult input. Ordinarily, when children spend a great deal of time spontaneously lugging one kind of material into a different area, it may be a tip-off that the teacher's ideas of what belongs where does not correspond to the children's. That may or may not lead to a new organization of space and materials, but it certainly opens up a topic of discussion for the class and the teacher. Children appreciate being consulted on matters that concern them, and I find that many times they have good ideas that had not occurred to me. Sometimes, of course, there is a basic difference of opinion, which the teacher may have to rule on. When Jay decided to keep "moving house" by piling up every item in the house corner into a grand mess, I let him do it a couple of times, but after that he was restricted on the grounds that other children needed to use the materials, and that we could not spend half our days on clean-up.

The relationship of the placement of materials to spaces and children is something on which I spend a great deal of thought, not always with predictable or positive results. The best lesson or activity can be ruined if the materials are not organized so that they are easily available to the children. A collage project that has a messy, mixed-up box of materials to use yields different results from an identical project that has materials arranged in separate boxes, compartments, or trays. If the glue or paste is in small individual containers, children can use it more easily and with less confusion than if they have large common jars to share. Reading a wonderful book to the class can be a disaster if the children can't see the pictures and are pushing each other to get a better view. Block building can be inhibited by too little designated building space; games and construction toys need clear floor and table space. Too many materials at once are confusing (especially at the beginning of the year); yet there should be a large variety of activities available every day so that all children can find things to do that are appealing to them and suitable. Where and how materials are stored can influence the way they are used by the children.

In these days of shrinking budgets and decreasing supplies, it takes even more thought, planning, and scrounging to have adequate materials. There are some sources of free materials, which teachers can draw on. Sometimes paper and printing companies are happy to have teachers pick up their scrap paper. Some museums or other centers provide recycled "junk" materials at minimal cost. Sometimes parents of older children donate outgrown toys and books to the class. The world around us offers acorns and chestnuts (great for counting and math!), leaves, seeds, shells, empty bird or wasp nests, insects and sometimes larger animals, all of which can be brought into the classroom to admire, observe, and study. The children like to bring in their own finds and favorite games and toys to share. Best of all are the human resources—the variety of family backgrounds and experiences of the children and their families, which supply much of the basic subject matter which dominates the children's thoughts and play.

CURRICULUM AND ASSESSMENT

Much of my curriculum is based on what the children bring to the group—their interests, enthusiasms, capabilities, ideas, and responses. From my observations of the children, I can gain some understanding of their ways of learning and their educational needs. Changes in curriculum are based on assessment of individuals and the whole group. To me, assessment is not evaluation, but a tool for making school more responsive to the needs of the children.

In the past 10 years or so, the suburban school where I teach has changed its population into a wonderful mixture of diverse nationalities. As much as a third or more of the children entering kindergarten do not speak English at all, and others speak minimal English as a second language. The mixture of cultures adds tremendous richness to the program. We count crackers in at least five or six languages every day, celebrate Chinese New Year, Japanese Children's Day, and other holidays, try food from other countries, read books about people all over the world, and make friends with people who may look and speak differently from us, depending on the backgrounds of the class members. Young children don't need too many words to engage in play together, and many of the non-English speaking children soon learn to understand and even speak the new language. But at some times of the day there are problems posed by the language barrier: Is it fair to make non-English speaking children sit through discussions or listen to book readings that they cannot understand yet? But is it fair to sophisticated English speakers to listen only to simple books or have curtailed group discussions? Should the group be divided for those activities, and, if so, who would supervise the other group(s)? Would separation by language only emphasize differences and thus negate the community we are trying to build all the rest of the day?

There are no definitive answers to any of these questions. Each group is different and needs its own solutions. One year my non-English speaking children decisively rejected sitting through difficult books and preferred to sit close by doing puzzles. Another year they quietly took on the challenge of trying to listen and stayed with the group. Yet another year, I had to deal with several little ones crawling in and out of the group circle, or chattering away loudly in Japanese during group meetings. What does help is to observe carefully to see how the children are reacting, be flexible about expectations and options for children, and keep looking for different ways of implementing the program so that the diverse needs of the children can be met.

Even when there are not so many cultural differences within the class, there are always drastic differences in personality, interests, levels of physical, social, and emotional development, uses of language, experience of other people and the world. The very diversity of the classroom, its unpredictability, is what poses the challenge of teaching. It is this challenge, the newness of every child and every school year that keeps me involved in teaching after some 30 years as a classroom teacher. I'm perpetually curious about who these children are, what they do and say, and how they find ways to learn.

While I am always fascinated by children's conversations, spontaneous stories, and dramatic play, I have learned increasingly over the years how to observe and listen carefully. In their eagerness to be active educators, beginning teachers tend to jump in too quickly, interrupt children's talk and play, correct mistakes, and take charge of all situations. It takes experience and trust in children to learn to stand back, allow gaps and silences while children think, let children help work out solutions to classroom problems, and accept children's inaccurate theories with respect for their process of learning. While, naturally, I am ultimately responsible for the safety of the children, the quality of instruction, and the social climate, I like to think of myself more as a constantly active consultant in the classroom than the big boss who controls everything. I try to set up a stimulating learning environment and make sure children remain involved and included, reflect on classroom events and make plans to further each child's development, and keep records of children's growth and learning. It is my role to be the memory for the class, to remind children of what we have done before and what has happened, so that we can forge connections to the present and look forward to the future. But I am happy to share my authority with the children who give me invaluable clues about how to make positive contacts with them and how to plan and carry out my curriculum.

While each year I may do similar projects or activities, they always turn out different in scope, emphasis, and intensity, depending on the group of children. And each new class engenders new topics of study or new approaches. The enthusiasm of a few key members, or even just one child, can pull a class into much more detailed work on something introduced almost casually by teacher or children. One year, we spent many weeks on castles, a topic that came up when a couple of children found a library book on knights and castles and eagerly studied the pictures every day. More children got interested in the castle book, and they all vied to look at it during reading time. That was my signal to search the library for more castle books, both factual and fictional, with elaborate illustrations. These books were greeted with delight. The children pored over their favorites for weeks, and we read many stories together as a class. For the house corner, the children made crowns and capes. I bought some small knight figures to go with a wooden castle block set to use for table play, to supplement the regular block building.

Gradually we ended up with detailed castle buildings in the block area, beautiful castle drawings and paintings, a large class book containing castle pictures (we studied books that had border designs around pages and adapted some), a group-composed fairy tale, several castle murals, an original castle song, and several castle dramas. No other class before or since has shown such sustained concentration and interest in this topic, which was initiated and promulgated by a few strong members, and then supported by my efforts to supply appropriate materials and activities to keep the topic alive.

In planning the curriculum, I need to take into account the children in the class—their strengths, interests, and vulnerabilities. In order to know the children better and understand more about them, I start to observe them carefully from the first day of school. I watch how they enter the classroom, how they react to other children and to me, what they say, which materials they use and how they use them, what they draw and paint, how they climb, run, sit with the group, how they look at books, and how they enter activities. Every week, all year long, I write down some observations about each child—anything that struck me. Sometimes I record an incident or a conversation, sometimes a description of something the child created, sometimes just a list of the child's preferences during activity time. These entries can be quite short, or more elaborate if special things were going on with a child. I try to use language that is very specific, descriptive, and nonjudgmental. Observing children carefully and describing them with as much unprejudiced precision as possible are skills that need to be honed by years of experience and the professional support of sensitive colleagues. It takes hard work, time, and practice to develop observational skills and the ability to translate what we see and know into clear prose.

During the year, I also keep a folder for each child and slip in any drawings, writing, or other work that the child has not taken home. The children each have a journal—a blank-paged spiral book—in which they work almost every day, dating their own work with a stamp when they have finished their page. In their journals, most children work on drawing, some add captions and words to their pictures, and a few write whole sentences. They are free to do whatever they like, but they must spend some time on it and not race through the empty pages with a scribble on each one. These journals, along with other work, form a fascinating record of the child's style, interests, subject matter, and approach to the world. I also try to have photos taken (by parents, student teachers, and myself) of the block buildings, constructions, and color patterns the children produce. The children's work in all areas, and my observations, provide me with material to build my knowledge of each child.

Gradually, my notes add up to several pages of observations on each child, which constitute a record of the child's kindergarten year. I use these notes frequently during the year to think about how to plan for children and to give me information for parent conferences or school meetings. At the end of the year, I study the notes and the children's saved work as the basic material from which to write narrative reports (one copy for the parents and one for the school) that attempt to give a detailed portrait of each child at this stage. Of course my knowledge is always incomplete—we can never know a child entirely—but since it is based on concrete observations, the report speaks to parents' own experience of their child, and there is usually immediate recognition on their part. I often include suggestions or my perception of how adults can support the child's learning and social development.

Assessing children's learning through observation, recording, and reflection are an alternative to the more common way of evaluation by checklists and testing. The advantage of narrative reports is that they are a thoughtful description of the whole child, whereas checklists only emphasize isolated skills that often seem unrelated to each other. It is hard to get a view of a child from a collection of checklist items that may miss the child's particular strengths and personality altogether or from a bunch of number scores from standardized tests.

The more we know a child, the more can we supply the materials and teaching approaches that make sense to the child. However, it is not always possible for a harried teacher in a large class to take enough time for observation or to see a child from enough perspectives. We all need the help of colleagues, student teachers, parents, volunteers, or other adults to see the classroom and children from many angles and thus broaden our view. For me, a sensitive student teacher who has time to catch and record conversations among children, to notice children's gestures and expressions, and to talk with individuals is an invaluable resource. Best of all, a good student teacher is someone with whom I can discuss the day's events and compare views of the minutia of the classroom. Perhaps the most useful learning for student teachers comes from such encouragement to focus carefully on the children, to reflect with the cooperating teacher on the possibilities for supporting children's learning, and to plan on the basis of the knowledge gained.

COLLEGIALITY AND CONNECTION

The traditional isolation of teachers in their classrooms is both limiting and a source of stress. To be alone constantly in a classroom of demanding young children without any contact with other adults is difficult for any teacher, new or experienced. There are not many schools that build in time for collegial contact, so teachers who are determined to reduce their isolation have to take action on their own. In my school for the past few years, we have maintained a voluntary Child Study Group for teachers. We meet once a month and generally follow the group processes for studying children, teaching, and classrooms that were developed at the Prospect Center in Bennington, Vermont, by Patricia Carini (1982) and others.

But there are many other ways to create more contact with other teachers, sometimes involving the children. In the latter half of every year, my kindergartners are paired up with 5th graders once a week, and the partners engage in various activities together, planned by both teachers in response to the children and in relation to current curriculum interests. This has always been a great success, and the devotion that develops between the older and younger children is touching to see.

In many areas, there are local teacher workshops, teacher centers, teacher research groups, and publications. In our system, there is a teacher publication named*Reflections* that comes out twice a year, originally conceived by a teacher and supported financially by a local, private foundation, to aid staff development. It contains writing and artwork by teachers and each year grows impressively in quality and in range of contributions. For the teaching staff throughout the community, it is exciting to read what colleagues are thinking, feeling, and doing. It has always been important for me to widen the boundaries of the classroom, to find supportive colleagues in and outside my school, to hear and read about other classrooms and teachers, and to get stimulation and new ideas. Being thrown completely on one's own resources is not tenable for most teachers for any length of time. Just as children need each other and learn from each other in the classroom, so teachers need to meet with colleagues to work through their ideas and learn different approaches.

In any teaching, there are bound to be discouraging periods when things don't seem to be going well. Teachers tend to blame themselves, become tense and unhappy, and thus worsen the situation. It usually helps to step back, reflect on what is happening in the classroom, and, especially, to talk with other people instead of holding all the problems inside. Good periods or bad, we all need to gain some perspective on that intense, self-contained world of the classroom. To do that, a lively sense of humor can be very helpful; in fact, that may be the one essential quality for teachers of young children. Laughter can instantly transform a small crisis into a viable situation, and a joke can often change the mood of a recalcitrant child or a bad day in the class. Talking to sympathetic colleagues honestly about our teaching takes us out of our guarded private realm into an open arena where humor and insight can help us overcome the paralysis of discouragement.

THE ART OF TEACHING, ITS DIFFICULTIES AND REWARDS

In thinking about what my own experience can contribute to ideas about deepening a teacher's understanding about children and teaching, I would probably point to the gradual shift of emphasis from "What and how do I teach?" to "What can I learn about teaching from children?" Watching children learn, studying them, documenting what we see and hear, and becoming researchers in our own classrooms gives us the raw materials from which to evolve our own ways of teaching.

In one sense, the longer I teach, the less I know about teaching. As a young teacher, I had much more certainty about what I expected from children and what I wanted to teach. Before I was a parent myself and experienced the complications of bringing up children, I easily blamed parents for problems in their children's development and behavior. Now, after many years of teaching, I see more ambiguities, possibilities, and uncertainties in a field that is surely more an art than a science, and always will be as long as we respect the complexity of the human mind and soul.

Perhaps the first requirement for growth as a teacher is the acknowledgment that there is no one right way to teach, that there are always unknowns, and that we need to remain open to children, new ideas, and new classroom approaches. No great new panacea will be the complete answer to classroom challenges, whether the movement is "school choice," "back to basics," "open education," "whole language," or whatever the next trend turns out to be, and no method is foolproof or suitable for all children. If we study the literature, attend workshops, learn more about the practices of current methods, and exchange ideas with colleagues, we can be profoundly influenced and may gradually change our own practice for the better. But we can only assimilate what is congruent with our own deepest convictions about children, teaching, and learning, and there is no gain in blindly following to the letter a particular system or methodology. For instance, many a good writing program has become fossilized by a rigidly orthodox adherence to "process writing"—an orthodoxy that far exceeds the intention of the originators of this approach. No matter how excellent the precepts and methods, no particular program can be accepted absolutely without thoughtful adaptations, additions, gradual change, and growth.

To deepen our practice, we first need to clarify for ourselves (and be able to articulate) the basic convictions that determine how we relate to children. For me, there have been some unwavering beliefs running right through from the beginning: that all children are learners, that all children have something to contribute to the group, that children are social beings who need other people and social acceptance, that children's integrity and dignity must be respected, and that children's potential for creativity and thoughtfulness must be given time, scope, and encouragement beyond all other aims in school. With these givens, I can try new materials and methods and have some basis on which to judge their efficacy or desirability, or reject others that I feel violate my own standards. For instance, I have steadfastly refused to give letter or numerical grades to children, or to assess them with checklists, even through times when there was much pressure to do so. I feel that the oversimplification of checklists and standardized test results are at best demeaning, insignificant, and inaccurate, and at worst extremely harmful when they stigmatize children.

One thing I have found is that, if you have strong convictions and are willing to put yourself on the line by expressing your opinions clearly both verbally and in writing, you often can persist in alternative practice (e.g., narrative reports on children instead of checklists) because others tend to back down in the face of such determination and passion. A certain amount of subversiveness may be necessary to good teaching at particular points in the vacillating climate of education in America. It is only comparatively recently that classroom teachers have begun to speak up and tell what they know from being in the front lines of education rather than at an administrative desk, away from every day classroom reality. Writing seems an especially powerful tool for teachers; teachers rarely have had the chance to publicly express their ideas before.

The idea that teachers have important contributions to make in the national debate on education, and that they should be included in educational decision making, has burst on the scene as revolutionary and quite surprising. For those of us who have struggled for years to find publication for articles about our teaching and to make ourselves heard, it seems wonderful and ironic that people are suddenly recognizing teachers as an important part of schools.

In spite of some change and movement, America still has a long way to go in truly appreciating contributions of teachers and making use of our hard-won insights and experience to change the organization and running of schools and classrooms. Teachers need to join with others to think about what is most important to them and try to find ways to communicate effectively with other teachers, administrators, parents, unions, community members, and legislators. There are many different ways to take an active part in becoming advocates for the children we know and teach, but it is incumbent upon us to do so at some level.

These are especially difficult times to be a teacher. Children in America more than ever are suffering from poverty, hunger, illness, and family problems. At the same time, school resources are being cut drastically, often with the most essential elements eliminated first, such as the arts, which I consider the basic paths to all learning. Even in the suburbs, some children come to kindergarten having experienced more sadness and disruptiveness in their lives than many of their teachers, and their needs may be hard (or sometimes impossible) to meet within a large class with no extra personnel. Schools cannot always compensate for children's hardships, and teachers may become exhausted physically and emotionally as they keep trying to provide for children who have already been deeply scarred in their short lives.

With the increasing challenge of more difficult classes and the bleak prospect for public schools, teachers nevertheless can get satisfaction out of a job that is perpetually interesting. How many other jobs offer close contact with people, constant variety, the tapping of all one's intelligence, creativity, and resourcefulness, endless new subject matter to explore, and the satisfaction of contributing to human growth? Being in the classroom means being utterly absorbed. For me, all personal matters vanish during school hours, as I lose myself absolutely in the flow of classroom life.

Being with young children always yields surprises and delight. In their eagerness to learn, the children come up with wonderfully novel ways to make sense of the world. I often find myself startled, touched, and amused. On the last day of the year in what was probably the most strenuous kindergarten class I ever taught, the children were taking turns showing their drawings and describing their summer plans. They said they were going to attend day camp, play outdoors, swim, roller-skate, etc. Then one little girl showed us a picture of herself as a princess. Solemnly she announced her plans: "I am going to use my imagination." Suddenly my hard year didn't seem so bad anymore. The transforming spirit—imagination—was alive and well, and perhaps I had managed to nurture it after all. It is the abiding pleasure of being witness to the endlessly divergent growth of young children that keeps us nourished as we look forward with suspense to the unfolding of next year's fascinating chapter of kindergarten.

REFERENCES

Carini, P. F. (1982). *The school lives of seven children: A five year study.* Grand Forks, ND: University of North Dakota.
Paley, V. G. (1981). *Wally's stories.* Cambridge: Harvard University Press.

CHAPTER **8**

Preserving Commitment to Teaching and Learning

Claudia Q. Tull

Twenty-five second-grade faces (smiling, apprehensive, and bored) look at me the first day of school. I contemplate their expressions, take a deep breath—and we're off! The students are unaware that the previous night I had had my annual first-day-of-school nightmare. As usual, it began with a totally disorganized room filled with unruly students who completely ignored me; then I start screaming and run out of the room.

Why, I ask myself, should I, an experienced teacher, continue to have anxiety attacks about teaching? I have been a teacher of young children for 13 years. I have worked for 4 years as a part-time education instructor for a local university and am now an adjunct faculty for the University of West Virginia College of Graduate Studies, where I occasionally teach graduate early childhood education classes. I have a master's degree and 30 hours of postgraduate work.

My particular elementary school only has about 2 children out of 10 below the poverty line, even though recent statistics indicate that 7 out of 10 West Virginian children live below the poverty line. My students live in rural communities or in suburban developments that have sprung up all over the county. Typically, one third of the children in my class are from single parent families or have stepfathers or stepmothers. Usually, one-third have mothers employed outside the home.

The Putnum County, West Virginia, elementary school where I teach and learn is on a narrow paved road in a rural setting. I hear roosters crowing as I go in every day, and children love to watch the horses on the hill across the road. I feel I confront few of the problems of crime, drug abuse, and poverty that many other teachers must face. So, then, what is the source of my anxiety?

I think the answer lies in an underlying, yet pervasive, fear that some day I may fall into the trap of using one of the following litany of excuses for not thinking about what I am doing, for not learning and teaching, or for not continually questioning my routine practices: "Children have changed. They're no longer interested in learning. Their parents don't help. I have too many students, so I can't do more interesting things"; "The state department has tied me up in red tape; so I can't teach the way I would like"; "I have to follow county curriculum; so there is no time to do more exciting activities"; "The teacher in the next grade expects her students to sit quietly and complete worksheets and workbooks neatly and quickly. If I don't teach my students those behaviors, I will be setting them up for failure"; "Why should I lug in materials, tolerate noise and confusion, frequently communicate with parents, attend seminars, use my money to buy professional journals and books, and spend hours planning and preparing when I'm paid so poorly, especially compared with people of the same educational level?"; "Why should I work hard when my profession constantly is blamed and criticized in the local and national media?"

I suppose that my yearly nightmares are symptomatic of my concern that I may become a victim of burn-out. How can I ensure that I remain a teacher and avoid becoming a school keeper (Jacobs, 1991)? I am held accountable for scores on standardized tests, which concentrate on basic skills. Yet I am striving to help children learn basic skills and develop their curiosity, problem-solving abilities, and critical thinking. Why don't I just go in on the first day and teach the first pages of reading, language, spelling, mathematics, science, social studies, health, and art books? It would be so much easier. So the question asked in the title of this section is obviously of more than academic interest to me.

I have concluded that teachers need to cultivate positive attitudes, fine-tune their skills, and deepen their knowledge base about learning and teaching if they are to grow in effectiveness and competence. I define a positive attitude as the desire to see the potential in any situation or person rather than focusing on limiting factors. Skills are those behaviors that enable teachers to construct learning environments, impart information, and encourage thinking. These skills include observation, organization and decision making, communication, and self-evaluation. Knowledge base refers to information about child development, learning, teaching strategies, and research on program effectiveness. As in any system, attitudes, skills, and knowledge are interconnected so that change in one area eventually influences all areas to some degree. Their coherence as a system, however, derives from the teacher's philosophy of education, which summarizes how an individual assumes learning occurs and how learning can be stimulated and encouraged based on those beliefs.

I think it will be helpful if I first chronicle my own growth in these areas. Then, I will discuss what I see as the implications of my experience for supporting teacher growth.

GROWING TOWARD INCREASED COMPETENCE AND EFFECTIVENESS

CULTIVATE POSITIVE ATTITUDES

I think positive, constructive attitudes towards self, children, their parents, colleagues, and learning enables most teachers to continue developing their teaching skills throughout their careers. Many competent teachers seem to demonstrate self-confidence and a feeling of pride. Usually, this is based on our perception of success as we observe our students. For instance, when a student says to me, "I didn't know that math could be so much fun," or when a quiet child bursts forth with new ideas, I feel validated.

Teachers must be able to balance these feelings, though, with an appreciation for the limitations of their situation. I cannot change a child's previous home and school experiences or control what will happen as he or she continues through school. But I can control my educational decisions, communication behaviors, and the teaching and learning environment that I establish.

Through the years, I have found the most used excuse for maintaining classroom situations where every student quietly completes assignment after assignment is the school principal who, reportedly, is opposed to more active, child-centered classrooms. Yet, I have worked with seven very different principals who have never made me change my approach, or even criticized it. I also always take the time to explain my philosophy and decision making to my principals and provide them with supportive research and professional articles. Frankly, I have had more difficulty coping with critical colleagues than oppositional principals. I find comments such as the following frustrating: "Well, when they get to third grade, they will have to learn to sit and work quietly. They have to learn that life is not always exciting."

Once a colleague suggested we begin a transitional kindergarten. I urged that we investigate the possibility further because research I had read gave mixed reviews regarding its effectiveness. Eventually, the school principal suggested that fewer children would have difficulty if teachers provided more appropriate activities.

Unfortunately, my colleague remained angry with me for quite a while. I have since tried to determine if a more tactful approach could have produced less defensive results. I now try to listen more carefully to negative comments from colleagues and consider whether they have merit. When their concerns have merit, I attempt to consider them when making decisions. At the same time, I've developed a higher level of confidence in my own ideas when they run counter to the norm.

On a different note, I find that the longer I teach, the more interested I become in exploring students' perceptions of our classroom life together. Now, I frequently ask them questions regarding their feelings about various activities and what they think they are learning. Sometimes our perceptions are very different, causing me to rethink my decisions. For example, I once asked my class why they thought we were studying dinosaurs. Many typical answers emerged, such as "They're fun"; "They were so big"; and "They're on the front of our science book." Eventually, one child articulated the type answer I sought. "Dinosaurs were big and powerful, but now they are gone forever. People have power over the world now but maybe some day we might be gone. If it happened to dinosaurs, maybe it will happen to us." But, then, another bright child suggested a relationship I had never considered. "Coal is important in West Virginia. Coal was formed by big plants dying and falling down. Maybe the dinosaurs helped knock down those plants." He had made a connection between rocks, an earlier unit of study, and our current investigation. These responses helped me to realize how continually important it is for students to link ideas. Following that comment, I began introducing new units by exploring why their study is important and investigating their possible relationship to earlier classroom activities.

Student comments, of course, are not always so constructive. So I also have to be able to look for the positive attributes of each student. I have to be able to look past rudeness, unruliness, and sometimes defiance. I don't overlook these behaviors, but I cope with them in the most positive way I know how, without disrupting learning. I strive, as well, to treat recalcitrant children with respect, kindness, and encouragement.

I also have to cultivate a positive attitude towards parents. Unfortunately, even though parent involvement is sought and encouraged, many schools create antagonistic environments. Because teachers are not paid well and are considered public servants, some parents seem to emphasize the servant function. As teachers, we naturally resent this attitude. I have had to learn to move beyond the resentment I feel when a parent uses foul language to discuss their child's progress. I have had to develop the ability to sift criticism with merit from meaningless aggravation. And, then I have had to learn to accord disgruntled parents the same respect, courtesy, and kindness that I give to more supportive families.

I feel positive attitudes towards self, children, parents, and colleagues are driven by a positive attitude towards learning. Because I am so interested in how children learn, I observe them closely and listen to them intently. This interest helps me to have a positive attitude towards my students—I see them as fascinating human beings, not just students. I also am interested in what motivates adults to continue learning. And, because of my curiosity about learning, I belong to professional organizations, read professional journals and books, attend conferences, complete classes, and teach graduate courses.

FINE-TUNING SKILLS

Observation Skills

As I acquired more experienced as a teacher, I needed to develop additional skills in observation, decision making, communication, and self-evaluation. Even though observation skills were part of my teacher preparation classes, I had to construct a system to meet my needs.

I begin by having parents complete a questionnaire about their children's likes, dislikes, strengths, weaknesses, and goals for 2nd grade. Then, I have students complete a questionnaire about their perceptions of school, favorite subjects, and their strengths and weaknesses. Armed with this data, I carefully observe five students for a week during direct instruction, group activities, individual activities, during individual reading and writing conferences, at play time, and during meals. I jot down notes and key words on note cards; then, at the end of the day I summarize on a file card my "findings" for each student. By the end of the first month of school, I have observed each of the children in my classroom, and established my anecdotal record-keeping system. Then, as the year progresses and I observe other important information, I add it.

My school district still clings to report cards and grades for 1st and 2nd grade. Because I feel report cards and grades are inadequate, I always attach a detailed letter that includes my observations of a student in various social situations and as a learner. When composing these letters, my note cards are especially helpful.

While developing this system of observation, I had to learn to recognize what were important characteristics in different learning situations. For instance, I have changed my attitude towards mistakes. As a novice teacher, students' mistakes threatened me. I felt that I was failing as a teacher. Now I view most mistakes as indicators of how a child is thinking or learning. Then I try to adjust learning and teaching strategies to accommodate this information. When a student misreads a word, for example, I observe whether the substituted word makes sense and how closely it relates phonically. This information permits me to determine whether a student is having decoding or comprehension problems. Earlier in my career I would simply have mentally noted that a child was unable to read a particular word.

Organization and Decision-Making Skills

The longer I teach, the more extensively I depend on my organizational skills. Before the beginning of each school year, I review my goals for students. Basically, these goals include: helping students establish reading, writing, and mathematical skills and understandings, encouraging independent thinking and learning, enhancing creativity, and developing positive communication skills and a sense of personal responsibility. Within the past few years, my county educational system, through a series of meetings involving teachers, administrators, parents, and business representatives has identified seven educational goals for the system that are similar to the goals I have developed for my class. My school's Faculty Senate wrote school-wide goals that also reflect these values. I keep a copy of these goals in view to help ensure that I don't lose sight of my overall goals for students.

I strive to organize my schedule, routines, and materials in a way that is consistent with my understanding of the learning process and allows students to work towards these goals. My class is divided into five groups whose composition changes every nine weeks. These teams rotate through various centers for math, reading, science, and social studies throughout the weeks. I use a central monthly theme (based on our reading series) to organize activities. Students also participate in individual reading conferences, writing conferences, direct instruction, sign language instruction, listening to stories and novels, physical education, and music. As part of a special state program, my class now is equipped with four networked computers and a printer which provide students and myself access to a wide range of educational supportive software and word processing.

This classroom organization reflects my desire to have students move around, be more interested in what they are doing, and have more choices; it also enables me to individualize. I have learned to think carefully through activities: Do they reflect classroom goals? Are they consistent with my philosophy? What materials are needed? What calamities are possible? How can I organize and arrange to maximize learning and minimize confusion?

Communication Skills

I teach in a large room divided into two classrooms by a bookcase. Because of my classroom organization, I needed to coordinate my schedule with that of the 2nd-grade teacher in the adjoining space so that noise and activity levels coincided. To accomplish this, I needed to persuade her that activities and teams working at different centers at the same time, even though noisy, were worthwhile. When I first approached her, I explained my decision making, and then encouraged her to observe and make her own conclusions. Fortunately, she had been dissatisfied with a more structured approach and was very open to change.

I use this same method when communicating with parents. I explain what I am doing, describe how my approach supports county and school goals, and then invite them to observe my classroom. Between student enthusiasm and my own, most parents seem supportive.

I also have had to develop my communication skills for coping with the school's Faculty Senate and other teacher organizations. Faculty Senates, as instituted by the state of West Virginia, consist of teachers and administrators, with each person having one vote. To encourage site-based management, Faculty Senates are responsible, within state guidelines, for all budgetary and instructional decisions. I often feel inadequate when working out compromises within these groups. And I am not alone in this feeling. Many teachers feel that, although a more collaborative model toward institutional decisions is being encouraged, participants lack collaborative experience and skills.

Through the West Virginia Council of Professional Development, teachers throughout the state have received training in understanding various interactive styles and communication techniques. We were given a small stipend, meals and lodging, and graduate credit hours. In addition, Putnum County now is offering training in communication skills through summer institutes. Because these trainings have helped me improve my abilities, I think training in communication and collaboration needs to be incorporated into teacher preparation and graduate programs.

As a beginning teacher, for example, I had avoided the teachers' lounge because I felt so irritated by the negativity expressed towards students, their parents, and administrators. Through observing positive teachers, however, I have learned that by initiating conversations on a positive note and by smiling and being cheerful, I can reduce teacher negativity. As I began to communicate more often with my colleagues, I learned that my colleagues can offer insight, positive teaching suggestions, and practical management skills. Now, I seek out these relationships. Summer classes offered through my school system and West Virginia's Professional Development Council have enabled me to meet teachers from other schools, exchange ideas and information, and appreciate the number of competent, exciting teachers who are in many different schools across the state.

Self-Evaluation Skills

I have found self-evaluation to be the most difficult skill to practice. I can assess students' progress and understandings, but I find it difficult to maintain objectivity toward myself. Once, an irate parent reported that her daughter said I raised my voice to embarrass her whenever I helped her individually. At first, I was struck by the absurdity of the accusation. Later, as I analyzed my behavior in other situations, I found that, if I am not careful, I do raise my voice, thus breaking the commonsense adage that "louder does not make it clearer." After this incident, I have tried to listen carefully to negative feedback and seek the element of truth. I use video tapes, oral tapes, and comments from observers. I also keep checking back to my goals to determine when what I am doing and saying enhances or detracts from their achievement.

Deepening One's Knowledge Base

Extending one's knowledge base is the third element needed to move beyond an initial level of competence. Thinking about child development, learning theory, research findings, and learning strategies stimulates me to continually fine-tune my art. I find sources for this information in professional journals and books, as well as at continuing education classes. As an example, Putnam County administrators received a Westinghouse Grant to provide a Mathematics and Science Institute in cooperation with a local university. In this class, we were exposed to whole language, writing across the curriculum, and Used Numbers (Russell & Corwin, 1990), an approach using classifying, charting, and graphing to communicate results of investigations involving numbers. My colleagues and I were encouraged to share understandings, curriculum practices, and classroom experiences.

In another example, because my husband receives publications from the Association for Supervision and Curriculum Development, I noticed a book entitled *Making Connections* by Caine and Caine (1991). *Making Connections* has long been my personal definition of learning, so I immediately began reading the book. It proved to be extremely relevant because it provided a research base that supported my philosophical approach while validating my learning and teaching experiences.

Another area where teachers can be exposed to research and theory is in teacher editions of texts. I know that manual bashing is very popular, but I have found that most of my current teachers' editions reflect recent research and make very appropriate suggestions for management and teacher practices. By having a philosophy of education, by thinking about teaching and learning, and by seeking discussions with others, teachers can move beyond cuteness or popularity as a basis for their instructional decisions and thoughtfully evaluate teaching practices and strategies found in journals, trade magazines, and teachers' editions.

PROMOTING TEACHER DEVELOPMENT

TEACHER PREPARATION

Most teachers need outside stimulation to avoid stagnation and burn-out and to help them continue developing their art. Teacher educators can help provide that stimulation through graduate programs and through working closely with state boards of education and local school systems. I believe excellent teaching has to be observed and then practiced with a master for a change in teaching practices to occur. Since teaching is not an isolated event but occurs in the context of a complex situation, reading about it or listening to a lecture seems an ineffective way to prepare teachers. Prospective teachers need to be able to observe competent teachers and then have opportunities to analyze and discuss their observations.

I have had student observers in my classroom for several hours a week, but I have never been given an opportunity to explain my instructional and communication decisions. Unfortunately, I also never have observed a teacher educator working in an early childhood classroom. I suspect that the lack of excellent practitioners among teacher educators explains why there has been little real change in teaching. Teachers tend to teach the way they were taught.

Consequently I believe every teacher education program should have a laboratory school where master teachers demonstrate their attitudes, skills, and knowledge. Then prospective teachers could learn their art in a controlled, positive environment before being thrown into the public arena. Ideally prospective teachers would observe master teachers in the laboratory classroom at the same time they were gaining background knowledge to help them understand their observations. Gradually students would become actively involved with teaching.

At the undergraduate level, I think students could complete the liberal section of their college education in the first 2 years and then spend another 3 years evolving to full-time teaching responsibility. Too often I have heard student teachers complain that what they were taught in their teacher education programs had no relevance to practices in public schools. Many times the only qualification of supervising teachers is a masters degree and experience in teaching their subject or grade level. Teacher educators rarely evaluate supervising teachers to determine if they provide an appropriate placement for their students, and little effort seems to go into matching philosophy and practice.

Encouraging Teacher Development

Assuming that beginning teachers enter teaching as competent practitioners, teacher educators encourage continuing development primarily through graduate programs. Based upon my own professional evolution, I think graduate programs should contain components that enable teachers to develop positive attitudes, teaching skills, a philosophy of learning, and a deepened knowledge base. Unfortunately, most graduate programs overlook the attitude and skill component or give it superficial treatment. To change negative attitudes or encourage positive ones, experienced teachers need to participate in seminars that help foster self-examination, and provide opportunities to observe other teachers and be observed.

Outside observers can help experienced teachers recognize problem areas, and constructive seminars, where problems and solutions are discussed in a nonthreatening manner, can facilitate change or development. For example, many classroom teachers unconsciously treat male and female students differently. I found that I tended to pay more attention to assertive students during discussions and review sessions. As a result of this insight, I now call on students during review sessions by randomly selecting sticks bearing their names. During discussions, I make sure I involve passive students by asking them what they think. I was unaware of the need for these practices until I recorded how frequently I called on individual students. This suggestion was offered to me by a teacher educator and, if he had actually observed my classroom, he might have helped me confront other negative behaviors based on beliefs that unconsciously control my behavior.

DEVELOPING TEACHING SKILLS

Developing skills in observing, organization and decision making, communication, and self-evaluation also can be enhanced by a combination of information and practice with an expert. Although these skills often are included in graduate classes, no opportunity exists to practice these skills and receive feedback. Consequently many teachers can discuss these skills for testing purposes but do not incorporate them into their way of thinking, behaving, or teaching. Many teachers, for example, are aware of reflective listening techniques but rarely practice them because they have never had the opportunity to try them in the company of a competent communicator.

EXPANDING ONE'S KNOWLEDGE BASE

Although a constructive educational philosophy or developmental interactionist philosophy now seems mainstream, most graduate classes continue to operate in a manner that reflects a behaviorist orientation. A constructive educational philosophy assumes that learners are actively involved in their own learning as they attempt to make sense of, or find meaning in, their environment. In contrast, a behavioral orientation emphasizes matching stimuli with responses. I don't feel a constructive educational philosophy is only appropriate for young children; it is a learning approach that matches what recent research is demonstrating about how the human brain functions regardless of the learner's age.

According to Caine and Caine (1991), the research on brain function suggests that sources of information should be complex, involving not only teacher-to-student and book-to-student interaction, but also social interactions, group discovery, individual search and reflection, role playing, and integrated subject matter. It seems to me, therefore, that much more emphasis should be placed on journal writing, taping and analyzing video recordings of graduate students' teaching, individual projects that can be applied directly to the classroom, and opportunities for graduate students to teach and learn in an exemplary classroom.

MATCHING PHILOSOPHY AND TEACHER BEHAVIOR

I think that the strongest barrier to continued positive development of the art of teaching comes from teachers' lack of a consistent philosophy of education. I have attended graduate classes with students who seemed to understand child development, who seemed to have a constructive approach to learning, and who seemed to have positive attitudes towards learning. But, when I observed their teaching, it didn't correlate with their stated beliefs. Obviously, if a philosophy is part of a person's way of thinking, it is part of their practice. Apparently, these teachers only were saying what they thought the professor wanted to hear.

Therefore, I think a primary task of teacher educators should be to help classroom teachers determine if their practice is consistent with their values, assumptions, and philosophy. Intense observation by a teacher educator in conjunction with video recordings could provide the raw material for teacher educators and classroom teachers to analyze and determine what values, assumptions, and theories of learning and development appear to underlie their practices. Then teachers could decide, with guidance and encouragement from a teacher educator, how well their beliefs and practice correlate and how changes could be made to produce more direct alignment.

The ability to articulate a philosophy of education and the way in which it is practiced in a classroom enables teachers to communicate with principals, parents, and colleagues. More important, it allows teachers to evaluate popular practices, suggestions, and activities to determine which ones reflect their philosophy and enhance classroom practice.

For instance, a whole language approach is currently very popular. I have observed teachers who proclaim to be using a whole language approach and found blackline masters that go with the books they are using. Students read books and then discuss and complete activity papers. I am unable to understand how that differs from using a basal approach.

In contrast, I use the eight units in my basal as the broad themes around which I integrate subject matter. My students read stories, discuss them, act them out, write summaries of them, practice relevant phonics skills, write their own stories and papers, read their classmates' stories, choose their own books to read, and keep journals. I feel that although I use a basal, I am implementing whole language activities. This kind of eclecticism is possible because all these activities are consistent with my philosophy and assumptions.

THE NEED FOR CHANGE

Putnam County Schools recently sponsored a week-long Mathematics Institute; the Institute, which was open to teachers from all grade levels, was organized to explore a new mathematics series and new state and local outcomes. Following the Institute, I overheard experienced primary teachers, who had their masters' degrees plus many more hours, complain about using manipulatives, planning cooperative groups, relying on fewer work sheets, and teaching children to think. I listened to these teachers and came to the conclusion that they felt children must first learn basic skills and that learning only occurs as a result of practice with paper and pencil. This belief was held in spite of excellent presentations using a variety of methods during the previous week.

From this experience, as well as others, I've concluded that teacher educators have had limited influence on the teaching practices of most teachers. Perhaps if teacher educators were able to observe teachers; provide them constructive feedback; help them evaluate their attitudes toward learning, self, children, and colleagues; assist teachers in developing their communication and observation skills; give teachers access to research and the skills to evaluate and apply it in classrooms; and help teachers determine their philosophy and its correlation with their classroom practices, more teachers would be excited by a challenge and eager to apply new ideas to their own classrooms.

I realize that this kind of collaborative approach may be impossible for most teacher educators. They have research responsibilities, institutional responsibilities, and publishing responsibilities that make attending to teacher education classes difficult. I wonder if it would be possible to have two branches of teacher educators. One branch could consist of researchers and publishers, and the other branch could consist of practitioners. Practicing teacher educators would teach in classrooms part-time so that prospective and experienced teachers could observe or participate. Practicing teacher educators also would be available to travel and observe classrooms.

Where this is impossible, video technology would be helpful. Teachers could videotape their classrooms, and their tapes could be analyzed and evaluated during seminars under the guidance of practicing teacher educators. Research teacher educators and practicing teacher educators would cooperate to make sure their students had access to research information that is applicable to decisions teachers and administrators are making. With such a program, perhaps there would be a much higher correlation between educational research and typical classroom practice. Then it may be possible for experienced teachers to become more positive, enhance their teaching skills, develop deeper understandings about learning, apply research, evaluate teaching activities and practices, and more effectively evaluate themselves throughout their teaching careers. Then, perhaps, I could lay aside my fear that some day I may unconsciously quit caring, quit learning, and ultimately quit teaching while suffering delusions of competence.

REFERENCES

Caine, R., & Caine, G. (1991). *Making connections.* Alexandria, VA: Association for Supervision and Curriculum Development.

Jacobs, L. (1991). The meaning of teaching. In J. D. Quisenberry, E. A. Eddowes, & S. L. Robinson (Eds.). *Readings from Childhood Education* (pp. 287–292). Wheaton, MD: Association for Childhood Education International.

Russell, S., & Corwin, R. B. (1990). *Used numbers.* Palo Alto, CA: Dale Seymour.

COMMENTARIES

Developmental Stages in the Lives of Early Childhood Educators

David C. Berliner

The essays by Hamilton, Martin, VanArsdell, and Tull contribute to an emerging literature on the growth of expertise among teachers. This literature is relatively new and much needed for two reasons. First, the general public does not recognize that increases in pedagogical knowledge are acquired by teachers through reflection on experience in precisely the same way that artists, physicians, and attorneys acquire their expertise. Second, the general public does not realize the great complexity of the knowledge that is acquired by experts in early childhood education or other areas of teaching.

FORMS OF KNOWLEDGE

Becoming exceptional at what one does is not automatic. What distinguishes the expert physician, sculptor, or early childhood educator from more ordinary practitioners in those fields is reflection on learning from *case* and *episodic* knowledge, and mastery of *procedural* knowledge. Case knowledge is acquired by physicians, aircraft pilots, or early childhood teachers as they experience and learn from actual cases. While a physician treats and learns from a case of an inflamed appendix, a teacher treats and learns from a case of overwhelming shyness.

Episodic knowledge is gained from the personally meaningful instructive events that are affectively laden, for example, the death of a patient one has cared for and treated or the failure to influence the physically punitive parents of a young child. Both teachers and physicians mentally replay these events for a long time, wondering what they could have done differently. Episodic knowledge derives from these small epiphanous events. What is learned and felt helps physicians and teachers to be more effective and more caring when they encounter similar events.

The sequence of motoric knowledge that every artist and craftsperson relies on is called procedural knowledge. Procedural knowledge for the physician entails taking blood pressure or removing warts. For the early childhood teacher it includes routines to get students to sleep, to serve food, to teach finger painting, or to line students up for field trips.

Case, episodic, and procedural knowledge are very different from *propositional* knowledge, the knowledge acquired by physicians and teachers in their course work and from professional reading. Propositional knowledge consists of facts, concepts, and principles. Facts about pneumonia and concepts such as homeostasis are learned by the physician. Facts about the kinds of toys that are liked by children of different ages and concepts such as the zone of proximal development, preoperational thought, or imaginary play must be learned by the teacher of young children. But propositional knowledge is not what moves the novice to a higher stage of development. As VanArsdell notes, to develop as a teacher requires "time and many children":

> My understanding of child development now has many children's names and faces attached to it. I am able to rely on experiences with children in my former classes to help guide my work with individual children. . . . I now feel more confident of my ability to handle challenging situations.

Tull recognizes the limitations of propositional knowledge when she comments that teaching is so complex that "reading about it or listening to a lecture seems an ineffective way to prepare teachers." Prospective teachers, she suggests, need to observe, analyze, and discuss real world teaching. Both Tull and VanArsdell describe clearly the need for instantiation of the concepts and principles learned about in course work. But the instantiation must be in the dynamic, complex, and messy real world of the classroom. It is there that propositional, case, and episodic knowledge are melded. Reliance on propositional knowledge alone—the plight of the novice and advanced beginner—leads to fright and feelings of ineptitude.

THE PATH OF DEVELOPMENT

I have described the stages of development of highly motivated and thoughtful teachers as a progression from *novice* to *advanced beginner* to *competent* teacher. This progression ordinarily takes about 5 years. A few teachers may then go on to a higher level, the stage of the *proficient* teacher, and a very small number of teachers eventually reach the fifth and highest level of performance, that of the *expert* (Berliner, in press). My research and that of others has given rise to a number of assertions about the thinking and behavior of teachers at different stages of development. These four early childhood teachers, as they reflect upon their own development, confirm many of those assertions. Some examples follow.

EXPERIENCE AND FLEXIBILITY

If you ask a novice what to do in a particular teaching situation they will often give you an answer. Expert teachers are much less sure of themselves, saying that what they do "depends." VanArsdell pointed out that better lessons than the one she had planned sometimes occur, and that such events call for flexibility about classroom rules and the use of materials. Hamilton pointed out that experienced teachers need to find the rhythm of a class, rather than adhere to a rigid schedule. The novice, however, often prefers to run with a script, and is relatively inflexible with regard to rules and regulations. Hamilton comments on this issue when she writes that beginning teachers sometimes "stick so rigidly to a schedule that individual children's needs are not met." The expert, on the other hand, has the experience and confidence to improvise and modify. Martin recognizes something the novice is terrified to learn, namely, the inherent unpredictability of the classroom. She comments: "The longer I teach, the less I know about teaching." In teaching, as in other areas, experts are usually much more flexible than novices.

EXPERIENCE AND RESPONSIBILITY FOR LEARNING

Expert teachers more often than novice teachers seem to pass the responsibility for learning on to students. Experts try to provide the conditions for learning to take place; they know that only the student can make the learning take place. Novices seem to think they must be in charge of the entire process. Both Martin and VanArsdell talked of relinquishing authority and letting students discover some things for themselves. It is this kind of attitude that lets Martin use cross-age tutors in her instructional program. Novices rarely do that because they are unfamiliar with the management of complex instructional settings and are unwilling to relinquish authority. Novices are much less likely to use cross-age tutoring programs or cooperative learning activities. Experience apparently diminishes authoritarianism and promotes the use of more complex instructional techniques.

EXPERIENCE AND DIVERSITY

Both VanArsdell and Martin note that diversity due to culture, language, or the mainstreaming of special education children into the regular classroom need not be debilitating for a teacher. Like some of the expert teachers that we studied, they recognized that individual differences are so large in most classes that adding a bit more heterogeneity changes little. Confident, experienced teachers are more often able to welcome all children to their classrooms. The novice early childhood teacher, like other novice teachers, is less likely to have the procedural, case, and episodic knowledge that provides the confidence to instruct special children.

CRAFT KNOWLEDGE AND DEVELOPMENT

Other similarities exist, but it should be clear by now that the development of skillfulness in pedagogy (or medicine) depends on the development of craft knowledge. Only the specifics of the craft knowledge differ across professions. As Hamilton notes:

> Competent teachers have all sorts of bits of information at their fingertips that they have learned through experience . . . experimentation and by learning from other teachers. It includes . . . which tippy cups results in the fewest spills, what kinds of stuffed animals are likely to wash well and not lose their eyes, and which baby gates are actually toddler-proof but not adult-proof. It also includes where to get materials and information: Are the Fisher Price people cheaper at Toys R Us or in the educational toy catalogue? . . . What's the best source for recycled paper? How do I find out which plants on the playground are poisonous?

In the organizational and management realm, Hamilton expresses the same need for craft knowledge to ensure that toys, tables, chairs, and babies are washed regularly, and that enough diapers, wipes, and food are available. The craft knowledge that separates the more-than-competent teacher from the less-than-competent teacher is also remarked upon by Martin when she discusses the normal contradictory nature of children, the design of space for their activities, and the set of observational skills that must be mastered to plan and communicate with parents about their children's progress. Craft knowledge is also what Tull accumulated as her attitudes and skills changed with experience.

CONCLUSION

All four of these writers inform us about learning to teach. They inform us that the craft knowledge they have developed is similar to the craft knowledge acquired by the highest paid and experienced management consultants, surgeons, trial attorneys, and accountants. The craft knowledge of the expert pedagogue is no different in kind, but it is clear that it is not always as valued by society. Nevertheless, it is a unique form of knowledge. It is complex, acquired slowly, and learned only through hard work and reflection on that work. As is clear from these essays, the expert early childhood educator, like experts in any other field of endeavor, possesses knowledge that a novice cannot even imagine!

REFERENCES

Berliner, D. C. (in press). Expertise: The wonder of exemplary performances. In C. C. Block & J. Mangieri (Eds.), *Creating powerful thinking and teachers and students: Diverse perspectives.* Fort Worth, TX: Harcourt Brace.

Knowledge of Child Development and the Competence of Developing Teachers

Lilian G. Katz

Many of the issues raised in the four essays in this part warrant the attention and concern of all teacher educators. Acquiring understanding of children, having clear goals, and becoming life-long learners, for example, are issues that apply to the education of teachers for all levels of education.

Knowledge of child development, another theme common to each of these authors, *is* of particular relevance to teachers of young children. In one way or another, each of the four contributors to this section argues that a thorough knowledge of child development is essential to the ongoing development of teachers of young children. I cannot recall teachers of the upper levels of education expressing a similar commitment to the study of child development. At least four factors may account for early childhood educators' emphasis on knowledge of child development in learning to teach young children: the age of the children served, awareness of exceptional patterns of development, educational goals, and the endemic uncertainty of teaching. (What follows should not be confused with current discussion regarding the role of child development knowledge as a source of early childhood curriculum.)

EMPHASIS ON CHILD DEVELOPMENT KNOWLEDGE IN TEACHER DEVELOPMENT

THE AGE AND NEEDS OF CHILDREN SERVED

Early childhood educators prepare teachers to work with children during the period of their most rapid development. This being the case, the extent to which children's growth, development, and learning are influenced by the environment or by maturational processes or by indeterminate mixtures of the two, cannot be known with certainty. In many important aspects of children's learning, progress may be attributed to rapid physical development that enables certain kinds of learning to occur (e.g., first language learning), and the specific contribution of the environment generally, teachers in particular, can only be guessed. It seems reasonable to assume therefore, that thorough knowledge of the maturational and environmental factors involved in very early development and learning may contribute to sound decision making concerning the curriculum and teaching practices.

Second, thorough knowledge of developmental norms during the early years can enable teachers to be alert to exceptional patterns of development. The ability to identify exceptional patterns of development can enhance the teacher's ability to access available services for children with special needs and thereby make an important contribution to a child's entire future.

THE GOALS OF EARLY EDUCATIONAL SETTINGS

It is tacitly assumed that the younger the learner, the less the coverage and mastery of a body of predetermined content and skills are emphasized in the curriculum. Given the absence of an emphasis on such content, the goals of the program are likely to be formulated in terms of developmental gains deemed important precursors of later learning. Perhaps, also, this assumption accounts for the notable absence in these essays of recommendations that a beginning teacher's competence should include knowledge of subject areas such as science, literature, or music!

All four essayists acknowledge the importance of children's thinking. Yet, the "nuts and bolts" of practice, as suggested by Hamilton and implied by Martin, for example, address the teacher's preparation of the physical environment and materials rather than the knowledge and skills to be acquired and constructed by the children. Are we to assume that there are no significant content areas to be mastered by young children or their teachers? Surely even young children have to think *about* something. Does this omission perhaps reflect a lack of agreement on the question of whether some things are more important than others to think about?

PHILOSOPHY AND UNCERTAINTY

Perhaps a reason these authors and many other experienced teachers reveal a strong commitment to a particular "philosophy" is because it helps to alleviate the endemic uncertainty of the teacher's role, which is especially acute for teachers of young children. For another reason, teachers' confidence in their interactions with children are likely to influence their effectiveness: minimal confidence may cause children to challenge them; maximal confidence may lead some children to defiance; and optimal confidence is likely to result in harmonious and cooperative relationships. Thus, teachers' confidence in the "rightness" of their decisions and actions may have important practical implications. Ideological conviction may be especially important for beginning teachers. Martin's introspective comments seem to support this conclusion.

> In one sense, the longer I teach, the less I know about teaching. As a young teacher, I had much more certainty about what I expected from children and what I wanted to teach. . . . Now, after many years of teaching, I see more ambiguities, possibilities and uncertainties in a field that is surely more an art than a science, and always will be as long as we respect the complexity of the human mind and soul.

IMPLEMENTING CHILD DEVELOPMENT KNOWLEDGE

There may be many good reasons to recommend, as VanArsdell does, to "begin with a comprehensive grounding in child development." Yet, this assertion begs many questions. Is all "child development" the same? Imagine, for example, that a group of teacher education departments of a variety of teacher education institutions decided to transfer credit to and from each others' child development courses. Would the negotiations concerning content and coverage be effortless? We may, for example, readily agree to cover the basics of physical development in the form of fine- and gross-motor development, but would we be able to reach similar agreement concerning social and intellectual development? Would we, for example, agree to take a Piagetian approach? Today one may even ask which Piagetian approach. Would some of us emphasize more than others the development principles derived from psychoanalysis, Erikson, social learning theory, and various approaches to social constructivism?

Even if consensus were achieved on what child development knowledge is worth having, it is not clear how knowledge of child development is to be implemented in practice. What practices, for example, can be derived from an investigation showing that children's understanding of calendar concepts matures at an average age of about 6 years (Zhang, 1993)? Should the standard calendar ritual in preschool and kindergarten programs be abandoned completely? Should the concepts be addressed only to those children tested as "ready"? Or should adults wait until children construct these concepts on their own? Inasmuch as all children eventually grasp calendar concepts, does the relevant child development knowledge even have significant practical implications?

Of greater importance, from my point of view, is the possibility that participation in an exercise like the calendar ritual, in advance of true understanding, may influence children's conceptions of themselves as thinkers or "understanders." I suggest that, in principle, when children are expected to behave as though they understand something when in fact they do not, their confidence in their own intellectual powers can be undermined and their intellectual dispositions weakened. This principle is based on a dynamic rather than just a normative approach to child development (Katz, 1991).

This discussion suggests that one potentially valuable exercise for early childhood teachers and teacher educators may be the exchange of views concerning what child development knowledge is most worthy of mastery. Exploration of such questions as "Is some child development knowledge more useful than others?" and "How much and what kind of child development knowledge can be learned in advance of actual teaching?" could contribute substantially to refining current practices in teacher education.

Of special relevance to these questions is Tull's assertion that at the undergraduate level students should have a liberal education, followed by another assertion that student teachers complain "that what they were taught in their teacher education programs had no relevance to practice in public schools." These two all-too familiar assertions are difficult to reconcile. Why is a liberal—and, presumably, impractical—education important, while impractical teacher education courses are not? Is it perhaps that the latter address the "wrong" practices while liberal studies make no pretense at being practical? Moreover, if it is the case that teacher education courses address practices that are discrepant from those actually employed in the public schools, is one of the two sets of practices more appropriate or more on the right track than the other?

Tull also concludes "that teacher educators have had limited influence on the teaching practices of most teachers." Although I am not aware of any firm empirical evidence to support this conclusion, impressions based on 25 years of experience suggest to me that Tull's point is well taken.

I suggest that all professional schools, whether preparing lawyers, doctors, teachers, social workers, or other professionals, have two main responsibilities. One is to create new knowledge by which the practices of the profession are improved. The second is to prepare the new recruits to the profession in the use of these improved practices. If this characterization of the mission of professional schools is correct, there *must* always be a discrepancy between practices advocated in professional preparation and the standard practices in its own field. Thus practitioners' wariness of the professors of their own professions is inherent and inevitable; it "comes with the territory." As teacher educators, therefore, we are likely to benefit from examination of how best to work through the unavoidable tensions created by our mission.

DEVELOPMENTAL STAGES OF TEACHERS

These essays support a renewed interest in the developmental processes of learning to teach (see Berliner, this volume). As these essays suggest, teachers do not begin their careers with the same insights and competencies as veterans. What may be added to these discussions is the "feedforward effect," a construct that helps account for two aspects of teacher education (Katz & Raths, 1992). The first aspect is that professional education courses provide students with answers to questions not yet asked. They therefore seem impractical at best, and tiresome at worst. The second and related aspect of the feedforward effect is that once employed graduates change the meaning and value of their training experiences when they view them retrospectively. These aspects suggest the hypothesis that many students in teacher education may find their study of child development impractical, but as real experience on the job accrues, they increase its value retrospectively. If the feedforward effect is viable, then it suggests that teacher education cannot be designed on the basis of what students value during their professional preparation because their evaluation is likely to change with later experience. This begs the question of what should serve as the bases of teacher education designs.

The issues outlined above suggest that longitudinal research on teacher development may be useful in determining appropriate designs for teacher education. As we search for some insights along these lines, perhaps an even more important issue, as suggested by all the essayists, is the question of how we can help our students to become life-long learners of child development and all the other learning that contributes to effectiveness as a teacher. Surely the least we can do is to provide models of continuous learners ourselves.

REFERENCES

Katz, L. G. (1991). Pedagogical issues in early childhood education. In S. L. Kagan (Ed.), *The care and education of America's young children: Obstacles and opportunities.* The Nineti-eth Yearbook of the National Society for the Study of Education (Part I, pp. 50–68). Chicago: University of Chicago Press.

Katz, L. G., & Raths, J. D. (1992). Six dilemmas in teacher education. *Journal of Teacher Education, 43*(5), 376–385.

Zhang, L. H. (1993). *The development of children's understanding of calendar concepts.* Unpublished doctoral dissertation, University of Illinois, ChampaignUrbana.

Reflections on the Growth and Development of Teachers in Early Childhood Education

Thomas Sobol

The four essays in this section provide a rich, well-rounded, and useful set of perspectives on the professional development of teachers of young children. They are firmly grounded in practice and rich with observations gleaned from that practice. They speak in readable and direct fashion to those of us who are deeply interested in the growth of teachers. Although each writer has her own perspective, their views of what is needed, of the nature of their jobs, and of how people can learn from and improve upon what they do converge to a heartening and instructive degree. And they serve as reminders of two salient facts about early childhood education today: (1) What works for early childhood education works for later levels, too. (2) We need broad public policy on the care and education of young children.

WHAT WORKS FOR EARLY CHILDHOOD WORKS LATER, TOO

Of course, developmentally appropriate practice differs at various ages. But the *kinds* of engagement with children that make educational sense at 3, 4, or 7 years of age make just as much sense for 10-, 13-, and even 17-year-olds. As noted by Martin, "All children are learners." This confidence is grounded in knowledge of child development, matures through careful observation of children as they learn, and helps to ensure that "I remain a teacher and avoid becoming a school keeper" (Tull, citing Jacobs, 1991). Nor are children only learners; Tull sees them "as fascinating human beings—not just students." Good teaching at any age is personalized and based on observation and reflection that allow teachers to fit new learning to students' learning styles and frameworks of existing knowledge (Darling-Hammond, 1992).

In order to do a good job and to grow in competency, all teachers—not just early childhood teachers—need to work with others. They need to work closely and mutually with parents, especially, but they also need to share ideas and experience with other teachers and staff members, administrators, teacher educators, teachers-in-preparation, and other professionals in "social services agencies, child care resource and referral offices, or political advocacy groups" (Hamilton). Tull recommends that teacher educators routinely observe practicing teachers to help them "determine if their practice is consistent with their values, assumptions, and philosophy." Since children are whole human beings whose lives are influenced by families and communities, we can really educate them only by joining forces. Again, these essayists' perceptions are borne out by much current experience and research, (e.g., Center for the Future of Children, 1992; National Association of State Boards of Education, 1989).

VanArsdell deals usefully and perceptively with the need for teachers of young children to be "prepared and supported" in working with both typical learners and children with special needs. Martin emphasizes that diversity among learners is a strength. She cautions against such harmful practices as "the oversimplification of checklists and standardized test results," noting that "to me, assessment is not evaluation, but a tool for making school more responsive to the needs of the children." Again, these recommendations are in line with much current thinking, in this instance about educating children with disabilities in the least restrictive environment, about developmentally appropriate exercises and assessments in the early years, and about the nature and uses of assessment generally.

WE NEED BROAD PUBLIC POLICY ON THE
CARE AND EDUCATION OF YOUNG CHILDREN

If we want children to learn what they need to learn throughout their growing years, then as a society we must pay more attention than we currently do to the quality of children's first years of life. We cannot assume that young children are having the experiences they need to grow and learn optimally. Research as well as experience confirm that it makes no sense for society to wait until children are 5 or 6 years old before beginning to help nurture them. According to the 1990 Census, almost 60% of mothers of preschool-aged children work outside the home (National Governors' Association, 1992). About 20% of children under 6 years live in poverty (Children's Defense Fund, 1992).

These changing demographics have led leaders of national and state government, business, and industry to join educators and parents in recognizing the importance of early childhood education. In 1990, for example, the first of the National Education Goals adopted by the National Governors' Association was that "all children in America will start school ready to learn" (p. 19). The next year the Committee for Economic Development (1991), an independent organization of business leaders and educators, called for the nation to "redefine education as a process that begins at birth" and to "recognize that the potential for learning begins even earlier, and encompasses the physical, social, emotional, and cognitive development of children" (p. 5). Early childhood education, therefore, figures large in the Committee's recommendations for improving the results of the American education system. In New York state, the Board of Regents (which oversees education in the state at all levels) has also made early childhood education a key component in its efforts to promote education reform (e.g., New York State Board of Regents, 1991, 1992).

Unfortunately, despite this public recognition, we still lack comprehensive national and state policies to provide good, broadly accessible, and reliable care and education for young children. Instead, we have a patchwork of providers: public and private preschools, Head Start, and formal and informal child care in centers and homes. These programs are governed by various laws and sets of regulations and financed by various funding streams. Some programs are readily accessible where they are needed; some are not. Some of the care and education provided is good; some is not. Large questions remain to be answered. Who should provide child care and early childhood education: the public sector, the private sector, families, or others? How can it best be organized? How should it be funded? Just as we are trying to arrive at a national policy for the provision of medical care, so must we, as a society, arrive at a comprehensive child care policy.

Such a policy must take into account the context within which early childhood educators grow in competence; for their growth is nurtured when they have resources, flexibility, and a structure that not only permits but encourages interaction with other providers of child care, teachers of children at later stages of development, teacher educators, parents and other family members, social workers, health care workers, psychologists, librarians—the entire set of actors whose contributions are too often fragmented, but must be focused if we are to give every child the start he or she deserves.

The four essays in this section allude to the need for a structure of support, for example, when Hamilton and VanArsdell describe the resourcefulness teachers need to put together an environment with whatever materials happen to be available, or when all four essayists stress the importance of learning with and from other teachers, teaching assistants, parents, prospective teachers, and teacher educators. And conversely, the lack of such a support structure may well lead to the burn-out of and failure to develop potentially excellent teachers—a phenomenon to which these essays also allude. The attention we pay to the quality of children's first years of life repays itself immeasurably in later years (e.g., the Committee for Economic Development, 1991). These four essays provide a rich store of ideas and advice for teachers, teacher educators, and all who are interested in raising and educating our children better.

REFERENCES

Center for the Future of Children. (1992, Spring). School linked services. *The Future of Children, 2,* 1. Los Altos, CA: Center for the Future of Children, The David and Lucile Packard Foundation.

Children's Defense Fund. (1992). *Child poverty data from the 1990 census.* Washington, DC: Author.

Committee for Economic Development. (1991). *The unfinished agenda: A new vision for child development and education.* New York: Author.

Darling-Hammond, L. (1992, April). Re-framing the school reform agenda: Developing capacity for school transformation. Invited address, Annual Meeting of the American Educational Research Association, San Francisco, CA.

National Association of State Boards of Education. (1989). *Joining forces: A report from the first year.* Alexandria, VA: Author.

National Governor's Association. (1990). National education goals. Washington, DC: Author. Reprinted in "America's Education Goals," *America 2000,* Washington, DC: US Department of Education.

National Governor's Association. (1992, May 29). New census data reveal redistribution of poverty. *The New York Times,* (p. 7).

New York State Board of Regents. (1991). *A new compact for learning.* New York: Author.

New York State Board of Regents. (1992). *Supporting young children and families, Policy Statement.* New York: Author.

PART III

What Is Needed to Become a Competent Early Childhood Teacher Educator?

CHAPTER **9**

Preparing Tomorrow's Inventors

Greta G. Fein

I have been asked to respond to the question "What is needed to become a competent early childhood teacher educator?" Let me say at the outset that the question is a daunting one. The answer can only be offered as a contingency: It all depends on the respondent's vision of the field. In my view, early childhood education is a cultural invention tied to the dreams, anxieties, and resources of the larger society (Kessen, 1979). As such, teacher education is an invention once removed. Who will teach, what will be taught, and whom, will be governed as much by larger circumstances as by the pedagogical principles and practices the profession holds dear.

The preparation of those who will teach infants and toddlers is especially controversial. The field's early inventors, including Comenius and Froebel, appointed the mother as the child's best teacher. Others, most especially Pestalozzi and Rousseau, had doubts about the mother's competence and set out to either improve her skills or replace her with a professional. Perhaps mothers could be trained; if not, the infant belonged in an alternative setting, one that was clean, healthy, and staffed by skilled individuals (Fein & Clarke-Stewart, 1973). Until recently, the cleavage between the mother school and the teacher school followed social class lines: leave middle-income infants at home and put poor infants in alternative environments (Fein, 1980; Singer, 1992). However, these alternative environments—whether day nursery, dame school, or foundling home—may have been little better than the child's own impoverished home. How best to save babies has never been settled.

When out-of-home care was in disrepute, strategies such as widow's pensions and social assistance emerged to keep the mothers of infants and toddlers out of the work force. As if to mock the public policy inventions of yesterday, maternal employment during the past two decades has tripled in this age group. Working mothers now span all social class groups and their infants receive care in diverse settings by individuals with little or no training and few educational credentials. Although especially acute in infant and toddler care, the problem is pervasive in the field (Caruso, 1991).

135

In the comments that follow, I first discuss some implications of the view that this field, its pedagogy, and its professionals are cultural products. I then argue that a multitiered system of professional development is needed to meet the demand for caregivers at a cost the community can bear. A crucial ingredient in the elaboration of such a system is the preparation of a sophisticated cadre of early childhood teachers from whom the leadership for multitiered training will come. Most important, from this cadre will come those who will invent an elaborated and coherent pedagogy for infants.

EARLY CHILDHOOD EDUCATION AS A CULTURAL PRODUCT

THE INVENTION OF THE FIELD

As educational historians often note, educational enterprises are informed by large world views that reflect the social urgencies and preoccupations of a particular historical epoch (Finkelstein, 1979). Even though a given view may fade in time, some aspects of its original suppositions tend to be incorporated into those views that follow. As a consequence, what is meant by early childhood education is more easily defined in retrospect than prospect.

The first inventor of early childhood education may have been John Amos Comenius (1592–1667). Comenius was in the forefront of the enlightenment, and his larger agenda was universal literacy (Fein & Clarke-Stewart, 1973). He envisioned a systematic sequence of educational experiences beginning in infancy and culminating in the pooling of all knowledge in multidisciplinary institutions of higher education. In Comenius's scheme, children below 6 years of age were to be taught at home by their mothers. Education at these ages was to consist of rich, playful encounters with real world events, along with gentle training in self-management, obedience, respect, and other socially valued traits. Then when children were ready for school, a single teacher, aided by books designed to bridge the mental distance between the concrete object and the graphic symbol, could bring literacy to hundreds of children at a time. The problem posed by Comenius has been with us ever since. What particular pedagogic strategies and tools are needed at each age level to bring about universal literacy?

Almost a hundred years later, Samuel Wilderspin attempted to apply selected aspects of the Comenian vision to children of the poor in England (McCann, 1966). Unfortunately, Comenius had not translated his insights into a practical pedagogy. Exactly what do you do on the first day of school? In Wilderspin's case, the pedagogical vacuum became dramatically evident when 38 children between the ages of 2 and 5 years turned up on the first day:

> As the mothers left, the entire group burst into crying, "Mummy, Mummy!" Wilderspin's wife endeavored to calm the children; but was forced to leave the classroom as it all became too much for her. Wilderspin also fled, exhausted by

his efforts. . . . He left behind a mass of screaming children kicking at the door. In desperation, Wilderspin grabbed his wife's hat, perched it on top of an old mop, and rushed back into the classroom. To his astonishment the children stopped crying. Before total chaos could break out again, he had an inspiration, and yelled: "Now we are going to play 'ducks' and I am the big duck." All the children started to quack in chorus. After that, they played "hen and chickens" and before they knew. . . it was twelve o'clock (Singer, 1992, p. 35).

Wilderspin concluded that learning in young children was embedded in active, playful encounters. His introduction of blocks for building and trees for climbing were concrete expressions of this understanding. But he also believed that the infant school should teach reading and writing. Towards this end, he created the "gallery," a small amphitheater designed to permit the teacher to watch his 50 or so pupils as he led them through various didactic exercises. Even though basic drills continued in smaller groups of 10, the children still were bored and restless (Singer, 1992). By mid-19th century, even Wilderspin was disillusioned by the dull and mechanical practices of teachers who claimed to use his methods. The invention of early childhood education could have ended there. Fortunately, it did not.

Friedrich Froebel (1792–1852) soon filled the pedagogical vacuum with specific, carefully described activities for children between the ages of 2 and 5 years. To ensure the proper transmission of his method, Froebel started the first training course in 1839. The movement grew so rapidly, that by 1850 Froebel was involved in the opening of the first college to prepare teachers. The Hochschule für Frauen was a women's college where prospective teachers received a liberal arts education as well as a thorough grounding in principles of Froebelian pedagogy. Froebel believed that women were suited by nature to teach young children. Even so, these natural talents required systematic cultivation. As the Froebelian movement spread, so did teacher education institutions. In the United States there were 10 kindergartens by 1870 and 1 teacher training institute. By 1880, there were 400 kindergartens and 10 teacher training programs (Cavallo, 1979). The rule seems to be that the invention of teacher education follows the invention of inspired pedagogy.

Yet a new generation of committed teachers rejected Froebelian methods (Pratt, 1948). By the second decade of the 20th century, this new generation invented a new pedagogy. The work of the progressivists was enlarged by the philosophy of John Dewey, sensitized by the psychodynamic theories of neo-Freudians, and heartened by the behaviorist optimism of Thorndike (Hewes, 1990; Lazerson, 1972; White & Buka, 1987). The child study movement fed the growing hunger of educators for information about children's development. Experimental nursery schools were established across the country, and, in many cases, these schools also served as teacher-training sites. What evolved over the next 2 decades was a mainstream, core pedagogy that filled classroom spaces with activity centers, diverse materials, and carefully planned teacher-led group times. As Lazerson (1972) notes:

The conduct curriculum, the project method, the activity movement, and free play all reflected somewhat differing approaches to early childhood education. . . . Yet classroom activities remained strikingly similar. . . . Although variations existed in practice, a pedagogical orthodoxy was being enunciated. . . . With their sand-boxes, paints, clay, dolls, and workbenches, most classrooms looked strikingly similar. . . . By the end of the 1920s, a common curriculum for nursery–first grade had evolved, with an increasing number of teacher training institutions offering a common preschool–primary school course of study (pp. 47–49).

A PEDAGOGY FOR INFANTS AND TODDLERS

Missing from this evolving consensus was a pedagogy for infants and toddlers. With publication of Spitz's (1946) studies of infants in foundling homes and Bowlby's (1951) report to the World Health Organization, abandoned and homeless infants were placed in adoptive or foster homes rather than residential homes or day nurseries. Schemes for the education of preschoolers in group settings were advanced with enthusiasm and promoted as psychologically wholesome and beneficial extensions of mother care. In sharp contrast, the presence of younger children in these settings was viewed with alarm.

Even though the 1960s saw a revival of programs for poor children (Provence & Naylor, 1983; Ramey & Mills, 1977), most infant intervention projects focused on parent education either through parent–child centers or home visiting programs (Clarke-Stewart & Fein, 1983; Gordon, 1972). Poverty programs for infants were built on the "mother school" tradition rather than the "teacher school" tradition. Songs and games for infants were collected, and some effort was made to add a developmental rationale for recommended activities (Gordon, 1972; Kessen, Fein, Clarke-Stewart, & Starr, 1975). Mothers were coached in styles of responsive, contingent, positive interaction deemed to be beneficial for infants. Yet the sum of these parts did not yield a pedagogy comparable in depth and richness to that which had emerged for older preschoolers.

Positive pedagogical inventions are not part of the tradition for infant and toddler care. This care, typically the purview of social welfare agencies, has been governed by a view of caregivers as warm, sensitive, responsive, loving, mother figures who engage in one-on-one, face-to-face interactions with a single child. But this model may not be the only one, or best one, for group care settings. Perhaps, group care requires techniques for promoting exchanges between infants who, research tells us, find other children fascinating. Or, perhaps, particular interactive patterns can engage several children at a time; and perhaps, inter-turn "wait time" has special significance in a group setting. The mother model represents a defensive, apologetic attitude toward group care for infants and toddlers. As a result, strategies for personalizing and individualizing interactions between children and adults in group settings remain unexplored. Such strategies will provide only some of the possibilities for a pedagogy yet to be invented.

Professional neglect of this age also may reflect economic realities. To meet adult–infant ratios (three or four infants to one adult), it usually is necessary to employ more caregivers and to do so at minimum wage, thus primarily attracting people with no training in early childhood education and little formal schooling (Hofferth, 1992). Professional expectations also are reflected in the kinds of teacher certification offered by different states (Cooper & Eisenhart, 1990). Only three states offer certification across the age range of birth through third grade and two others offer certification for birth to 4 years of age. Admittedly, the age boundaries of birth to 8 years cover a period of tremendous change. Yet wide boundaries offer professionals trained in early childhood education great opportunities for impact, especially if one can argue that a coherent view of teaching and development can be applied to these diverse ages. Thus, I would argue that certification across the age range is in the best interests of children.

PREPARING A SOPHISTICATED CADRE OF EARLY CHILDHOOD TEACHERS

THE INVENTORS

It is clear that the training and supervision of child care providers is a multilayered enterprise. Fewer than 45% of child care workers in centers have college degrees, and fewer than 50% of those providing family day care have more than 1 year of college. Of those who have degrees, only 10% to 17% have degrees in early education. Even though efforts to improve the quality of practice are urgently needed, these efforts must be designed for a diverse population with varying levels of commitment to the field and varying types of academic skills (Roupp, Travers, Glantz, & Coelen, 1979).

I think we need two models of professional preparation for teachers of infants and toddlers. In the supervisory model, caregivers receive on-site supervision by center directors or lead teachers. The problem, however, is that the directors and lead teachers often lack academic degrees or training in the field (Caruso, 1991). The solution to this dilemma is to insert a second training tier to provide training for potential on-site supervisors (Perry, 1992).

But who will train the trainers of supervisors or the trainers of trainers? At some point, not too far away, the field will have to prepare a cadre of well-informed, highly expert early childhood teacher–generalists who will some day invent a pedagogy for our youngest children. Only through such a pedagogy can we make the case that infant and toddler education and care can offer special opportunities for child growth and personal development. Some elements of the pedagogy may enrich children's lives at home with their mothers; but in its totality, this new pedagogy should describe the means by which the lives of infants and toddlers in group settings can be made optimally stimulating, sociable, and affectionate.

The primary responsibility for training this cadre must be borne by colleges and universities. To meet this responsibility, teacher preparation programs need to have a strong infant and toddler care component within a broader developmental configuration.

EDUCATING THE INVENTORS OF TOMORROW

Early childhood teacher education is a fairly new area of study. Much of current practice rests upon studies of the preparation of those who will teach in the elementary and secondary school. In my opinion, too much of this research deals with didactic methods and structured, teacher-centered classrooms. Even so, there are some emerging notions that can be used when thinking about the preparation of early childhood educators equipped to invent tomorrow's pedagogy; we attempt to use these notions in our teacher preparation program at the University of Maryland.

In my own work, I find a transformational view of professional education most helpful (Fein & Schwartz, 1982; Jackson, 1986). According to this view, professionals are people who examine educational situations in a special analytic way (Kennedy, 1987). First of all, professionals "see" these situations with unusual vividness; they have a heightened sense of what is relevant to learning for a particular individual or group at a particular moment. Then, they are able to transform their "insight" into actions that may consist of doing nothing at all. How does such a person think? Vivian Paley's wonderful books—all of them—provide an on-line account of such thinking in an unusually talented teacher and pedagogical inventor. The question, of course, is how can such transformational thinking be developed in teacher education programs for infants and toddlers? I have identified four characteristics as essential—though not sufficient—to teacher preparation programs desirous of achieving a transformational view of professional education.

A Situated Knowledge Base

I would argue that the knowledge base for early childhood teachers consists of principles of child development and education, admonitions about good practice distilled from 200 years of experience, and a set of ethical standards that govern relations with children, parents, and colleagues. Much of this knowledge can be found in books, but it does not become the property of the student until it is actively used to understand individual children and particular classrooms. In our teacher preparation programs, theoretical principles are applied to particular classroom events as these events are observed and recorded by our students.

Observational Fluency

It is generally understood that the generalities of educational psychology, child development, or even philosophy, must be translated into terms appropriate to specific cases. Even more because the richest early childhood teaching is done at the teachable moment, teachers must be able to do on-the-spot diagnoses of classroom events and quickly decide what to do. The quality of teacher decisions is necessarily tied to the quality of information entering into the diagnosis. For this reason, teacher education programs are obligated to teach observation skills.

Reflection

Reflective practice has become a major theme in recent discussions of teacher education (Kennedy, 1987; Schon, 1983). The reflective practitioner, according to these discussions, is one who thinks about classroom events in an effort to understand them. A major task facing prospective teachers, therefore, is learning how to analyze particular classroom situations, connect their analysis to general principles, and then arrive at conclusions about the possible consequences of a specific course of action. This view has led our teacher preparation program to a model of teaching as deliberate action.

Interactive Routines

Successful deliberate action as a teacher requires a set of routines likely to engage the interest of infants and toddlers, along with practice in situations in which these routines may apply. All together, prospective teachers

> need experiences upon which to draw, the ability to conduct mental experiments, the ability to critically evaluate their outcomes, and the ability to revise their definition of the situation if not satisfied with the solutions the mental experiment yielded. . . . Professional educators must not only provide their students with these things, but do so in a way that transforms the students into thinkers capable of deliberation and of deliberate action. (Kennedy, 1987, p. 149)

SOME PROGRAMMATIC FEATURES

From an institutional perspective, the easiest way to prepare prospective teachers is to require a particular set of courses taken in whatever sequence suits the student. Then, after meeting certain prerequisites, the student participates in a supervised teaching experience.

We do not follow the easy way at the University of Maryland. Rather, we use a cohort model in which a group of students enters the program, takes blocked and carefully sequenced courses for two semesters, and concludes with student teaching. Even though the use of cohorts is an administrative nightmare, the cohort system makes it possible to achieve a level of programmatic integration not possible with the more conventional, free-wheeling credit-count arrangement. It also offers prospective teachers the beginnings of a stable, professional peer network. Finally, even though our students, like Sam Wilderspin, worry about the first day of school, we stress concepts, principles, and reflective decision making. Our approach is characterized by four programmatic elements.

Vertical Integration

The ideal sequence for course work and student teaching has been a long-standing debate among teacher educators (Kennedy, 1987). If student teaching comes last, students must call upon what was learned months earlier in an abstract form. And if student teaching comes first, students have a rich perception of the classroom, but the fit between theory and these perceptions is unclear. Vertical integration means that field experiences and course work are concurrent. We orchestrate this integration in our program through a systematic sequence chosen to underscore important theoretical issues.

Developmental Sequence

The teacher preparation program at the University of Maryland roughly follows an infancy to school age sequence. For 6 weeks, students study infancy in their child development and method classes (currently, Children's Literature and Creative Activities). Concurrently, they are involved in an infant placement either in a child care center, a family day care home, or a home with a mother who is not working. Students are in their placements twice a week, for 6 hours a week. They then move on to a preschool placement, and course material shifts to this age level. In the second semester, they spend one day a week in a primary classroom. Concurrently, course work covers the development of school-aged children, and methods in domains such as language arts, reading, and mathematics.

Orchestrated Field Analysis

It is generally agreed that prospective early childhood teachers must be good observers. But observation can be defined as field notes, journal entries at the end of a day, or the 30-second noting of predefined behavioral events. I believe that the best training "to see" comes from narrative specimen records, structured probes derived from classical child development paradigms, interpretive commentaries, and synthesizing case studies. I do not believe that observations using predetermined behavioral categories are nearly as valuable as those that capture moment-to-moment behavioral change using objective, yet vivid, descriptive language. In our program, students complete fairly elaborate field assignments in which naturalistic observations and more structured probes serve as the data base for interpretations of child, teacher, and classroom characteristics, using principles derived from material studied in their courses.

The question then becomes: How do the principles, admonitions, and social norms I have learned in class apply to this particular set of events? Preconstructed "cases" may serve a similar function and these, too, have a place. Nevertheless, personally observed, authentic situations provide a closer approximation to the actual teaching context. In evaluating this material, students can come to grips with the need to impose flexible, conceptual order on the complexity, subtlety, and inherent ambiguity of what happens in educational settings.

These assignments each require a description of the setting, a 15- to 20-minute narrative specimen record, and an indepth evaluation of the connections between observed behaviors and principles of child development or early education. In addition, the assignment may include several structured probes linked to particular developmental phenomena, for example, students are asked to assess object permanence, mother–infant interaction style, or linguistic development. These data are used as the basis of a case study, that is, an indepth study of a particular child in a particular setting. Here, again, students are asked to reflect on observed events, to consider their implications for development and education, and then to propose modifications of the setting that would better meet the target child's developmental needs and educational potential.

Interdisciplinary Integration

Because we use a cohort plan, it is possible to assemble teaching faculty into teaching teams. At their best, these interdisciplinary teams support our program's position that integrated learning environments are good for adults as well as young children. During their second semester, students apply this approach by creating an integrated unit that systematically introduces classroom activities for language, arts, science, math, and social studies through a unifying theme. Frankly, in our present program, there are far too many domain-specific methods courses that, by their very position in the program, create a force for fragmentation. A controversial aspect of our proposed post-baccalaureate Holmes-inspired program is that some of these are eliminated.

FROM THE RANKS OF GENERALISTS

Currently, teacher preparation at the University of Maryland is a 4-year program, with a year and a half of professional work, leading to a bachelor degree in education. In order to make sure that prospective teachers have some contact with the liberal arts and sciences, there is a host of prerequisites. Unfortunately, these prerequisites amount to a fairly shallow general education. Our students get little more than a "101" college education, even though by our requirements they do so with a 2.5 or better grade point average (GPA).

Although the path has been bumpy, our program is moving toward post-baccalaureate certification with a master's degree for those who choose to complete the remaining requirements. This program should be especially attractive to mature students who already have an undergraduate degree and wish to be credentialed in the field. I believe that it is from among these individuals that the inventors of tomorrow's pedagogy for infants and toddlers will emerge. They will be generalists in the sense that they are comfortable with a wide age range and appreciate subtle features of classrooms and schools.

The sociocultural context of infant and toddler care currently does not favor pedagogical invention or specialized teacher education. Even though the presence of infants in center and family care settings has increased in the past decade, this increase happened in the midst of a debate among professionals about whether nonparental care is potentially harmful for young children (Fein & Fox, 1988). Guides for the management and education of infants and toddlers in group care have been published (Goodwin & Scrag, 1988), and specialized caregiver training programs have been designed for individuals caring for infants and toddlers (Perry, 1992), all good signs of efforts to strengthen the program quality of infant and toddler care. Even so, we do not have good evidence for whether or not it is better to assign infants to a stable caregiver or leave responsibility for a particular infant more open (Wilcox, Staff, & Ramoine, 1980), even though our implicit family model supports the former. Without a well-formed and empirically supported pedagogy, quality-of-care indicators will remain limited to structural variables, interactiveness, and some ad hoc judgments of physical or administrative amenities.

The pressure for infant and toddler care is intense and cultural views about child care at the youngest ages is changing. If a pedagogy is to be invented, who will be the inventors? In this essay, I have argued that universities, colleges, and professional training schools must assume front-line responsibility for preparing tomorrow's educational leadership. In early childhood education, this leadership will need a broad background in the care and education of children from birth to 8 years. With a little luck, some graduates will gravitate towards infant and toddler care, develop deep experiences in this area, and, one day, invent the pedagogy and training needed to make schools for infants and toddlers into places good enough for my grandchildren.

REFERENCES

Bowlby, J. (1951). *Maternal care and mental health.* Geneva: World Health Organization.

Caruso, J. J. (1991). Supervisors in early childhood programs: An emerging profile. *Young Children, 46*(6), 20–26.

Cavallo, D. (1979). The politics of latency. In B. Finkelstein (Ed.), *Regulated children/Liberating children.* (pp. 158–184). New York: Psychohistory Press.

Clarke-Stewart, A. K., & Fein, G. G. (1983). Early childhood programs. In P. H. Mussen (series Ed.) & M. Haith & J. Campos (Vol. Eds.), *Handbook of child psychology* (Vol. II, pp. 917–1000). New York: Wiley.

Cooper, J. M., & Eisenhart, C. E. (1990). The influence of recent educational reforms on early childhood teacher education programs. In B. Spodek & O. Saracho (Eds.) *Early childhood teacher preparation* (Vol. I, pp. 176–191). New York: Teachers College Press.

Fein, G. G. (1980). The informed parent. In S. Kilmer (Ed.), *Advances in Early Education and Day Care* (Vol. I, pp. 155–185). Greenwich, CT: JAI Press.

Fein, G. G., & Clarke-Stewart, A. K. (1973). *Day care in context.* New York: Wiley.

Fein, G. G., & Fox, N. (1988). Infant day care: A special issue. *Early Childhood Research Quarterly, 3,* 227–234.

Fein, G. G., & Schwartz, P. M. (1982). Developmental theories in early childhood education. In B. Spodek (Ed.), *Handbook of research in early childhood education* (pp. 82–104). New York: Free Press.

Finkelstein, B. (Ed.). (1979). *Regulated children/Liberated children.* New York: Psychohistory Press.

Goodwin, A., & Scrag, L. (1988). Setting up for infant care: Guidelines for centers and family day care homes. Washington, DC: NAEYC.

Gordon, I. (1972). Instructional theory approach to the analysis of selected early childhood programs. In I. Gordon (Ed.), *Early childhood education: The seventy-first yearbook of the national society for the study of education, Part II* (pp. 203–228). Chicago, IL: Chicago University Press.

Hewes, D. (1990). Historical foundations of early childhood teacher training: The evolution of kindergarten teacher preparation. In B. Spodek & O. Saracho (Eds.), *Early childhood teacher preparation* (pp. 1–22). New York: Teachers College Press.

Hofferth, S. (1992). *The demand for and supply of child care.* In A. Booth (Ed.), *Child care in the 1990s: Trends and consequences* (pp. 3–25). Hillsdale, NJ: Lawrence Erlbaum.

Jackson, P. W. (1986). *The practice of teaching.* New York: Teachers College Press.

Kennedy, M. M. (1987). Inexact sciences: Professional education and the development of expertise. In E. Z. Rothkopf (Ed.), *Review of education* (Vol. 14, pp. 133–168). Washington, DC: American Educational Research Association.

Kessen, W. (1979). The American child and other cultural inventions. *American Psychologist, 34,* 815–820.

Kessen, W., Fein, G. G., Clarke-Stewart, A. K., & Starr, S. (1975). Variations in home-based infant education: Language, play, and social development. (Final Report No. OCD-CB-98) New Haven, CT: Yale University.

Lazerson, M. (1972). The historical antecedents of early childhood education. In I. Gordon (Ed.), *Early childhood education: The seventy-first yearbook of the national society for the study of education, Part II* (pp. 33–54). Chicago, IL: Chicago University Press.

McCann, W. P. (1966). Samuel Wilderspin and the early infant schools. *British Journal of Educational Studies, 14,* 188–204.

Perry, J. (1992). A review of infant/toddler issues in supervision and mentorship. In E. Fenichel (Ed.), *Learning through supervision and mentorship* (pp. 56–60). Washington, DC: Zero to Three.

Pratt, C. (1948). *I learn from children: An adventure in progressive education.* New York: Simon & Schuster.

Provence, S., & Naylor, A. (1983). *Working with disadvantaged parents and their children.* New Haven, CT: Yale University Press.

Ramey, C. T., & Mills, P. J. (1977). Social and intellectual consequences of day care for high risk infants. In R. A. Webb (Ed.), *Social development in childhood: Day care programs and research* (pp. 79–110). Baltimore, MD: The Johns Hopkins Press.

Roupp, R., Travers, J., Glantz, F., & Coelen, C. (1979). *Children at the center: Final results of the National Day Care Study.* Cambridge, MA: ABT Associates.

Schon, D. A. (1983). *The reflective practitioner.* New York: Basic Books.

Singer, E. (1992). *Child care and the psychology of development.* London: Routledge.

Spitz, R. (1946). Hospitalism: An inquiry into the genesis of psychiatric conditions in early childhood. *The Psychoanalytic Study of the Child, 2,* 313–342.

White, S. H., & Buka, S. L. (1987). Early education programs, traditions, and policies. In E. Z. Rothkopf (Ed.), *Review of Education* (Vol. 14, pp. 43–92). Washington, DC: American Educational Research Association.

Wilcox, B. M., Staff, P., & Ramoine, M. F. (1980). A comparison of individual with multiple assignments of caregivers to infants in day care. *The Merrill Palmer Quarterly, 26,* 53–62.

CHAPTER **10**

The Value of Developmentally Appropriate Practice for All Children

Betty L. Hutchison

What does it take to teach someone else to teach young children between birth and 8 years competently? My short answer is training, experience, and a point of view. Advanced study in appropriate disciplines plus actual experience with real children in a variety of situations ensure validity to teacher educators' recommendations, but it is the philosophical underpinnings that supply coherence.

In this essay, I integrate discussion of these three facets of a competent early childhood teacher educator, drawing heavily on my personal experiences with young children, their families, and adult early childhood students. My experiences in early childhood education primarily have been in programs for children under age 6. In my opinion, however, the principles of effective teaching with young children up to age 8 are no different.

My teaching experiences have been extremely diverse. I began my career as a kindergarten teacher in a large urban school system. Because my kindergarten teaching career included numerous school settings, I had the opportunity to teach children of many racial and ethnic backgrounds and from all socioeconomic levels. Additionally, I have worked as a supervisor in a Head Start program and have been the administrator of campus-based child care programs that provided full-day early education for the young children of students, staff, and community parents.

My experience with adults includes teaching and supervising students in early childhood programs in suburban upper-income communities in two metropolitan areas. I also have taught predominantly black low-income community college students who work in inner-city programs for children. As a program designer, I have developed and administered programs that provide training for family child care providers, foster parents, and students seeking the Child Development Associate (CDA) credential to work with infants and toddlers, preschoolers, or parents as home-visitors. Many of these CDAs were awarded to bilingual and bicultural stu-

146

dents, including students who were predominantly Spanish-speaking and Mandarin Chinese-speaking. Currently, I am an associate professor and coordinator of the Graduate Program in Early Childhood Education on the Evanston, Illinois campus of the National College of Education, which is part of the National-Louis University system. My work and my life, therefore, have encompassed children, parents, and early childhood students in all their splendid diversity, and I have arrived at certain conclusions that seem to me to have the aura of both universality and inevitability. These experiences lead me to assert that early childhood students must

- Become students of human development
- Base their practice on developmental principles
- Recognize that, with young children, care and education are not dichotomous, but aspects of the same process
- Extend their practice beyond cognitive concerns to include the familial and social aspects of the lives of children in their programs

These tenets, in turn, suggest that early childhood teacher educators have a special responsibility to

- Provide early and continuous experience with young children under a variety of conditions
- Provide experiences in programs that are models of good practice
- Introduce students to the broad aspects of the teacher role, including
    Acting as a partner with parents as well as an educator
    Becoming an informed actor in the realm of social policy

KNOWLEDGE OF THE DEVELOPMENTAL PROCESS MATTERS

A society that stresses freedom and individuality makes knowledge of human development imperative for its educators. Early childhood teacher educators should help students think less about becoming "teachers of children" and more about becoming "students of children."

As improbable as it may seem to others, the early childhood profession places its reliance and faith on children as originators and responsible actors in the educational process. Within this context, teachers become facilitators, participators, and translators, but rarely sole purveyors of received truths. Although teachers usually have the social knowledge that children lack, they need to accept their limitations when it comes to defining individual educational goals. Enacting this role requires prospective teachers to become expert in knowing normative behaviors of children and the conditions that foster their development. Concurrently, they must be able to detect programmatic practices that are symptomatic of disregard for the developmental levels of children.

I first taught in a public school kindergarten in the era before Head Start. The program was a traditional half-day kindergarten enrolling children who would be 5 years of age before December 1 of their enrollment year.

Although I held a generic K–8 teaching certificate, I had the good fortune to attend a teacher preparation program that provided specialized courses for kindergarten majors. My kindergarten methods classes emphasized progressive educational theory and experience in nursery schools. As I studied progressive education with its strong overtones of John Dewey (l938/1981), I became more convinced that kindergartens, which, at that time, were basically external to the 1–12 educational system, were the only places in the public school system where progressive educational principles could be put into practice.

Even so, once assigned as a teacher in my own classroom, I had much to learn that I had not encountered during my laboratory teaching experience. A striking example was my introduction to "the test" administered near the end of the school year. This instrument was designed to assess a kindergarten child's overall readiness to learn how to read. It contained the usual vocabulary items, plus matching and copying tasks. During the test, children who all year long had been free to move about, talk, and help each other, were expected to sit apart with no talking allowed, keep their eyes on their own papers, conform to timed sequences, and pick up and lay down pencils on command.

I was absolutely the wrong person to be given the power to test young children. As much as I believed in progressive, child-centered principles, I also thought that tests were fun and that high test scores were important. As a black child raised in the tradition of the necessity for over-achievement, I was a test "junkie."

Today, as I look back, I wonder about those children. I assume the majority of them survived the experience, but what about the ones who performed poorly? I remember one child who probably had an undetected vision problem. No matter how hard he tried, even after placing his fingers on the matching symbols, he could not draw the connecting lines. He was made to try over and over by a disbelieving, ignorant young teacher.

With experience, I eventually came to despise "the test." I came to realize that my own first-hand and cumulative knowledge of children strongly correlated with most test results. Even more important, my knowledge of a particular child was often a better predictor of subsequent school performance. The point of this personal anecdote is that, as a new teacher, I had neither the information nor the backbone to question the well-established practice of testing.

Three factors contributed to serious deficiencies in my preparation to teach: (1) lack of study of holistic human development; (2) continual emphasis on strategies for classroom instruction and management of groups of children in order to "teach" them; and (3) the general lack of exemplary programs outside the university system.

The trend toward enrollment of younger and younger children into formal programs, in conjunction with recent legislation mandating adaptation of environments for children challenged by physical and mental anomalies, reinforces my belief regarding the importance of having appropriate baseline expectations for all children. I try to emphasize to my students that the first question of an early childhood teacher is not "What does the child know?" but "How does the child feel, both physically and emotionally?"

USING DEVELOPMENTAL PRINCIPLES TO INFORM PRACTICE

During my kindergarten career, I worked with children from the most privileged economic backgrounds as well as children who lived in desperate circumstances. They came from a range of ethnic and cultural backgrounds. Probably none of them experienced the extremes of violence that seem so common today, but the differences in their experiences were still so great that it could be reasonably imagined that they might need to be taught in very different ways. However, in the majority of cases, I became more and more aware that my most successful days (years) were those when the children and I planned our classroom proceedings together.

At the end of the day, with labeled, big block structures still intact, a cooperative mural half completed, and play dough animals waiting on the table for the next day's construction of a jungle, the room was a custodian's nightmare and a child's haven. I became a resource to the children, pulling from my reserve of experiences to contribute information or suggestions to keep their projects going. Even before the educational jargon contained the term *developmentally appropriate,* children of many backgrounds were demonstrating to me that they could be trusted to want to learn and become the agents of their own instruction.

However, since schooling and intellectual functioning are synonymous in the minds of most prospective teachers, the notion of surrendering learning to children is akin to an oxymoron. Thus, I have found helping potential early childhood teachers develop the trust and needed background to respond to children's initiatives to be a very complicated challenge.

First, there is the methodological paradox. Beginning students need to do extensive planning for even the most mundane tasks in order to ensure that materials are ready, their techniques sound, and their goals achievable. When more ambitious activities are being planned, I require students to submit detailed outlines and evaluate them on the basis of the thoroughness of their preparation. Then, I tell my early childhood students to *abandon* the plan if something else more relevant to the children presents itself. Not surprisingly, confounded students express disappointment that their carefully honed activities must be discarded on account of some "childish impulse."

Then, after abandoning their plans and "going with the flow," students must learn to control and direct the spontaneity to prevent degeneration into chaos and to meet children's learning goals. Abandoning the plan, of course, does not relieve students from making preliminary preparations for succeeding days. As a result, two needs immediately surface.

One need is for information on the new topic. It is this need that makes liberal education so important to early childhood majors. The interests of children are so diverse that no student can ever expect to be fully prepared, yet the importance of reading widely and being conversant with current events is rarely discussed as an essential requirement for competent teaching in early childhood.

Furthermore, "playing with children" is seen as an anti-intellectual task. I have maintained that even though we say we are non-academic in nature, early childhood education does, in fact, have very stringent academic goals. Literacy is one goal which enters into almost every early childhood activity. Basic understandings of mathematical concepts, physical science, and the social sciences are ubiquitous in early childhood curricula. Activities that are rooted in emotional expression, such as art and music, also are consistent with advancing literacy and math skills. As a result, when children express various interests, early childhood teachers, acting as personal resources, must be able to supply accurate information, strategies for finding additional information, and suggest activities that expand understanding of the subject at hand, as well as advancing basic skills.

In addition to finding needed information, prospective teachers need to ensure that the topics pursued are as inclusive as possible. Strategizing to find a role for the shyest child, devising a method of adapting activities for the physically challenged, helping the most capable child take on tasks which are sufficiently stimulating, and making sure that the least capable child makes a meaningful contribution are examples of the forethought teachers must engage in while pursuing children's expressed interests. Children's play is multifunctional in an early childhood classroom and helping prospective early childhood teachers master its uses is a major goal of a competent early childhood teacher educator.

Intellectually limited or intellectually lazy persons cannot help children perform optimally. Teacher educators, therefore, need to include opportunities for prospective early childhood teachers to pursue and share with their classmates some esoteric interest. Their choices, even if far removed from the content of their education course work, should be recognized and validated in order to be consistent with this ideal of intellectual inquiry.

Some may question the relevance of this discussion to primary grade educators. The processes by which children construct knowledge of written language (DeVries & Kohlberg, 1987/1990) and master math concepts (Kamii, 1985) are examples of academic tasks that children have demonstrated they can be trusted to pursue much more independently than previously imagined. From birth, there seems to be a human need to experiment, reflect, and devise one's own idiosyncratic rules and meanings.

EXPANDING THE TEACHER ROLE: EDUCATION AND SOCIAL POLICY

A contributing factor to my eventual disgust with formal testing was test makers' assumptions regarding the basic information possessed by children at certain ages. I distinctly recall a kindergarten achievement test item that required the identification of a tree house. Yet the children taking the test lived in public housing where swings were missing from their poles and the grass had been paved over.

This incongruity is symptomatic of issues in public education that occupy a prominent position in my instruction of potential early childhood teachers. Early childhood teachers need to understand that schools and their programs only partially inform the education of young children. Teachers must be cognizant of the broad social context influencing children's lives.

Concerns with these issues, however, propels teacher preparation programs into the arena of social policy and advocacy. Yet the history of early childhood education has been linked inextricably with social change, as exemplified by the accounts of Pestalozzi (1894), the founding of the kindergarten in America (Weber, 1969), and the saga of Head Start (Lombardi, 1990). The current effort to confront bias and expand acceptance of diversity of all kinds (Derman-Sparks, 1989) is yet another example of the use of early childhood programs to advance social causes.

Because early childhood programs are positioned on the edge of social movements and often are in the forefront of evolutionary or revolutionary thought, the role of advocacy is uniquely central to the early childhood professional. This means that early childhood teacher educators are faced with the challenge of helping usually gentle and caring individuals to forge an identity as resolute, articulate, and effective spokespersons and actors on behalf of children and their families. My own growth as an advocate was not the result of a predictable, professional evolution, but was prompted by particular circumstances, especially my experience with Head Start.

During one summer, quite by accident, I decided to work as a district supervisor for a Head Start program. During my orientation to the program, I became increasingly annoyed by a phenomenon that had begun to aggravate me when I was a teacher. It was the experience of being talked down to—patronized. Public school teachers were always being "inserviced" about some new instructional method or some new textbook. These inservice sessions were notorious for decreeing actions unrelated to the realities of individual schools and disregarding input from participants.

During the Head Start orientation, my annoyance was directed toward the session's content. Poor people, we were told, suffered from cultural deprivation. Their inadequate thought processes resulted from the "restricted code" of their language (Bernstein, 1961). Even though poor people in the large metropolitan area where I worked were not overwhelmingly black, the personification of poverty was that of black children and their families. Clearly, I personalized the message because I still remember my disbelief, dismay, and anger.

My reaction, however, was not shared by many of my colleagues. And, as the concept of cultural deprivation gained currency, its application was not limited to minorities who happened to be poor. It was framed in a way that allowed the devaluing of all minority experiences, regardless of economic circumstances. The concept of cultural deprivation gained such currency that I suspect it may have propelled development of the ethnocentric Black Power movement. Another, more directly educational, result may have been teacher dismissal or unawareness of cues "culturally deprived" children provided that indicated their knowledge, experiences, and interests.

This particular inservice experience provided the impetus for my return to school for doctoral study in early childhood education. During my doctoral studies at the University of Michigan, I pursued my concerns with the concept of cultural deprivation. I felt keenly my lack of knowledge about human development and recent research. It was an exciting time of discovery and recognition. I found confirmation and valid reasons to support my practice and to challenge such absurdities as "cultural deprivation."

Having a basis for my assumptions and practices was like an emancipation. To be able to articulate reasons within coherent frameworks of thought was like being given a road map to places where I had traveled all my life without realizing how close they were to each other, the short cuts to getting there, or my way around the detours. I believe teacher educators have a responsibility to give students this same kind of liberating knowledge. But I received this knowledge at the *end* of my teaching career, and prospective early childhood teachers should receive it at the very *beginning* of theirs. Such knowledge provides the basis for teacher practice; it provides the information and beliefs that form the basis for advocacy. As a brand new teacher, my social vision had been naive and uninformed.

My first teaching position had been in a school located in a lower-middle-class, predominately black neighborhood. In the school's hallway, experienced teachers explained Aid to Families with Dependent Children (AFDC) to me and pointed out some of the recipients. There was much merriment one day when it was recounted how an elderly, puzzled grandmother had come to school to enquire about her grandchild's failure to advance from kindergarten to 1st grade and the "reading readiness" class to which the child had been assigned.

This anecdote is recalled to explain my insistence on discovering the influence of social policies. What was it like to be on AFDC, and what implications did it have for children's and parents' school experience? How did it feel to come to school to ask about a grandchild and leave feeling either more puzzled or humiliated? What were the residual effects on the family of a child who had been tested and failed? How did all of these situations translate into school achievement? How can the school or individual teachers act to modify standards or practices to compensate for, or even eradicate, the effects of practices outside their spheres of authority? Such questions were asked even then, but assumption of the responsibility not only to *ask* but also to *act* in order to change such circumstances was not seen as an appropriate role for educators; nor is it today.

Questions of school–community–parent interaction did not loom large in my teacher preparation, but I consider their investigation and analysis indispensable to prospective early childhood practitioners. Students need actual experience with families to begin to understand the need for analysis of social policy. They also need to learn to view parents differently. Traditional teacher training tends to restrict classroom or program authority to that of the professionals in charge.

Parents and teachers in early childhood programs, however, need to develop different authority relationships. Partnership is the term glibly encouraged, but it should be understood as a partnership with changing foci and roles. In some matters, the wishes and authority of the parent may be supreme. In other instances, the early childhood educator must claim and retain the role of expert and define policies and practices that reflect the best of current educational and psychological thought. This type of relationship speaks to aspects of power that rarely are shared between professionals and non-professionals. Achieving skill in maintaining such complex relationships necessitates actual experience with children and families of many varieties in diverse communities.

The ethics of early childhood practice demand concern for the overall condition of children. Yet it is irresponsible to suggest that individual early childhood teachers can effect radical social change on their own. Therefore, introducing prospective teachers to professional organizations and movements dedicated to improving the lives of children and families is yet another task of early childhood teacher educators, along with modeling participation in organizational activities. Finally, competent early childhood teacher educators also help their students realize that mastery of communication skills, oral and written, is required if they are to be effective as parent educators and spokespersons for children and families.

USING EXEMPLARY PROGRAMS: THEORIES BROUGHT TO LIFE

There were few, if any, visible exemplary programs serving normally developing children during my classroom career in public schools. Most teachers attempted to implement recommended practices within the boundaries of official policy. The kindergartens we dreamed about were nowhere to be found.

After leaving the public school system, I worked with community college students seeking associate degrees and classroom aides from Head Start programs who were seeking the CDA credential. In both instances, I found that students' acquaintance with developmental theory provided validity to their decisions and reliability to their ongoing practice. While depth of understanding and ability to engage in articulate discussions varied considerably, consistent references to children's developmental levels and relevant theory helped students advance in their thinking beyond the regurgitation of lectures. This was particularly important for CDA students.

Students often would confess their disbelief that the children most familiar to them could learn anything if teaching occurred in a developmentally appropriate fashion. To the untrained eye, children in such programs "played all day." One student observer predicted that the children would "grow up to be convicts" since they did not have to sit down and be still often enough! They most valued directive methods of group control and instruction, using worksheets and other tangible evidence of the occurrence of teaching and learning.

Fortunately, a way existed to challenge their opinions. Child care centers on the campuses of the community college system where I worked served as laboratory schools and were invaluable instructional resources. These laboratory schools and their exemplary programs provided opportunities to *retrain* experienced practitioners by providing direct contact with developmentally appropriate early childhood programs. These centers enrolled children from all socioeconomic levels and tended to reflect the surrounding communities. As a result, students could observe and participate in programs serving bilingual or non-English speaking children, and white, black, low-income or middle-income children. As a result of these placements, early childhood students became convinced that poor children also deserved the opportunity to learn through play.

Laboratory school experience is often criticized as poor preparation for the "real world." However, the real world too often provides few examples of excellent practice and rarely furnishes cooperating teachers who can create the intensive and extensive mentorship found in campus-based centers. The availability of exemplary programs and supportive relationships is crucial to retraining individuals who already are experienced in *the real world*. While the presence of good models does not guarantee understanding or even acceptance of the practices that help children develop and learn, their existence makes it more difficult to take the position that inappropriate practices are the only way to teach in *the real world*.

CONCLUSION

In final response to this part's title question, a competent early childhood teacher educator is one who, as a student of children, knows how to support children in their natural quest for knowledge and provides opportunities for prospective teachers to attain that skill with children living in real-life circumstances. Furthermore, the competent teacher educator provides these experiences in optimal surroundings in order to reinforce the efficacy of good practices.

Yet, in today's world, more and more children are less likely to have optimal childhoods. Competent early childhood teacher educators, therefore, help their students understand that early childhood teaching encompasses a breadth of activities not commonly perceived as being within the teaching domain. The profession's holistic view of early childhood education demands a holistic response by early childhood practitioners. Consequently, competent teacher educators discuss relevant issues and practices in health, social services, and social policy, in addition to early childhood theory and practice in their instruction of prospective teachers.

Further, competent early childhood teacher educators help their students understand that teaching young children is only partial fulfillment of their professional responsibilities—that work with adults will always be a major component of their jobs. Thus, prospective early childhood teachers need to be prepared for their roles as members of a classroom team, peer and educator of parents, collaborator with professionals outside the field of education, and advocate and spokesperson for early childhood practices and policies with program administrators, decision makers, and the public at large. Finally, a competent early childhood teacher educator sets an example for students by actively supporting and participating in early childhood organizations, for these activities enhance the services children receive and make possible a strong, collective voice on behalf of young children and families.

REFERENCES

Bernstein, B. (1961). Social structure, language and learning. *Educational Research, 3,* 163–76.

Derman-Sparks, L. (1989). *Anti-bias curriculum.* Washington, DC: National Association for the Education of Young Children.

DeVries, R. & Kohlberg, L. (1990). *Constructivist early education: An overview and comparison with other programs.* Washington, DC: National Association for the Education of Young Children (originally published in 1987 by Longman).

Dewey, J. (1938/1981). *Education and experience.* New York: Macmillan.

Kamii, C. (1985). *Young children reinvent arithmetic: Implications of Piaget's theory.* New York: Teachers College Press.

Lombardi, J. (1990). *Head Start: A nation's pride; a nation's challenge.* Alexandria, VA: National Head Start Association.

Pestalozzi, J. (1894). *How Gertrude teaches her children.* Trans. by R. Holland & F. Turner. London: Allen & Unwin.

Weber, E. (1969). *The kindergarten: Its encounter with educational thought in America.* New York: Teachers College Press.

CHAPTER 11

Viewed Through a Prism: The Multifaceted Enterprise of Early Childhood in Higher Education

David E. Fernie and Rebecca Kantor

We have been asked to address several questions related to the enterprise of early childhood teacher education in a research-based university: (1) "What is required to be a competent early childhood teacher educator?" (2) "What is the essential character of an effective early childhood teacher preparation program?" and (3) "What are the necessary conditions for effective early childhood teacher education?" Each of these questions raised for us a central problem that we believe all early childhood teacher educators in research-oriented universities must face and resolve.

WHAT IS REQUIRED TO BE A COMPETENT EARLY CHILDHOOD TEACHER EDUCATOR?

The major problem raised by this question is the constant press to meet multiple demands related to the diverse activities expected of us. These demands include creating and delivering effective teacher preparation programs at both undergraduate and graduate levels; conducting research to advance the field's theoretical and practical knowledge; creating research apprenticeships with students at all levels; and fulfilling community and campus service commitments.

The difficulty of meeting these multiple demands has become more intensified by current sociopolitical conditions experienced within higher education. These conditions include a climate of continuing fiscal restraint and cutbacks combined with a heightened public demand for accountability and increased hours of

156

direct teaching. In response, universities struggle to do more with less or to transform themselves while maintaining their stability and guiding visions.

Our personal response to this problem has been to try to create unity through the integration of teaching, research, and service activities. Central to this unity has been a preschool ethnography—a starting point for a range of collaborative activities—and a laboratory school, a locus for teaching and research activities. We present this version of professional life, which we have created as collaborators across two early childhood departments in two colleges at The Ohio State University. We will show how this unity creates coherence for ourselves as teacher educators, for our undergraduate and graduate students, and for the experienced teachers and young children with whom we work.

This is not a self-conscious "model" we have designed and tested. Rather, it is what has emerged in our "doing" of teacher education as we worked to meet the multiple demands of a higher education agenda. Now reflecting on our experiences for the purpose of writing this essay, we present this post hoc examination as a working model.

To begin, we present a brief history of the emergence of this unity over 8 years. Our collaboration began in 1985 in the early years of our respective tenures at Ohio State. We shared a basic early childhood training in individual psychology and child development and constructivist early childhood education but had distinctive specializations. A third colleague with interests in cognitive constructivism began the ethnography with us but moved to another university.

At the time we began, the activities of the respective faculty members were idiosyncratic. We see in these early histories the dilemma we each faced to fulfill multiple roles and to meet diverse and separate expectations within our respective lives as professors of early childhood education.

Kantor had several roles linked to the early childhood program in the Family Relations and Human Development Department within the College of Human Ecology. She was hired into a tenure line position with the usual assistant professor responsibilities, including creating a tenureable research record. In addition, she had part-time lead teacher responsibilities in the department's laboratory school. This professor–practitioner configuration was the department's strategy to model from within a new way of doing preschool, with the specific goals of introducing more constructivist-oriented programming and creating a more visible research program in the laboratory. The laboratory school had its own fragmented identity, too—the traditional schism between the goal of high-quality programming and the need to meet conditions as a research site.

Within the Department of Educational Theory and Practice in the College of Education, Fernie faced his own set of diverse and separate demands. These included teaching responsibilities, primarily at the master's and doctoral level, supervision of undergraduate certification programs, the press to create a tenureable research record, and to serve the wider campus and public communities. At the time, he had traditional relationships with community programs, that is, "visitor researcher" with limited involvement in the ongoing daily life of any particular setting.

Our early dialogue as collaborative researchers centered around our common interests in how the classroom functioned as a social group. We shared a belief that classrooms are inherently social places, and that the field's dominant emphasis on individually oriented child development knowledge was inadequate to describe and explain the classroom as a social place. As we socially constructed our ideas and formulated our questions about life in the preschool, we searched for a paradigm that would allow us to explore our interests.

Simultaneous to our search for a new mode of inquiry, the lead teachers in the laboratory school were conducting their own inquiry about the classroom and the process of undergraduate teacher apprenticeship. Led by Kantor, the laboratory school staff worked to articulate their practice in a formal curriculum document (Kantor & Elgas, 1986) to share with their undergraduate practicum students, who spend a 10-week quarter in the laboratory school.

As part of this task, they, too, were struggling to find the language within their existing constructivist framework to capture and make visible to students the more social aspects of a curriculum—what happens "between the heads" as opposed to "within the heads" of children and teachers as they engage in curricular experience. In retrospect, the teachers were searching for the framework that we, both researchers and teachers, would later call "social constructionism" (Gergen, 1985; Rizzo, Corsaro, & Bates, 1992). A passage from the foreword to this curriculum document illustrates this search:

> I truly believe that our curriculum is the result of a negotiated process—teachers and children construct and negotiate the curriculum together. . . . Thus, we can only share with the reader some beginning ideas, basic guidelines, examples, anecdotes, and ways to choose activities, experiences and materials that match our curricular framework. From there the children take over, take the curriculum content in unforeseen, unpredictable directions which the sensitive, skillful teacher must go along with, carefully guiding, facilitating, probing and exploring. . . . The motto of our program is "Working from the Ideas of Children." (Kantor & Elgas, 1986, pp. 1–2)

At this point, we, the researchers, began to learn about ethnography as a research lens for making visible the social aspects of both the emergent curriculum and daily classroom life. This led, in 1987, to the start of an educational ethnography conducted from a sociocultural perspective in the laboratory school. Over time, our research collaboration has brought together undergraduate, master's, and doctoral students, faculty from our respective departments, and the teachers, practicum students, and children in the laboratory school. The laboratory school has served as a central setting for creating a unified whole out of our diverse higher education activities. In complementary fashion, the research project has provided the social structure from which the unity, the essential character of our enterprise, has emerged.

WHAT IS THE ESSENTIAL CHARACTER OF AN EFFECTIVE TEACHER PREPARATION PROGRAM?

The major problem we see embedded in this question is how not to reduce knowledge for young children, students, or professors to static information to be transmitted from "knowers" to "learners." In response to this problem, we have searched for ways to create learning experiences that are transformative for ourselves and our students and, in so doing, to create dynamic knowledge inductively through these experiences. This approach to knowledge creation applies across teaching, research, and service activities. To answer the question, we turn to a description and explication of the essential character of our early childhood enterprise across these activities.

The image of unity evoked as we reflect on the full spectrum of activities in our early childhood and higher education enterprise is that of a prism, with multiple and parallel facets facing a solid center. The solid center of our particular enterprise is made up of a research collaboration and a laboratory school. The four facets of our prism are:

1. *Educational possibilities,* a disposition to go beyond traditional practice to explore diverse sources for the curriculum and thus, to generate new and better informed practices for young children.
2. *Collaborative inquiry,* a process involving all members of our community—children, teachers, undergraduates in training, graduate students becoming researchers and ourselves as teachers and researchers.
3. *Social constructionism,* our theoretical view that group life and knowledge are given meaning as people interact and build on their interactions (whether in research or classroom contexts).
4. *Ethnography,* a research paradigm that serves to uncover life in the classroom for both researchers and practitioners.

In order to describe this essential character in specific terms, we examine a small, preschool group activity conducted daily in the life of the laboratory school.

The preschool class is divided, roughly by age, into two stable ongoing groups, each one consistently led by one of two teachers. For the younger group, all of whom are typically new to school and group experience, the teacher's goals for the year can be described as a developmental progression: first, they must become a group, and then they can engage in collaborative projects.

THE PRISM AND ITS FACETS

For the teachers in this preschool, a small group began as an *educational possibility*. At the time there was little evidence within the extant child development literature that egocentric 3-year-olds could engage in collaborative group activity. In fact, there was accepted theory and research (Piaget, 1932/1965; Parten, 1932) to the contrary; that is, that egocentric young children would not be able to participate regularly or successfully in interdependent group endeavors. Yet the teachers believed that to nurture and enhance children's cooperation and collaborative abilities within the small group would serve children well in this classroom, in later schooling, and in life beyond the classroom.

At the core of this educational possibility is a commitment to inquiry, both as individual exploration and as group collaboration. Reflecting the classroom's commitment to social construction theories, children's ideas are elicited and acknowledged in small group activities as they explore diverse materials and learn to represent their experiences across different media and symbol systems.

Recognizing that the establishment of group identity is prerequisite to *collaborative inquiry,* the teacher and undergraduate student teachers spend the early part of the year helping the children establish a sense of group. They present diverse, open-ended materials to provide a vehicle for each child to explore his or her own ideas within a group context. As children do so, the teacher makes public comments about each student's ideas, asks students to describe to each other what they are doing, and works alongside them. In this incipient togetherness the focus is on experiencing "group," and on learning how to share space, materials, and ideas.

Over time, the teacher facilitates the children's continuing progress as a group by helping them to choose a name for their group using a democratic process; suggesting and creating a group display of their individual art products; and using conversation to help children become aware of their responsibilities to the emerging group and of their individual rights within it. Eventually, the children are able to engage in collaborative activity and, in turn, to participate successfully in new and more socially involved curricular formats. By the latter part of the year, group projects (Katz & Chard, 1989) such as murals and group wood constructions become the focus of collaborative inquiry.

This development of inquiry within a small group is a *social construction* to which lead teachers, undergraduate student teachers, and children make distinctive contributions. The teacher uses talk and social action to help children first to become a group and then to act as one. Undergraduate student teachers collaborate with children during this activity and, over time, take over the planning and leadership for the group. In weekly seminars led by the lead teachers of the classroom, undergraduates reflect on the development of children's collaborative inquiry processes and of the small group curriculum. Consistent with the social construction theme, the undergraduates' process for planning the curriculum content of the small groups is now shifting from lesson plans developed by individual student teachers, to lesson plans generated collaboratively in small group discussion.

Although the lead and student teachers in this setting have activities and goals in mind as starting points for the small group activities, they primarily follow the lead of the children, who often take the group in new and unanticipated directions. The children generally infuse their "peer culture" (Corsaro, 1985) interests into the group's art work and literacy activities (Kantor, Miller, & Fernie, 1992). For example, the lead teacher once brought in a variety of construction materials (e.g., toilet paper rolls, cardboard, wood, and industrial junk), with the idea that the small group might want to create a city. But, after her deliberately neutral introduction of the materials ("I thought we could use these to build something today"), the children worked together to build a Teenage Mutant Ninja Turtle sewer, following their intense interest at that time in these popular media characters.

For many years, the teachers in the laboratory school worked to develop this educational possibility of collaborative inquiry with 3- and 4-year-olds against prevailing, conventional wisdom, guided by their intuition that this experience was meaningful and developmentally appropriate. In the process of conducting our classroom *ethnography,* one of the lead teachers conducted a systematic analysis of the small group activity time for her master's thesis (Williams, 1988). Her work validated these intuitions and detailed the process of social construction. Williams's thesis work revealed the nature of group developmental process and confirmed for us that young children can engage in meaningful group experience. It provided a description of the social construction of the small group, which informed both our research and practical understanding of this daily event.

This example demonstrates the value of inquiry in teacher education. On one hand, it makes classroom life and teaching practice the object of research, which yields new educational and developmental knowledge for the field; on the other hand, its yield informs and enhances the practice it analyzes, providing teachers with a sharper lens to examine their own practice and a language for describing it. In this case, Williams used her new understanding of small group curriculum in her undergraduate teaching. Moreover, she has come full circle in her development as teacher and researcher and supervised an honors undergraduate student who reanalyzed and reinterpreted the master's thesis data from a gender perspective.

We can see in the small group example a microcosm of how all four facets of the prism are linked to create a unity within our early childhood enterprise:

1. Small group has been an educational possibility for the teachers who believed in it, the preservice teachers they mentored, and the researchers who thought this educational possibility could be clarified through research.
2. Small group was a context for *collaborative inquiry* for children and teachers as they explored materials, for undergraduates as they learned to "see," guide, and plan for children's group processes, and for researchers and teachers as they together uncovered patterns of interaction and growth.
3. Small group was a process of *social construction,* as curriculum was generated through, by, and within the group as they engaged in daily group social action.
4. Small group and the other analyses within the preschool *ethnography* occasioned the construction of new knowledge and new teacher and researcher roles, transforming how each member thought of the experience itself and of her- or himself as teacher and researcher.

In the above example we see not only the integration of the four facets of our essential character, but also a microcosm of the interrelatedness or unity created across teaching, research, and service activities. A curriculum topic in the laboratory school became a research topic for a lead teacher and master's student and, thus, a part of her professional development and continuing education; the knowledge created through her ethnographic research informed her teaching of young children in small group, as well as her mentorship of undergraduate teachers in training; as undergraduate students tried out small group in the laboratory school practicum, their explorations were supported by lead teachers now better informed through research; lead teachers and researchers together ventured into the community to explore the possibilities of small group collaboration in other preschool and early primary school settings; in master's level courses with largely elementary teachers, preschoolers' small group accomplishments were related to possibilities for further social development and educational continuity during the elementary school years; within the research team, this analysis informed our overall understanding of the classroom, and the conduct and interpretation of analyses focused on other aspects of life in this classroom. This spread of new knowledge across activities was made possible because potentially separate groups (professors, undergraduate and graduate students, laboratory school teachers, and children) had been brought together through the laboratory school and the ethnography to create both a social network of mentorship and collaboration and a synergy of ideas and experimentation.

THE ETHNOGRAPHY

The ethnography we have been conducting in the laboratory school over the past 5 years (Fernie, Kantor, Klein, Meyer, & Elgas, 1988) has contributed more broadly to each of the activities within our early childhood enterprise than we had originally anticipated. In terms of our faculty research agenda, it has given us a coherent program of research centered on an indepth understanding of a single classroom. At the same time, it has greatly influenced our teaching to both undergraduate and graduate audiences, giving us the sociocultural lens we had been searching for to explicate and communicate our ideas about social life and educational possibilities in preschool classrooms.

We have used our conceptualizations and our systematic data analyses within our teaching as heuristic tools. Within university undergraduate and graduate courses, as well as within workshops and presentations to community educators, we have used the ethnographic perspective to help teachers see their own classrooms as complex, yet patterned, social worlds. The ethnography gives us convincing real-life examples (and video illustrations of them) for purposes of demonstration and discussion. It has been our experience that teachers within the wider community and students at all levels relate well to ethnography as a perspective and methodology, perhaps because ethnography "bears a close resemblance to the routine ways in which people make sense of the world in everyday life" (Hammersley & Atkinson, 1989, p. 2).

Further, we believe that the parallelism of ethnography to everyday life serves to demystify the discourse of research by defining it as inquiry not so distant from what teachers do as "child-watchers." The words *transformative, evolving,* and *inductive* apply to the inquiry processes of both interpretive researchers and reflective teachers. At the undergraduate teaching level, the search for and identification of patterns within the complexity of daily group life, a central feature of ethnographic research, fits the preservice teacher's need to clarify and get a handle on this seemingly overwhelming complexity. Through our teaching within the university and wider community, we have discovered that the sense-making of ethnographic research connects easily to the sense-making of novice and experienced teachers in their classrooms. Thus, ethnography can be better described as research *related to practice* than as research *translated into practice.*

Over time, this mode of inquiry has become collaborative and has grown among the laboratory school teachers and in the training of undergraduates. Laboratory school teachers now often present local, state, and national workshops and presentations based on their socially constructed understanding of the classroom and are even embarking on their own extended writing venture—a book about classroom guidance informed substantially by the sociocultural perspective and the conduct of the ethnography.

Furthermore, undergraduate student teachers engage in collaborative inquiry with children. We hope these educational experiences dispose them to collaborative inquiry and "action research" as continuing features of their work with peers and with children. For all of us, integrating the research process with teaching and program development has forever changed what we see, think about, and can describe in the classroom.

Educational Possibilities

Before the ethnography, we held a conventional interpretation of the theme of educational possibilities, that is, to move the program in more constructivist-oriented directions as outlined in such work as Kamii and DeVries (1978/1993) and Forman and Kuschner (1977). Over time, however, the idea of educational possibilities, even within the classroom, moved in new and more social constructionist directions consistent with the wider enterprise described in this chapter. Thus, we were led to topics that were beyond the typical purview of cognitive constructivism (e.g., small group development, group conversation, peer culture dynamics) and to envision traditional topics (e.g., literacy, rejected children) through an ethnographic lens.

From the departure point of curriculum for young children we have come to see educational possibilities more broadly. And, having been an integral part of the creation and analysis of educational possibilities within the preschool curriculum, the laboratory school teachers are now creating new educational possibilities for themselves. As a result of all of the experiences described in this essay, a main function of the laboratory school has become to envision and explore educational possibilities. Often, laboratory schools are criticized for being "ivory tower," "ideal," or even irrelevant. We would agree that they are ideal, for laboratory schools generally do not have the chronic problems of other child care settings (e.g., staffs with high levels of turnover and low levels of training). But we disagree that they are irrelevant; without "real-world" pressures and with optimal conditions, laboratory schools are in a unique position to take a lead in exploring educational possibilities for children, curriculum, and programs.

Classroom-focused research, we contend, is a very relevant and useful kind of research for a laboratory school. It simultaneously creates new knowledge for the field and informs and enhances local practice. Within this perspective, laboratory schools are defined as places of experimentation, inquiry, and research, which do not conflict with, and indeed, enhance the program agenda. Such an approach bridges the schism between laboratory schools as research sites and as programs serving young children and their families.

The most summative (and unanticipated) educational possibility that has emerged from our collaborative agenda is the one for ourselves as higher educators. In the collaboration described here, we have experienced new ways of working with students within and across our departments, and with colleagues within and across research and teaching activities. As the mutual benefits of such collaboration to ourselves, our students, and our respective departments has become more clear, the dialogue we started with each other has widened to include other colleagues in our respective departments. Most recently, our two faculties have begun the process of formalizing an interdepartmental PhD in Early Childhood, which would build on both departments' common interests in educational and developmental processes, yet respect distinctive traditions, program requirements, and faculty profiles. Thus, the work in our collaboration has provoked, by example, an educational possibility for an ongoing PhD program.

WHAT ARE THE NECESSARY CONDITIONS FOR EFFECTIVE EARLY CHILDHOOD TEACHER EDUCATION?

This last question turns out to be the most difficult because it implies that there are discrete and positive conditions that support the provision of effective teacher education. On one hand, we can (and will) identify some positive aspects of the conditions we experience; on the other hand, we are equally convinced that our enterprise is also a response to negative aspects of conditions experienced within research-based universities. In this last section, we note both aspects as they have affected us, and speculate about the form the positive conditions may take in other settings.

We begin with the negative conditions because, as we described in our early history, the first of these was the original impetus motivating us to transform our enterprise. Research-based universities (and particularly "land grant" institutions with a strong public service mission) impose a multiplicity of simultaneous research, teaching, and service demands. In our case, efforts to meet these demands provided a momentum toward unity. The alternatives, it seems, are either to do "more less well," or to specialize in some way, for example, to define one's responsibilities exclusively within a graduate program, to choose only to do research, or to choose not to do research.

Each of these versions of professional life has its benefits and costs in terms of personal satisfaction and the positive regard of peers, but only the research-focused faculty profile typically brings university rewards and status. Consequently, it is difficult to make high-quality teacher education the highest priority within the culture of research-based universities.

The current public clamor over the mission of universities, though not without its positive side, is a second negative condition influencing early childhood teacher education. In counterpoint to the traditional valuing of research within universities, a consumerist public now demands time accountability and cost efficiency, pressing for universities to prioritize teaching and service over seemingly esoteric research. The unity of research, teaching, and service that we have described is one viable response to reconcile these two competing conditions.

A third and final negative condition is more subtle. Within universities, academic subcultures often clash and vie for status: ethnography and other interpretive methods are decried as soft by "hard scientists"; a commitment to collaborative inquiry may be seen as an inability to work alone; and the social construction of knowledge is often misinterpreted when judged by individualistic standards. Thus, the four facets of our enterprise that are so valuable to us may not be valued by others.

For us, the convergence of these three negative and related conditions define this question's central problem: How to fit effective early childhood teacher education compatibly within a research-based university, given shifting and sometimes conflicting institutional and public priorities and divergent notions of what counts as an effective faculty profile. Yet, ironically, the very negative conditions that constrained our professional lives also impelled us toward the creation of more satisfying ones; and there were institutional attributes that supported this possibility.

First, working at a research institution invites experimentation and supports the educational possibilities we have created for our students, young children, and ourselves. At a pragmatic level, we could not have initiated our classroom ethnography, a catalyst for the unity, without a substantial university seed grant. We would have been hard-pressed as young researchers to find external support, especially for the non-mainstream research program we were developing.

Fortuitously for us, both collaborative inquiry and educational ethnography became more prominent during this time within our own university community and within the national research community. Thus, we were in the right place at the right time to be supported for a collaborative program of ethnographic research—support which was vital to two pre-tenured assistant professors.

Another favorable condition inherent within a research-based institution is the opportunity to combine various levels of students and to integrate multiple settings and programs within a single enterprise. The strong association among the layers of students, the social synergy we have described, is a central feature of our unity and made it possible for us to meet our multiple demands.

As we have demonstrated in several ways, the laboratory school has served a highly integrative function as the locus of our early childhood enterprise. While we contend that it is necessary to have such a locus for the many activities described in this essay, it is not critical that the setting be a laboratory school sponsored by an academic program. We envision similar educational possibilities when an academic faculty shares a close relationship with a community-based early childhood program.

As we have reflected in this essay on these three guiding questions, we have come to realize that the influences on our lives as early childhood teacher educators are complex. The problems we have described concern features of institutional setting and historical circumstance, personal choices and more impersonal forces, beliefs and values that interacted to shape our early childhood enterprise. We do not presume ours to be the only configuration of conditions nor the only meaningful response to them for early childhood teacher educators in research-based institutions. We do imagine that others in similar settings will resonate with the same problems we have identified in this reflective essay and with the need to address them in some personally satisfying way. Our goal in this essay parallels the goal in our preschool ethnography—to create an indepth description of, but not a prescription for, everyday life from the perspective of the participants. As readers look at early childhood teacher education through our prism, we hope it will shed light on their own experiences.

REFERENCES

Corsaro, W. (1985). *Friendship and peer culture in the early years.* Norwood, NJ: Ablex.

Fernie, D., Kantor, R., Klein, E., Meyer, C., & Elgas, P. (1988). Becoming ethnographers and becoming students in a preschool. *Journal of Research in Childhood Education, 3* (2), 132–141.

Forman, G., & Kuschner, D. (1977). *The child's construction of knowledge: Piaget for teaching children.* Belmont, CA: Wadsworth.

Gergen, K. (1985). The social constructionist movement in modern psychology. *American Psychologist, 40,* 266–275.

Hammersley, M., & Atkinson, P. (1989). *Ethnography: Principles in practice.* New York: Routledge.

Kamii, C., & DeVries, R. (1993). *Physical knowledge in preschool education.* New York: Teachers College Press. (Original work published 1978)

Kantor, R., & Elgas, P. (1986). Unpublished document from The A. Sophie Rogers Laboratory for Child and Family Studies, The Ohio State University, Columbus, OH.

Kantor, R., Miller, S., & Fernie, D. (1992). Diverse paths to literacy in a preschool classroom: A sociocultural perspective. *Reading Research Quarterly, 27*(3), 184–201.

Katz, L. G., & Chard, S. (1989). *Engaging children's minds: The project approach.* Norwood, NJ: Ablex.

Parten, M. (1932). Social participation among preschool children. *Journal of Abnormal Psychology, 27,* 243–269.

Piaget, J. (1965). *The moral judgment of the child.* New York: Free Press (Original work published 1932).

Rizzo, T., Corsaro, W., & Bates, J. (1992). Ethnographic methods and interpretive analysis: Expanding the methodological options of psychologists. *Developmental Review, 12,* 101–123.

Williams, D. (1988). *The complexities of small group process for beginning preschoolers.* Unpublished master's thesis, The Ohio State University, Columbus, OH.

CHAPTER **12**

Accomplishing My Work as a Teacher Educator: Hopes, Practices, Supports, and Constraints

Margaret V. Yonemura

My charge is to write about what it takes to be a competent early childhood teacher educator. I find myself thinking once again about what I do and why, and of the conditions necessary for me to work well despite the inevitable constraints. Competency for me means that my very specific hopes and expectations for students are at least partially realized. After a brief biographical sketch about my past and present work, I begin the essay with these hopes, moving on to ways that they can be realized in practice. I conclude with the supports that give me encouragement and energy to continue despite the constraints.

I began my professional life as a case worker, but in my mid-twenties I realized that I wanted to teach young children; so I entered the preservice master's program in early childhood education at Teachers College, Columbia. I left there to spend the next 10 years teaching in and administering schools for young children. I spent most of those years at a children's institution working with inner-city children who affirmed some basic beliefs about children, teaching, and curriculum that I had consolidated in my graduate studies. Even though battered by poverty and separated from family, the children had the same strong need to make sense of their worlds that I had met in privileged children; they had abilities to concentrate and imagine, and energy to play with joy and vitality. They also had anger and rage from the pain of being separated from their families. Nevertheless, they responded warmly to teachers who recognized their need for some autonomy and respected their initiative and full human capacities. They learned when the curriculum made sense to

167

them, in terms of helping them understand their present, it worked as well in open-ing up new intellectual and social vistas. The impact of poverty on the lives of these children in our rich, technologically advanced society brought home to me ways in which social class and race handicap human potential. My eyes were not at this stage open to the influence of gender, class, and race. But my limited awareness made me conscious that teaching cannot ignore life beyond the classroom walls any more than curriculum can neglect the world children directly experience.

I would not have lasted without a strong support system. My reflections on that support have influenced my work as a teacher educator, as I will describe later. Those years of working directly with children and their teachers demonstrated for me the validity and complexity of holistically focused education and the social and interactive nature of teaching and learning.

My work as a teacher educator has engaged me fully for the past 27 years. Dur-ing this time I have worked with undergraduate and graduate student teachers in private and public universities. From 1969 to 1973 I was chairperson of Graduate Programs at The Bank Street Graduate School of Education. In 1973, I joined a new school, which later became the School of Education and Human Develop-ment of the State University of New York at Binghamton, a research center.

The Division of Education where I work offers only master's degrees. I work with experienced teachers and preservice liberal arts graduates, most of whom are in the program for at least two years. Being together in a small program of about 50 students in early childhood and elementary programs with a small faculty has potential for getting to know each other well, which is important for my work, but I have also worked in large teacher education programs where subgroups created a sense of closeness for faculty and students.

The program draws on aspects of the developmental and social reconstruc-tionist traditions of teacher education as described by Zeichner and Liston (1990). We believe that what students bring as persons, inseparable from their develop-ing professional selves, will deeply influence how they teach. The writings of Dewey convince us that a reflective stance toward teaching is essential if personal–pro-fessional growth in a favorable direction, rather than stagnation, is to occur. We agree with Greene (1989) that teachers must understand the social and political contexts in which their setting is embedded.

Early childhood students[1] begin the program by taking courses in "Child Growth and Development," "Developing Curricula for Young Children" (both of which I teach), and reading. In the spring, the preservice students engage in student teaching, mathematics, and science education. In the remainder of their program, students take courses in a foundations area, applied research, special education, and literature for children, as well as workshops in drama, music, and art. Through-out the program, field work is concurrent with courses. The program concludes with a semester-long seminar and practicum, which I lead for my advisees. I visit their classrooms during this time. Either through a comprehensive examination or an integrative project, students are required to demonstrate their ability to artic-ulate their philosophy of education through merging theory and practice.

MY MAJOR HOPES

The courses, workshops, and field work are vehicles for learning many aspects of teaching, including theories, research findings, and technical skills. However, I focus on four major hopes for students as they move through the program and the program responses needed if these hopes are to be realized.

My first hope is that students continue to develop themselves fully throughout the program as persons and as responsible members of society. I hope that they will be supported in making a deeply rooted commitment to work toward elimination of the prejudices that hamper many of us, and that they will grow in their respect for cultural diversity. I believe this is possible only if they explore freely and deeply what it is that they believe and value. My second hope is that students recognize and welcome working with children's emotions, intuitions, imaginations, and intellects. To do this, they need, within the teacher education program, to expand their own imaginations and receive recognition of their own emotions, intuitions, and intellects. My third hope is that they believe a degree of autonomy and the ability to take initiative are as essential for children as for themselves and people of all ages. For this to occur, they must experience this empowerment as part of their own professional preparation. My fourth hope is that they see children as complex, active, informed learners with their own knowledge. When students experience themselves as knowledge generating, I believe that they will be enabled to nurture this capacity in children. I will elaborate on each of these.

VALUES AND BELIEFS

I need to know my students as persons, their values and beliefs, the knowledge they have stored away, and the feeling they bring to their teaching. This means being willing to go beneath surface behaviors to take time to explore, reflect, and recognize feelings together. We have been through a period influenced highly by behavioristic thinking in which emphasis has been placed on overt behavior, such as movements or questions in the classroom.

One experience with a student stands as a reminder to me how easy it is to be deceived by surface events. I had occasion to observe a student over 2 semesters. At the end of this period, I commented, not for the first time, how much I enjoyed seeing her engage in private, almost whispered, one-on-one mini-conversations with children even in the hurly-burly classroom with too many young children and too little space. The student smiled as she recalled the very different meaning for her of these whispered exchanges as the year progressed. "At first, I was afraid I was saying the wrong things, so I didn't want you or anyone but the child to hear," she told me. Now, however, she wanted personal face-to-face moments with each child in order to learn from and with them. Seemingly identical surface behaviors had such different underpinnings—the first reflected her view of the teacher as one who ought to have the "right" answers in contrast with her later understanding of a teacher as a fellow learner.

Since I value personal, one-on-one fleeting conversation between teacher and child, I attributed my own values to this student and neglected in our conference to pursue what was beneath her surface behavior, thus missing an early chance "to increase the person's awareness of his [sic] beliefs and preferences about teaching and to have him expose them to personal examination" (Lortie, 1975, p. 231). I learned about myself in this encounter and about my need for greater openness and sensitivity.

Bussis and her colleagues (1976) and Connelly and Clandinin (1988) in their research make a strong case for the powerful nature of values and beliefs in determining action. In my collaborative study with Jean (Yonemura, 1986), a teacher for 4-year-olds, I observed many ways in which her deeply held and espoused values and beliefs found expression in the lives of the children in her classroom. I believe, that as a teacher educator, I must work in a way that brings values and beliefs forward for critical exploration.

EMOTIONS, INTUITIONS, IMAGINATION, AND INTELLECT

In addition to holding values and beliefs, students also possess emotions, intuitions, imagination, and intellect, and, in my work, I hope to support their development in all these domains. Although we talk a great deal about feelings, as R. D. Laing (1959) pointed out, we seem to have difficulty getting in touch with them in ourselves and in others. Popular culture, including the representation of children on television and in movies, usually cheapens and sentimentalizes emotions, relegating them to the category of "warm fuzzies." All children need teachers who reject sentimentality and attend to their emotions, young children especially because they are particularly vulnerable during these early years when they must cope with a complex world at a time of great dependency in their development. Teachers need support in recognizing and coping with their own feelings if they are to accomplish such demanding work. I believe that I must attend to my students' feelings if I am to be effective at my work.

I view emotions, intuition, imagination, and intellect as interdependent. As adults, we need to use our imaginations to build our intellects just as children need imaginative play to build, as Dewey (1910) said, "a world of meanings, a store of concepts" (p. 161), which he points out are fundamental to intellectual achievement. Cobb (1977) cautioned that without intuition, intellect alone results in "mechanized, computerized memory—colorless and dehumanized" (p. 49), I believe that I must respond to the students in ways that do not isolate them into fragments of cognition and affect. Unless I do this, I will also fail in my third objective, which is to help them experience some autonomy and initiative.

AUTONOMY AND INITIATIVE

I agree with Gruen (1986) who says that our sense of autonomy depends on "having access to life-affirming emotions, to feelings of joy, sorrow, pain—in short to a sense of being truly alive" (p. 2). Healthy children remind me of what it is to be truly alive as they assert themselves as persons who know who they are. Some student teachers have arrived at adulthood with a strong sense of autonomy. They know who they are and what they believe. Others are more prone to being what the person in authority wants them to be. As a student, Coles (1989) recalls his encounter with one supervising psychiatrist who helped him to do his own thinking. He writes: "He wanted me to hold off the rush to interpretation, to restrain myself from trying to get him to give me *his* interpretation, which for me would become the definitive one, at least until the next supervisor came along" (p. 14). His supervisor cared enough about him to want him to develop his own ideas. Teachers have for years expressed resentment against the shaping imposition of supervisors in colleges and schools who need to be in control.

A study of student teachers in England highlights the significance of addressing the need for building autonomy and freeing initiative in students. Lacey (1977), swimming against the trend to see student teachers as passive recipients of education, chose to see them as possessors of social strategies, carefully selecting this term "because it implies a purposive, guiding, autonomous element within individual and group behavior" (p. 67).

He described three strategies students brought to classroom situations in which their cooperating teachers asked them to teach in a way that went against the grain for them. One strategy was simply to comply—those who go along, get along. The still, small voice was silenced. The second strategy was to adjust one's thinking, bringing it in line with the cooperating teacher. One's own beliefs were stilled by the cooperating teacher's voice. The third strategy involved redefinition of the situation in which the student held on to her or his own beliefs but searched for a way in which the situation could be perceived differently, freeing up new options that might avoid either confrontation or capitulation. Lacey calls these three approaches strategic compliance, internalized adjustment, and strategic redefinition, respectively. He found that when students who used strategic redefinition had the skills to support alternative actions in the classrooms, they could be effective in having their ideas listened to. Such students are one source of re-invigoration of the classroom. They also hold on to themselves and grow as persons, in contrast to the students who go along or cave in. It seems reasonable to assume that students capable of strategic redefinition have a healthy sense of themselves and that they are likely to take initiative as well as to grow in many dimensions, including morally. They do not have to become clones of what the supervisor views as an effective teacher, but they can feel free enough to risk being themselves.

Bucher and Stelling (1977) in their study of residents in psychiatry found that these students discounted feedback from faculty and supervisors when it was incongruent with their own images of themselves. I do not want my students to have to play concealment games with me. Understanding who my students are in their own eyes is a priority for me in order to comprehend, for example, why they respond to children as they do or why they accept one option over another.

PERSONAL PRACTICAL KNOWLEDGE

My fourth hope has to do with helping my students value the knowledge, which they are capable of continuing to generate, that they bring with them to the teacher preparation program. This personal practical knowledge, as described by Connelly and Clandinin (1988), is a composite of values, beliefs, memories, and images built up over time and cohering, not without stresses and strains, so that we come to recognize characteristic ways of responding at work and in student teaching. This personal practical knowledge, however, is not static, but dynamic, even contradictory, but capable of being reformulated and expanded.

In early childhood education, we have worked toward helping children know what they know, as well as what they need to know, in the belief that they have generated knowledge out of their experiences. I believe that it is essential to help students to recognize and value the knowledge that they bring with them to the teacher education program as well as the knowledge they generate in their studies. My students have largely been women, some new graduates, others returning after having raised a family. They all bring a reservoir of knowledge with them based on formal studies and their experiences in life.

Anne entered the program at the end of raising her seven children through their early and middle childhoods. One evening, as we were walking out of class together, she told me about an experience with her twin girls when they were 2 years old.[2] Anne had had several trying nights with her new baby and she was determined that the baby and the twins would take an afternoon nap together. The first day she tried this it did not work. The second day, increasingly frazzled, she spoke sternly to the twins about remaining quiet in their cribs for a nap. They were silenced by her unusual stern manner. As she crept away downstairs, she overhead her less verbal twin chatting away to her verbally advanced sister who replied firmly: "Quiet now. Wait 'til mama go downstairs." Anne's anecdote, one of many in her repertoire, tells much about the complexity, intelligence, and moral sensibility of a 2-year-old. Anne's first-hand experiences and knowledge of her children's grappling with moral events surfaced in class to complement knowledge from formal theories such as Piaget's and Kohlberg's. But Anne and many of my students feel doubt about the validity of what they know and see themselves initially as consumers, not generators of knowledge. All the more reason for awareness on my part, as a teacher educator, for the need to build supportive relationships and structures in which their personal practical knowledge can surface and interact on an equal footing with the formal theories and research of the courses.

Knowledge growing out of experience that has been explored, reflected on, and distilled is forming part of the newly recognized human sciences that differ from such sciences as physics, engineering, and behavioral sciences because, as Van Manen (1991) put it, they focus on "the subjectivities rather than just the external behavior in human life" (p. 220).

I learned to think in new ways about teaching after reading Sylvia Ashton-Warner's (1980) *Teacher* and Carolyn Pratt's (1970) *I Learn from Children*. Their rich stories, full of personal practical knowledge, suggested similarities in my own experiences, giving me energy to follow paths that I was not seeing taken by many. They spoke to my emotions as well as my mind, inspiring as well as instructing. They provided different knowledge that was complementary[3] to the findings of traditional research and theory. Let me turn now to the ways in which, with my colleagues and students, I try to work toward attainment of these four hopes.

WORKING TOWARD ATTAINING MY HOPES

Colleagues in public and private schools have contributed powerfully toward at least a partial fulfillment of my hopes. Cooperating teachers who have allowed students to invent part of the curriculum and test it out have demonstrated their belief that students should have some autonomy and can produce as well as take in knowledge. Their acceptance of students' feelings, as well as ideas, are especially significant. It is one thing to reflect on practice in a seminar and another to put theories, values, and beliefs into action.

One's vulnerabilities are on the surface when one teaches. Because our program is small, we can draw to some extent on the classrooms of our alumnae who are aware of our objectives. This brings the added benefits of keeping us close to their development as mature professionals. We also work with cooperating teachers who are not our alumnae, and this calls for more time and effort to interpret our objectives.

Clearly, I am just one part of a program but, because this essay centers on my work, I will not try to do justice to the considerable efforts of my colleagues except in passing. I hope that I will have made clear my view that I function as a team member. Teacher education is a complex and difficult undertaking that cannot be undertaken with a "Lone Ranger" mentality.

I believe that an essential part of my work as an early childhood teacher educator and as an advisor to my students lies in the relationships I build with and between students. My role as advisor is part counselor and part tutor, but it is also much more. Foremost, I see myself as a learner engaged with the students in mutual inquiry.

ADVISOR AS LEARNER

The dominant ethos places students as learners and faculty as teachers typical of the prevalence of dichotomous thinking. But the relationship need not be cast in this way. Without discounting my knowledge and experience, I need to be learning and renewing myself in my work. Vygotsky and Bruner have opened our eyes to the interactive nature of learning, in which neither teacher nor child in isolation can achieve what they are able to as a unit. Similarly, adult learners are not solitary atoms but social beings who hold the potential to expand each others' personal practical knowledge. Oliver (1990) provides a dynamic interactive metaphor to unburden us from the mechanistic cause–effect thinking derived from the out-moded physics of the 19th century. He asks that we see "learning–knowing" from the biological notion of "collapse," which occurs "when a photon of light and a green leaf participate in photosynthesis" (p. 69).

In this interaction all participants are changed. Thinking about teacher education programs and their participants in these terms makes the possibility of expanding development of one's ideas and feelings a reality for all in exchanges of knowledge that are multidirectional. In this exchange, change, too, is multidirectional. Perhaps this is why I do not conceive of myself as anyone's mentor. Mentor, after all, is not known for learning anything from Telemachus. I see my advisees and myself as potential teachers of each other, colleagues who have different kinds of expertise, who are not locked in the typical dependency of a supervisor–supervisee relationship, which reduces chances for autonomy and risk-taking initiative that contribute to empowerment.

To explore values and beliefs, our relationship needs to be based on mutual trust, but in a dog-eat-dog world, this is not easy. After all, I am not only their advisor; I am also their instructor for two courses, which are graded. When I can—as in the seminar and practicum—I do not grade, preferring to use qualitative ways to assess learning. When I have to grade, I try to be open about my grading and to work out with students a variety of ways that they can demonstrate their understandings. I share my own feelings and beliefs about grading, which I see as a hurdle, but one that is not insurmountable. I also share with students the contradictions I experience and the compromises I make, as well as my efforts to bring about change. I would like to see more independent study without grades, so I work to see that each advisee has some "free" credits—a small beginning.

TIME FOR REFLECTION

Like most teacher education programs, ours is packed with courses, workshops, and practica. Time must be rigorously carved out for reflection. I try to create time for reflection in my courses, but I look on the seminar with my advisees, which accompanies their last field placement, as a special time in which their values, beliefs, ideas, imaginations, intuitions, and feelings hold center stage. In this seminar, I raise questions based on the personal anecdotes they share and their relationship to research, theory, and wider social and political realities. I need much time after the seminar to reflect and think through my questions for the following week in the group or one-on-one, depending on my resources and understandings of what serves the students best.

Students are often hungry for technical skills and become impatient of reflection. I believe that it is important for me, from the start, not to separate the how–tos from the whys of teaching. Occasionally, a student whose schedule is packed will look at the seminar as a waste of time. Many of my students bring relatively little personal experience of reflective conversations. It is hard but important for me to work through their impatience, until they begin to see the significance of a reflective stance to them as persons and professionals. I need my colleagues' support to do this.

GETTING TO KNOW OURSELVES

In the seminar and in the courses I teach, we share aspects of our life stories together. Memories of the past bring to consciousness values and other food for reflection. Ayres (1989) has pointed out that "Autobiography is a process of self-formation and self-declaration; it is a process that pushes back memory, revealing not only entanglements but also choices—it is a method that connects the inner self to the public self. Autobiography widens the scope of choice and in the process enlarges, hopefully, both the autobiographer and the reader" (p. 126). And our choices must be viewed in the context of our moral development, our sense of responsibility, which, with some degree of empowerment, prevents us from feeling victimized and helpless by the injustices surrounding us.

There are no substitutes for reflection on practice and getting to know ourselves in ever deeper and varied ways as we search our practice for ways in which we enact or violate what we say we think, believe, and feel. We are all engaged in making our worlds, which is a form of learning—Edith Cobb (1977) says, " . . . a search for higher levels of synthesis, self, and world drawn from the recognition that outer and inner worlds are interdependent aspects of reality, rather than independent states" (p. 66).

In the course on child growth and development, students follow a young child through a semester with the child acting as their teacher. The approach I encourage them to take is phenomenological so that they enter a child's world through his or her eyes. Recently, I have asked students to interview family and friends and study photographs and old drawings or writings that they made at the study child's age. This has seemed to open up for some students parts or their lives and themselves that they have not thought about. We think about roots of their present values, beliefs, feelings, and ideas that may be there.

This centering on the student as a person, this concern with the self, should not be confused with narcissistic self-absorption. Just as young children become more themselves as they interact with others, so do I and the student teachers grow through social interactions. As we think about ourselves and our development, new awareness of forces that define who we can be and how we are perceived can be brought in.

We do not get to know ourselves in isolation. We are a part of society, and society has a say in how we are viewed in terms of such categories as gender, race, and social class. In the pursuit of self-knowledge, we have to come to terms with the multiple meanings others attribute to us and we to them. This is part of the hard quest to face prejudice and bias, to acknowledge its pain to us from others' ignorance and to others by our ignorance. We look at the seeds of so much prejudice in young children, drawn from any sources. We also share experiences of their capacities to move beyond prejudice, their abilities, and ours, to be compassionate.

THE ARTS

In the seminar and the courses I teach, I draw on the arts in addition to the professional literature. I do this to bring imaginations and intuitions and feelings, as well as intellects, into our work. I feel that discussions take on a different tone and acquire rich nuances when literature, poetry, or film are the centerpiece of a session. We have a few sessions when we focus on materials they have made. These are always times of playfulness and learning. When we work together at self-sculptures, there is a mix of high seriousness and fun, and I see the students in new ways. This is true after a session when students have danced, a too rare occurrence in our work together.

PEER LEARNING

I support students' learning from each other. By creating planned opportunities for students to work with each other—doing a child study or an integrative project together—I believe that I demonstrate a belief that they are holders of personal practical knowledge as well as a belief in their capacity to learn from each other. I see these opportunities of learning how to learn from peers as an important preparation for students' continuing professional development. When they are certified teachers, in many situations, they are dependent on their peers for intellectual stimulation and emotional support. When we can induct students into researching their own practice together, Schon (1983) points out, we have given them a means of engaging "in a continuous process of self-education" (p. 298). We have supported their growing sense of autonomy and their abilities to take initiative.

Time is built into the program for students to work together. A major assignment in the final seminar focuses on learning in dyads about each others' beliefs and values and then exploring video tapes or actual observations of each other's teaching in order to see how these beliefs and values find expression. Students are encouraged to converse together. Such conversations, as those in advisement and the seminars, are not easy or frivolous but attempt to address the complexities of teaching and of teachers as persons.

PERSONAL PRACTICAL KNOWLEDGE

Midway in the program, my advisees and I discuss their ideas about the integrative project they will complete at the end of the program. It is their work and their ideas; their seriousness and commitment emerge from this. A few students want it "over with," and they do have the option of a comprehensive examination. But I spend time talking with them before they make this choice because I have seen the potential of an integrative project as a major support of professional development. Basically, the integrative project demonstrates that the student is capable of both acquiring and generating knowledge. The whole experience of studying what one has chosen to study because of its personal meaning is one I value for children and teachers.

It is my job to open up for students the validity of conducting grounded interpretive studies. Students need reassurance to do this. In the recent past, I have found
several intellectually very able students who expressed a sense of guilt because I have
encouraged them to do an integrative project that they want to do in a way that
makes sense for them, for example, describing the integration of a child with hand-
icapping conditions into the classroom using a weekly log as the basis for reflective
exploration, or recording for a year anecdotes that portray how the educational program was influencing the subgroups in the classroom and the class as a whole.

I draw on my own hermeneutic, interpretive research to support the importance of this option for students. One year I worked collaboratively studying Jean,
an experienced teacher, in her work with children and with her student teacher,
Jeff. This opened my eyes to their strengths and to the stressful, as well as the
delightful, complexities of teaching. I later spent two years working collaboratively
with three of our preservice student teachers exploring their work in the program
(Yonemura, 1991). My personal practical knowledge as a teacher educator was
deepened and my work has become more interesting and more of a challenge to
me through the complex intermingling of our reflections on their teaching and
mine. I recognize that such research does not lead to generalizations for teacher
education—those who engage in such research will not be able to formulate generalizations about large populations—but it has other strong values.

I find this part of my work very satisfying. It offers an intellectual and imaginative challenge to me to dig into my mind for ideas and references to feed into the
integrative project. I am often led into areas of inquiry that I would not have
explored by my own initiative. Working with students on their integrative projects is one well-defined source of support for my growth and development. Since
at least one other faculty member, Wendy Kohli, is involved, this further enhances
my learning. I am aware and appreciative of the many supports I receive in my
work. I turn to those now and touch on some of the constraints, too.

SUPPORTS AND CONSTRAINTS FOR MY WORK

COLLEAGUESHIP

So much of what I am trying to do as a teacher educator hinges on getting to know
my students well. This is where colleagueship and the structure of the program
combine to support me. (The structure of our program is helpful for maintaining
a student–advisor relationship that is continuous throughout, although I am sure
that there are many other ways of achieving this objective.) After their first
semester, I have a still hazy sense of my advisees as persons.

The following spring the preservice students work with an adjunct faculty member[4] who supervises their student teaching. She and I work closely together so that
she is aware of the broad outline of ideas I have covered in the fall. She revisits some
of the same ground, bringing her own rich experiences and knowledge to expand
on this. We learn from our discussions of each student, and this is a great support

and stimulus to me. My feeling at the end of the first semester "Where is all this going?" finds an answer as my colleague describes the emergence of higher levels of professional development she is seeing in the students, and areas where we need to focus differently. At the end of this first spring semester, I meet with the students to review the year. By this stage, they stand much more clearly in mind as the persons they are. (Students who are experienced teachers usually study part-time so that I have more than two years, often four or five years, to get to know them.)

Not all my work with students is enjoyable. I regret moving too quickly or too slowly in a relationship, for example. We struggle together as students work through their needs to dominate children, the "control" theme emerging often. Their enthusiasm to share what they know and, against their better judgment, to "fill up the empty vessels" is at times problematic. And their culturally reinforced urge for techniques that work, measurable outcomes, and certainty brings us into conflict as they sometimes seem to believe that I am holding back on telling them what works.

Even though I understand intellectually what is happening, I sometimes feel defensive. They are, like the rest of us, soaked in the negative criticisms of education and teacher education. Initially, this creates a wobbly floor for theoretical and philosophical discussions. Many of the students are not used to having their values and beliefs find a central place in their education, and this can be threatening when juxtaposed with student teaching in which actions at times belie espoused values. The program is rigorous and, at first, the demands for written work are perceived as an additional burden—until the students see the benefits. Colleagues provide me with release from my tensions as we talk, lament, and laugh together about our work. The support I receive from our biweekly program meetings in indispensable.

A CLIMATE OF CARING: THE INSTITUTION

I made reference at the beginning of the essay to how important my support system had been to me when I began teaching in the children's institution. I had a supervisor to whom I could reveal my feelings openly (not easy for me), sure that I was in safe, intelligent, and honest hands. I did not always hear what I wanted to, but, on reflection, I knew I was learning. Time for reflection was built into my job. Each Friday morning, for 2 hours, an interdisciplinary team discussed the children. In the school, we had weekly meetings for thinking about programs and the children. I worked in what Noddings (1986) describes as a community of caring. She makes the point that if we are committed to educating caring moral persons "we cannot accomplish this purpose by setting an objective and heading straight toward it. Rather, we approach our goal by living with those whom we teach in a caring community, through modeling, dialogue, practice and confirmation" (p. 502).

The climate of the institution significantly determines its impact. In a visit in May 1991 to the schools for young children in Reggio Emilia, Italy, I was impressed by the ways in which environments and time were planned so that people of all ages could feel comfortable and at home, as well as intellectually alive. Teachers had 6 hours of their 36-hour week for their own development, exemplifying a climate of caring for them. In this community of caring, high standards of education are expected and realized. I expect teachers of young children to be caring persons. They and we who work with them need to experience caring ourselves if this is to become a more widespread reality.

My four years of experience as an administrator and faculty member at Bank Street Graduate College gave me first-hand knowledge of what it means when an institution makes a commitment to caring. Each Friday, the faculty advisors met together for two or three hours with either a group dynamics specialist or a psychiatrist. Attendance was a priority for all of us. I heard none of the criticisms of "another meeting." The group dynamics specialist was available for furthering the discussions about working effectively with small groups. The psychiatrist helped expand understandings about students as persons. It was a forum for all of us to express our professional concerns and doubts. As an administrator and faculty member, I felt included. Bank Street faculty, known as advisors, hold no rank and there is no tenure. The expectation for advisors was that they would give themselves wholeheartedly to the work of advisement. Pressures to publish were minimal.

We are all familiar with the hierarchical structure of our universities with rewards geared to individualistic ends. The person who invests major energies in program development and teamwork with colleagues in the schools and the universities can very well be jeopardizing his or her own promotion and tenure. The demands to do everything excellently—research, teaching, grant-writing and program development—exist, and they are draining to most. And the particular nature of the research demanded has followed a conceptualization of knowledge that marginalizes that which grows from personal practical knowledge.

Nevertheless, I have received two sabbaticals in my work life in universities, and these have supported the writing I have found very hard to do while immersed in the teacher education program. Time away from the voracious committee demands has been supportive of my development. I feel advantaged, too, to have been in at the start of a small, relatively new school where administration, faculty, and support staff have worked at minimizing the bureaucratic rationalism present in our university, as in all other large organizations, for example, each division has a director, a faculty member who functions as a coordinator and facilitator jointly with, not "above," faculty—one less layer of bureaucracy.

In my bleaker moments, like King Canute, I feel as if we are trying to turn back the bureaucratic tide, but I hold on to a feeling of hopefulness. This does not have the euphoria of optimism for, as Havel (1991) points out: "Hope is definitely not the same thing as optimism. It is not the conviction that something will turn out well, but the certainty that something makes sense, regardless of how it turns out" (p. 49). My hopes as a teacher educator make sense to me for many reasons, including great potential I see in young children and the urgency for a better world I find expressed by so many of the student teachers with whom I work. Putting these hopes into practice, however, continues to be a challenge. The challenge is met, and I am effective, to the extent that I think and teach in ways that encompass and foster the diversity and breadth of human development. I must not let the wizardry of our amazing technological advances subvert the centrality of humanistic concerns in my work. I am effective when I can join with my students in seeing beyond the classroom walls of today to the classrooms and society of tomorrow and how our work helps to determine what form they will take. I am effective when I pay attention to the need to build, maintain, and nurture authentic relationships with all those involved and influenced by teacher education. Paying attention is not done on the fly, but is a consequence of time given to reflection and to interactions. And, finally, I am effective only when these interactions, contrary to the hierarchical structure of the university, take place as mutually beneficial encounters in which all are seen to have the potential to make distinctive, valuable contributions.

ENDNOTES

[1]The experienced teachers have a program of 36 hours. The liberal arts graduates complete 52 hours, which include a student teaching semester each Spring.

[2]I am indebted to Anne Clune for this anecdote.

[3]My colleague, Wendy Kohli, coordinator of our program, who teaches a course on "Teacher as Researcher," commented to me that at first some students cannot grasp the validity of qualitative, interpretive research based on personal practical knowledge. After several sessions, their puzzlement turns to anger as they realize that they have been educated to value only one kind of "hard" science research.

[4]Nancy Ziegenhagen taught mathematics in an inner-city setting prior to founding and then directing The Susquehanna School in Binghamton, New York, for 20 years. It has served as a major center of inquiry for the program.

REFERENCES

Ashton-Warner, S. (1980). *Teacher*. London: Virago.

Ayres, W. (1989). *The preschool teacher: Six teachers reflect on their lives.* New York: Teachers College Press.

Bucher, R., & Stelling, J. G. (1977). *Becoming professional.* London: Sage.

Bussis, A., Chittenden, E., & Amarel, M. (1976). *Beyond the surface curriculum.* Boulder, CO: Westview Press.

Cobb, E. (1977). *The ecology of imagination in childhood.* New York: Columbia University Press.

Coles, R. (1989). *The call of stories: Teaching the moral imagination.* Boston: Houghton Mifflin.

Connelly, F. M., & Clandinin, J. D. (1988). *Teachers as curriculum planners: Narratives of experience.* New York: Teachers College Press.

Dewey, J. (1910). *How we think.* New York: D. C. Heath Co.

Greene, M. (1989). Social and political contexts. In M. C. Reynolds (Ed.), *Knowledge base for the beginning teacher* (p. 143–154). New York: Pergamon Press.

Gruen, A. (1986). *The betrayal of the self: The fear of autonomy in men and women.* New York: Grove Press

Havel, V. (1991). Havel on hope. *New Perspectives Quarterly, 8*(2), 49.

Lacey, C. (1977). *The socialization of teachers*. London: Methuen.

Laing, R. D. (1959). *The divided self*. London: Tavistock.

Lortie, D. (1975). *Schoolteacher: A sociological study*. Chicago: University of Chicago Press.

Noddings, N. (1986). Fidelity in teaching, teacher evaluation, and research for teaching. *Harvard Educational Review, 56,* 496–510

Oliver, D. (1990). Grounded knowing: A postmodern perspective on teaching and learning. *Educational Leadership. 48*(1), 64–69.

Pratt, C. (1970). *I learn from children*. New York: Cornerstone Library.

Schon, D. (1983). *The reflective practitioner: How professionals think in action*. New York: Basic Books.

Van Manen, M. (1991). *The tact of teaching: The meaning of pedagogical thoughtfulness*. Albany: State University of New York Press.

Yonemura, M. V. (1986). *A teacher at work: Implications for professional development*. New York: Teachers College Press.

Yonemura, M. V. (1991). Glimpses of becoming an early childhood teacher: A teacher educator's perspective. *Curriculum Inquiry, 21,* 397–418.

Yonemura, M. V. (1992). Teacher conversations: potential source of their own professional growth. *Curriculum Inquiry, 12,* 239–256.

Zeichner, K. M., & Liston, D. P. (1990). Traditions of reform in U. S. teacher education. *Journal of Teacher Education, 41*(2), 3–20.

CHAPTER 13

Early Childhood Teacher Educators in the Context of Professional Change

Joan Isenberg and Shirley Raines

Our goal in this essay is to describe what we believe competent early childhood teacher educators need to know and understand. We rely on our combined 28 years of experience as early childhood teacher educators to portray the character and conditions that enable and support what we call competent teacher educators. We also heavily rely on our recent experiences in helping transform George Mason University's clinically based approach to teacher education to one framed by the creation of Professional Development Schools (PDS).

Writing about the characteristics of competent teacher educators in times of political and economic unrest, dissatisfaction with public education at all levels, and educational restructuring poses challenges and frustrations for us. The public perceives that schools today are not working and need to be transformed. By definition, transformation of schools demands a dramatic change in teacher preparation. Early childhood teachers must be able to work knowledgeably, skillfully, and collaboratively in changing school environments.

We believe this achievement depends on early childhood teacher educators who (1) critically reflect on their practice; (2) are knowledgable of child and adult development; (3) understand the "learning to teach" continuum and the differences among novice, expert, and mentor teachers; (4) possess an ability to build new realities about teacher preparation; and (5) advocate for children and the profession. These key beliefs and their implications for practice, in turn, inform our vision of competent early childhood teacher educators (Calderhead, 1987; Holmes Group, 1986; Schön, 1983).

In addition, our answers to the following three questions have helped shape our thinking about our roles as early childhood teacher educators in a climate of professional change: What unique institutional demographics contribute to or inhibit us from implementing our beliefs in exemplary ways? What dilemmas, frustrations, and stark realities confront us in our struggle to ensure that future early childhood teacher candidates enter the profession prepared to meet the demands, realities, and vicissitudes of public schools? How do we strive toward more effective early childhood teacher education?

OUR UNIVERSITY

George Mason University (GMU), a member of the Holmes Group, is a rapidly expanding, suburban university, which enrolls more than 20,000 students. Our institution is complex, fast-paced, future-oriented, and values nontraditional, innovative programs and leaders. Situated in a highly sophisticated, mobile community surrounding the nation's capital, the university aims to be internationally known for its interaction with external communities.

The Graduate School of Education (GSE) has 17 programs, which prepare teachers, counselors, administrators, and related instructional personnel in state, regional, and National Council for Accreditation of Teacher Education (NCATE) accredited programs. Its outward-oriented mission is consistent with that of the University. Most of the 36 full-time faculty are senior level. The early childhood program has two full-time faculty and a cadre of part-time early childhood faculty in two initial and one post-certification early childhood program.

As part of Virginia's 1988 state-mandated restructuring effort, the faculty voted to move to a graduate-level certification program and reduce by 50% the number of early childhood degrees to be awarded. Currently, our initial state-approved certification program prepares teachers who already hold degrees in a liberal arts discipline. Henceforth, we plan to award about 50 master's degrees each year to early childhood teacher candidates.

The restructuring of teacher education at George Mason University is based on the premise that teachers must be broadly educated and informed professionals. In accordance with the Holmes Group principles, a major facet of our restructured teacher education program is the implementation of a Professional Development School Model. Our decision to develop a PDS model was based on the belief that developing a teaching profession requires "thoughtful, long-term inquiry into teaching and learning by school and university faculty working as partners" (Holmes Group, 1986, p. 4).

CLIMATE

We work in an entrepreneurial climate which rewards innovation. We find ourselves constantly facing changes in a shifting landscape, adapting to internal changes, and responding to schools and the school community. Such a pace has implications for our programs as well as our own professional growth and development. For us to be effective in such an environment, we have to be risk-takers.

Being faculty members in an innovative university has meant moving from a traditional view of teacher preparation as an applied science to a newer view of teaching as clinically based. Traditionally, we taught prospective teachers on campus in university courses with a field experience component. Students completed student teaching during which they applied the practices studied in a university classroom. This approach to teacher preparation has consumed most of our professional lives as teacher educators.

A newer approach to learning to teach focuses on a clinical apprenticeship in a Professional Development School. The graduate teacher-preparation program, which had strong university administrative support, was developed in response to state licensure requirements, the call for liberal-arts backgrounds for teacher candidates, and the university community's perception that graduate preparation is superior. The program changes were conceived with the understanding that the public schools would act as full partners in the preparation of future teachers. These partners, however, had yet to be courted and convinced.

Faculty

Both of us are full-time, early childhood faculty who are tenured, full professors[1]. We teach courses in all three early childhood programs, supervise interns in the public schools, work in partnership with classroom teachers, chair doctoral students' programs and dissertations, and chair committees. Each of us is well published in the early childhood arena and actively involved in early childhood professional organizations at the local, state, and national levels. Moreover, both of us engage in professional development and renewal activity and are committed to a constructivist perspective on learning and the establishment of a community of learners in all learning contexts.

We are committed to a graduate model that integrates theory and practice because we believe we can make a difference in public schools through our preparation of early childhood teachers who view education holistically, think critically, make informed decisions, work effectively as team members, and live healthful and productive personal and professional lives. This challenge keeps us striving to become better early childhood teacher educators, but the dilemmas, frustrations, and realities associated with change to a PDS model have stretched our commitment in new ways. It also has provided a new lens for our response to the question of what is needed to be a competent early childhood teacher educator.

DILEMMAS, FRUSTRATIONS, AND STARK REALITIES

Our new direction in teacher education naturally evokes dilemmas and tensions that have ramifications for our programs and for us as teacher educators. Some of these tensions are conceptual in nature (e.g., inquiry-oriented practice versus technical practice, philosophy and reality conflicts, and full- versus part-time faculty to supervise interns and work with clinical faculty). Others are technical (e.g., scheduling classes and clinical experiences, time, calendars, and selection of both mentors and sites for placements). Still others are cultural (e.g., school versus university cultures, behaviors, expectations, and the roles and responsibilities of teachers and university faculty).

Still others are political. Our lofty goals and high ideals of reflective practice, increased professional knowledge and professionalism, the creation of new educational cultures, and a shared community of inquiry are certainly worthy pursuits, but the stark realities of the university and public school stall many efforts. We continue to be plagued by time constraints and competing loyalties in our effort to break the mold to create a new design.

TIME USE AS AN INDICATOR OF COMPETING LOYALTIES

The amount and intensity of time and the differences in time schedules between public school life and university life on a daily, semester, and summer basis have been significant issues. The labor and time needed for any new project competes with other responsibilities and loyalties. As expressed by one kindergarten teacher, "I can't take that much time off to collaborate on a Professional Development School Model. I teach 50 children a day, 25 in the morning and 25 in the afternoon. My priorities are the kids." A university professor was heard to say, "How can I afford to invest this much time in a venture that I'm not sure the system will reward me for doing?"

In addition to the decision to commit the time needed to develop a model when there are competing responsibilities and rewards, there are other complex time constraints. Public school teachers who teach in the day time and university professors who work in the schools during the day and teach other courses at night find simply scheduling a meeting a significant problem. Negotiating large blocks of time with public school teachers is a monumental task requiring secretarial assistance. Often, numerous permissions from administrators are needed, along with funding to pay for substitutes. University professors, with loaded calendars of service to numerous committees and task forces, as well as teaching, research and scholarship endeavors, find the calendar a major obstacle. One principal coined the word "calendaring" to describe the significant portion of every meeting spent finding a time to meet again.

In our naiveté at the beginning of the project, we believed if developing the PDS model were given priority by university and public schools, there would be enough time. However, creating a new project, establishing different communication avenues, establishing trust, managing and solving conflicts, and forging new relationships becomes more than a priority. It is a pervasive, consuming force—a major "change effort." We found ourselves at the university juggling all other responsibilities around the PDS model. And, our early childhood colleagues in public schools, while desiring more time to devote to the project, were lost in the daily routines of their teaching.

BREAKING THE MOLD OF THEORY VERSUS PRACTICE

We found ourselves enmeshed in theory versus practice issues. Continuing arguments about the "knowledge base in teaching" or whether expert teachers' actions can be recorded, coded, and principles extrapolated as the teacher effectiveness literature proposes kept this issue alive.

Teacher educators often quote to prospective teachers the old axiom, "There is nothing so practical as good theory, nor is there anything so theoretical as good practice" (Merseth, 1991, p. 13). In our initial deliberations regarding the PDS model, we often heard teachers laud their experiences as the practical and our courses as the theoretical. We know, though, from our own teaching experiences and the best of the clinical faculty classrooms that good practice is very sound theory. Practice and theory often meld in classrooms where teachers have strong child development backgrounds, emphasize whole language, and operate with an integrated curriculum. Our interactions with those clinical faculty and interns fit what we believe are both good practice and good theory.

Conventional views of theory and practice, however, are now being joined by the views of researchers such as Clark and Lampert (1986) and Calderhead (1987). They posit that teacher thinking can be analyzed in terms of looking at "contextual knowledge," which is situation specific; "interactive knowledge," which involves the teaching acts; and "speculative knowledge," which means dealing with the uncertainties created by so many variables which influence what is taught, how it is learned, and the flow of the ever changing world of the classroom (Clark & Lampert, 1986, p. 29).

For the intern, learning the "contextual knowledge," the "interactive knowledge," and the "speculative knowledge" of the classroom life is a tremendous challenge. Why does it work so well for some interns and so poorly for others? The knowledge, attitudes, skills, and "certainty" of the clinical faculty in their practice appear to be significant influences.

Despite our best efforts to prepare teachers who think about all aspects of teaching, we find ourselves as partners with teachers whose primary focus is the day-to-day management of children and curriculum. The emphasis on the technical "how" of managing a classroom work load, the mechanics of procedures, and the obligatory fit with the public school system as it presently operates too often define the measure of a "good" intern.

Yet the technical is far from the goal to which we aspire. Our challenge has become achieving the triangular match of the right classrooms with exemplary practice, belief systems that match those of the early childhood program at GMU, and highly qualified applicants who can survive the intense demands of heavy course work and a full-year internship.

The dilemma of theory and practice, of the triangular match of beliefs and practice, and the selection of the interns and clinical faculty escalates the problem of achieving our vision and fulfilling our commitment. We believe our responsibility as early childhood teacher educators is to dialogue often and tirelessly with those with whom we work. We continue to address the tensions created by competing loyalties, the support for sustaining the status quo in practice, and the absence of vision regarding professional development. We must continually find ways to communicate the fundamental principles and constructs of our early childhood program.

But hard issues still remain: dealing with conflicting views of teaching and learning; complicating the already complex life of the classroom teacher by asking him or her to mentor a neophyte; devoting the reflection time needed for a look at the "big picture" of the model; struggling with the "schooling" issues while protecting an intern's almost paper-thin self-concept as a teacher; and targeting the child, not the school, as the focus of our joint endeavors.

STRIVING TO BECOME EFFECTIVE
EARLY CHILDHOOD TEACHER EDUCATORS

In our striving to be more competent teacher educators, to actualize the five attributes identified at the beginning of this essay, we have identified four overarching programmatic beliefs as essential for prospective early childhood teachers:

1. a belief in reflective practice
2. a belief in collaborative programs that provide a coordinated and cohesive set of experiences with carefully selected mentors
3. a commitment to inquiry-oriented practices
4. a commitment to life-long learning and development as a professional

Although we believe that teacher development occurs in stages, our discussion focuses only on the initial stage of the learning to teach continuum.

A Belief in Reflective Practice

Teacher education is accused of failing to prepare teachers for the complexities of the teaching task and the realities of today's schools, and of failing to create a culture of professionalism. Reflecting on one's practice allows both prospective and practicing educators to examine each of these accusations. Nurturing reflective practice is a basic tenet and a recurring theme in our work together as teacher educators, in our collaboration with schools, and in the design of courses and field experiences.

Reflective practice is derived from the constructivist view of learning. We believe that learners actively synthesize knowledge and select critical features of information gained from their experience, environment, and inquiry. Being reflective, however, is new for many mentors, and most of our clinical faculty do not know how to probe an intern's thinking and practice or are too tender in their approach. We accept it as our responsibility to assist mentors in learning how to become more reflective and how to lead interns to a reflective posture. We must be quick to point out, however, that the clinical faculty role has come easily for many teachers. They were already reflective practitioners, and the step forward to mentoring based on their reflection evolved admirably.

We know the difficulty student teachers and other novices have reflecting on their practice. We have also painfully witnessed the effects of university teaching being "washed out" by experience. As student teacher supervisors, we are troubled by the difficulties of novice teachers in applying principles "learned" in the university classroom when confronted with conflicts found in student teaching. Yet, asking student interns to reflect on classroom practices that we find unacceptable can be interpreted as the university trying to direct practice in a teacher's classroom. When perceived as an intrusion, these incidents cause tension between teachers and the university.

Deciding whether or not to question some classroom practices is a major dilemma for us. Frankly, many times we avoid the issue, turning instead to the advice, "Wait until you have your own classroom; you can do it differently." Our ability to question practice in a nonthreatening way, focus on the reflection process, and move the cooperative nature of the PDS venture along is a troubling and continuing issue and challenges our commitment to advocacy for children and the profession.

A BELIEF IN COLLABORATIVE PROGRAMS WITH COORDINATED EXPERIENCES

Given our commitment to the preparation of "broadly, deeply informed" teachers who can critically analyze their practice and our institutional commitment to thoughtful, long-term inquiry into teaching and learning, it is important to find ways for collaboration that have the potential to create new school and university cultures. For us, this means finding new ways to bridge the gap between our university's entrepreneurial, innovative culture and that of the public schools, which are essentially conservative, embrace academic programs, experience intense parental pressure for student achievement, and have competitive and sophisticated teachers.

Effective collaboration between our university and the public schools has been difficult to achieve because of differences in existing cultures, orientation, and working conditions, which can lead to stereotyping, breakdowns in communication, and conflict. Bridging the cultures has meant spending more time in the schools, attending school functions, compromising university service commitments, and spending hours on the telephone at night for professional communications.

We found that, like all professionals, teachers want to be appreciated. Some of the incidentals of the planning process for PDS proved as valuable as research and curriculum inquiry. Inviting classroom teachers to well-planned, campus meetings to contribute to the program design, for example, removes them from their school setting and affirms their professionalism. Professors sharing the dilemmas of the university's annual review process, budget woes, lack of support services, and "shared misery stories" lead teachers to see the realities of university life. Conversely, sharing our own professional breakthroughs with interns and their breakthroughs with children and families cemented the reality that we all struggle and need to celebrate our successes.

Our fundamental belief is that working collegially, particularly on research and development activities, can create a culture of collaboration that contributes to personal growth and improved practice. We found that involving public school clinical faculty in reviewing university course work helped to build a sense of collaboration between these two cultures. We also found it essential to bring all clinical faculty together at the beginning and end of each semester to discuss students' university course work, appropriate field experiences, and the philosophy undergirding our program. As a result of these discussions, we are beginning, in all our professional courses, to align more closely the clinical experiences with expected university course requirements and outcomes.

Through these large group encounters with clinical faculty from all seven PDS schools, we are attempting to provide a more consistent, cohesive, and coordinated set of experiences that can achieve our programmatic goals. While the primary goal of such interaction is curriculum alignment and program improvement, a side benefit has been a deeper understanding and respect for the roles and responsibilities of teachers and teacher educators.

A COMMITMENT TO INQUIRY-ORIENTED PRACTICE

We highly value inquiry-oriented practice, particularly through reflective journal writing and case studies. Analyzing teaching through these sources can help students begin to define themselves as developing professionals with a self–other orientation. For us, the "hard issues" of philosophy and reality questions, teacher-directed versus teacher-facilitated instruction, child-initiated versus teacher-centered classrooms, and play versus work are dialectics that embrace the best of early childhood practice. Many teachers also embrace these practices but feel they should teach in other ways because of real or perceived pressures from testing, curriculum guide interpretations, textbook adoptions, parental pressure for academic success of children, and mandates from administrators. Confronting these issues in the PDS school moves them from being talked about in the university classroom to being lived in the school culture. There are no quick fixes to these "hard issues."

Rather than seeing the issues as "fixable," we have chosen instead to use them as the substance of teaching cases and use case method as a way of presenting the dilemmas. Epistemologically, the case method fits our expanded view of the teacher knowledge base, but the question then becomes whether or not the case can be the vehicle for preservice teachers to acquire the knowledge to begin to deal with the complexities of the issues. While there is limited research on case methods in teacher education, insights can be gained from the wide experiences and long tradition of case methods in other fields. The case and the study of the case, including analysis of context, patterns of interactions, and speculations of solutions, may lead to some guiding principles but resolutely leads to critical inquiry of sometimes competing principles (Kennedy, 1987).

We are optimistic about the potential of case methods. They encourage reflective practice and deliberate action, provide practice in critical analysis and action in complex problem-solving situations, involve and empower students in their own learning, and promote a community of learners (Christiansen, 1990; Merseth, 1991). This approach to cases and case methods, which focuses on critical analysis and possible actions, leads teacher education closer to Schön's (1983) reflective practice model.

We believe that early childhood teacher educators must begin to include teaching cases as an integral part of teacher preparation programs. However, the success of the case method in teacher education is dependent on the following factors, among others. To be effective users of cases:

1. Teacher educators must recognize the possibilities of cases as a major delivery system for course content. For example, we use cases to help students examine the complexities of whole language, solve problems with real social and multicultural dilemmas, and plan for hands-on science, mathematics, and technology experiences.
2. Teacher educators must build a collection of cases which meets the needs of their particular population of prospective teachers. We use cases to deal with the struggles of white middle-income monolingual teachers in classrooms with children from various racial, ethnic, and linguistic backgrounds.
3. Teacher educators must research the effectiveness of case methods versus other methods and in interaction with other methods. We are piloting the use of cases and researching our own practice with them.
4. Teacher educators must refine case presentation and discussion. We are taking the necessary risks to learn how to present cases in ways that ensure they engender substantive discussion of critical issues.

Cases are appropriate pedagogical techniques because they require learners to be active, apply their understandings rather than accept ideas passively, and wrestle with real world problems of human relationships and high incidence cases indicative of today's schools. Cases are needed which are common occurrences that expert teachers are familiar with but new teachers have yet to experience by working within the system. Cases also help develop a mind set that the real world of teaching necessitates ongoing problem analysis and decision making. Using cases helps prospective teachers develop responsibility for examining their own school problems rather than placing responsibility on outside factors (Silverman, Welty, & Lyon, 1992).

A COMMITMENT TO LIFELONG LEARNING

Our guiding principles set a tone and a standard for early childhood teacher preparation at GMU. We know that many teacher educators need to change their pedagogy, and that many early childhood teachers need to change their pedagogical practices. Case method may be only one of the many changes we need to make. As we look to teachers of the future, we support the notion that has permeated the field of early childhood education from the beginning—that learning to teach is a lifelong process and that teachers as well as students must become lifelong learners. This reality has certainly been reinforced for us during our transition to the Professional Development School Model.

A VISION FOR OUR FUTURE

Larry Cuban (1992) titled his presidential address to the American Educational Research Association "Managing Dilemmas While Building Professional Communities." The title is appropriate for us, two early childhood teacher educators struggling to discern which dilemmas to manage. We are idealists in our beliefs and almost constantly feel the opposing forces of idealism and pragmatism. Our view is long term, but courses come to an end each semester and internships end each year. The first class of PDS interns taught us a great deal. The first intense year of working together in new relationships with teachers and administrators finds us a few steps closer to taking on the hard issues, rather than simply fixing the schedule or adjusting the course requirements.

We find ourselves purposefully walking into the fog of creating a new culture where teachers and teacher educators truly collaborate. We cannot yet see clearly, but sunlight is beginning to stream in and we are willing to keep struggling along the path to becoming effective early childhood teacher educators.

ENDNOTES

[1] This essay was written when Shirley Raines and Joan Isenberg were both faculty members at George Mason University.

REFERENCES

Calderhead, J. (1987). *Exploring teachers' thinking.* London: Cassel Educational Limited.

Christiansen, C. R. (1990, May). *Teaching a case.* Paper presented at Case Methods Conference, Commonwealth Center for the Education of Teachers. Charlottesville, VA.

Clark, C., & Lampert, M. (1986). The study of teacher thinking: Implications for teacher education. *Journal of Teacher Education, 37* (5), 27–31.

Cuban, L. (1992). Managing dilemmas while building professional communities. *Educational Researcher, 21* (1), 4–11.

Holmes Group Executive Board. (1986). *Tomorrow's teachers: A report of the Holmes Group.* East Lansing, MI: Author.

Kennedy, M. (1987). Inexact sciences: Professional education and the development of expertise. In E. Rothkopf (Ed.), *Review of Research in Education* (Vol. 14, pp. 133–167). Washington, DC: American Educational Research Association.

Merseth, K. (1991). *The case for cases in teacher education.* Washington, DC: American Association of Higher Education and the American Association of Colleges of Teacher Education.

Schön, D. A. (1983). *The reflective practitioner.* New York: Basic Books.

Silverman, R., Welty, W., & Lyon, S. (1992). *Case studies for teacher problem solving.* New York: McGraw–Hill.

CHAPTER **14**

Reflections of an Early Childhood
Teacher Educator In-the-Making

Catherine Wilson

The occasion for writing as a "teacher educator in-the-making" has been 3 years of teaching introductory courses in early childhood education in a large, urban university. As a doctoral student seeking to understand what kinds of experiences may be important in learning to become a teacher of young children and how the teacher educator can contribute to that process, my thoughts are the tentative notions of a newcomer, fragile and often fragmented. They reveal my struggle to discover all the pieces of the puzzle, with only a glimmering of how they fit together. Hoping to place my efforts to learn about early childhood teacher education within the context of my institution of higher education and the students enrolled in its early childhood program, I begin with an autobiographical account of my early semesters of teaching, describing the painful as well as the cherished discoveries of a novice. From this personal rendering of teacher and students learning together, I attempt to explore what seems to be the necessarily interdependent nature of the questions, "What is needed to become a competent teacher of young children?" and "What is necessary to become a competent teacher educator?" These emergent understandings, as well as an investigation of the support I continue to find crucial to, and in some cases missing from, the process of learning to become an early childhood teacher educator, form, in conclusion, a set of queries I will pose to more experienced colleagues.

FIRST STEPS: IN THE COMPANY OF MENTORS

Having been a teacher of 3- and 4-year-old children, I was apprehensive of the challenges I would face as the instructor of an introductory course in early childhood education. But I also felt great excitement, for I had found my own preparation for teaching to be invigorating and highly relevant to my work in a middle-income nursery school program. And, as a cooperating teacher with students in their final practicum, I welcomed the renewal a teaching relationship usually brought to my own learning. So now, with a growing curiosity about how one learns to become — and continues becoming — a good teacher of young children, I was about to take on an expanded role as a teacher educator.

To prepare for teaching the course, my mentor gave me Elizabeth Jones's *Teaching Adults: An Active Learning Approach* (1986b). Without this framework, I would have surely followed the model of earlier "apprenticeships" (Britzman, 1986), for my years as a student provided powerful images of teachers as dispensers of information and grades, and students as consumers and reproducers of information. Overlooking all I knew about learning in young children, I envisioned college teaching to be a replication of many of my own experiences as a student. But, as I was to discover, Jones (1986a, 1986b) and others before her (Katz, 1974, 1977; Mitchell, 1931) had looked problematically at the relationship between how teachers are prepared and how they are expected to teach, arguing for a "consistency, harmony, or concordance between the way we teach teachers and the way we want them to teach" (Katz, 1977, p. 4).

Jones (1986a, 1986b), Lilian Katz (1974, 1977), and my university mentor were steadfast guides in the first semesters, assuring me that my experiences as a teacher of young children not only could, but *should* inform my thinking about early childhood teacher education. But how was this kind of teaching, grounded so firmly in a carefully nurtured community of social and intellectual activity, to be translated into the impersonal environment of an urban–commuter university?

Students in our program came to the university from a widely spread metropolitan area. Occasionally, some would enroll for a course with a friend or colleague, but often they arrived as strangers to the university. Moreover, most students in early childhood courses were women who worked long hours, both in and outside the home, some driving as much as an hour to reach campus. Arriving for a 3-hour evening class, fatigued from a day of work or preoccupied with concerns about child care meant that rejuvenation was essential before we could even begin to think about teaching and learning.

Another, smaller group consisted of full-time undergraduate students, separated by age and life experiences from the older students, and struggling to form friendships in a loosely configured social world of a university where most students returned to live with their families at night. The few students who did live on campus appeared isolated from the other students by living on a predominantly nonresidential campus.

If we were to create a learning community with interesting things to think about and a network of supportive relationships to lessen the risks of learning, it seemed important to address these constraints in the student life of the program. My energies in the first semester of teaching, therefore, were committed to diminishing the isolation and anxiety of an unfamiliar institution or program—reflecting, perhaps as well, my own personal need for affirmation and support in my new role as instructor.

We began by simply making many occasions to know one another, both in class discussion and in informal conversations extending during breaks and after class. We also used communication journals, unevaluated and open to student agendas, for further personal conversations between student and teacher. While these efforts did not create the kinds of relationships developed between teacher and student in early childhood teaching, they helped, as one student wrote, in "feeling free to discuss our changing ideas and thoughts."

The confidence many students felt to express "changing ideas" also gave me a window into how what was learned in the course was being understood by students. Having abandoned the lecture format and, instead, "covering" the course syllabus through conversations centering on students' field observations, I could hear students think about the course through *their* questions.

Finally, hoping to harvest understanding from our experiences as learners in a university classroom, we talked often about the course itself, and the decisions we were making as teacher and students. When students were impatient with not having lecture notes, frustrated with the questions of other students, or uneasy with the open-ended nature of the observation assignments (several students even wrote longingly for the "certainty" of quizzes), we talked about those questions as part of our exploration of learning and teaching.

As the semester progressed, the barriers that made learning a solitary affair seemed to be lessening. Our discussions became more developed and inclusive of greater diversity of students, and my spirits were buoyed by the energy brought to the course by the students. Now, even with a clock reminding us that 10:15 P.M. had arrived, small groups of students often remained another half hour for continuing conversations.

Those were the good nights. Other nights I went home to very little sleep, with lingering questions about what students were learning. The class format and journals provided glimpses of how students were understanding the intended content of the course, but we often seemed to be riding a juggernaut of discussion with no one at the helm. I was discovering that giving support to the learning embedded in discussions took considerable expertise; pedagogical decisions were complicated by the need to preserve social comfort, while simultaneously pursuing intellectual conflict. And, the specter of departmental expectations for content students would "know" on completion of the course—as well as the visions of children who would live under the care of these students—made it difficult for me to "trust in the learner" (Jones, 1986b) to create understandings out of our loosely shaped discussions.

NEW AWAKENINGS: MORE THAN PROCESS

This point of uncertainty was an important juncture in my own learning, for I had been given the expanse of working space to explore how the process of learning and teaching might unfold, but now it was crucial to have a mentor to assist in bringing critique to those experiences. My own emergent views required dialogue with a more experienced teacher educator—one who would question, as well as encourage—and who would provide continuous debate to my thinking. To form the focus for this dialogue, I kept a record of my thoughts and questions about teaching, and this journal became the basis of both written and conversational inquiry with my mentor.

The topics of our conversations were wide-ranging. Sometimes we probed possible views of the students, searching for understanding about the process of learning; other times, we would consider the challenge of pedagogical judgments and interpersonal skills necessary for such a process-oriented approach to teaching. Often, the response of my mentor would be the proposition of another question, as an invitation to a continuing investigation of an issue. Just as frequently, I would find great comfort in discovering my doubts as a novice were shared by a more experienced teacher educator.

But, I think most important for moving my thinking beyond the *process* of teaching were our shared discussions of the writings of other teacher educators and the resulting expansion of our conversations from questions about the dynamics of learning, to the *purpose* of teacher education. For example, one of our dialogues came from reading Barbara Bowman's (1989) thoughts on the role of personal knowledge in teaching—for I was very excited about the use of childhood memories as a means for bridging the gap between an adult teacher and child.

To counter this view, my mentor shared the work of Floden, Buchmann, and Schwille (1987) proposing a break with experience as a necessary element of education, and it was the debate arising from these writings that led us to probe beyond the questions of "how" teachers should be educated, to the more problematic questions of "what" are the roles of teachers—and teacher educators—in society.

The opportunity for ongoing personal dialogue with a more experienced colleague was essential—and continues to remain so—in learning to become a teacher educator. Importantly, it has been a relationship that encourages me to take risks as a teacher and serves as a resource in that process. But, just as often, it acts to challenge and disassemble the tidy conclusions I create from my own experience, and I think, necessarily complicates and enlarges the process of learning to become a teacher educator.

THE WIDENING CIRCLE: LEARNING FROM STUDENTS

During the first semester, my focus was almost entirely on my own teaching, with little room, despite my efforts to attend to the needs of students in the university classroom, for thinking about what students were learning. But, with the broader perspectives gained from conversations with a mentor, I began to take more notice of the students and the issues they brought to the course.

This was a second juncture in the process of becoming a teacher educator. My awareness raised a new set of challenges that transformed my understanding of teaching what had been a "generic" introductory course in early childhood education, to a very particular course, given shape and vitality by the prior experiences, present lives, and anticipated teaching sites of the students. For, unlike my own work as a teacher of young children, almost half of the students in this introductory class were teachers in various public school districts in the metropolitan or suburban areas. Returning for additional certification, or preparing to teach in the burgeoning early childhood programs in the public schools, these graduate students brought distinctive questions to our discussions.

Another smaller group of undergraduate students were concurrently enrolled as elementary education students and often bewildered by the differing educational philosophies of the two departments within the School of Education. This strong elementary school orientation in both the graduate and undergraduate students meant that each topic on the course syllabus was an occasion for great debate. These highly dynamic discussions allowed me to feel successful at encouraging "active learning," but, for the students, it was more than an academic exercise; years of beliefs and work as teachers (and as students) were challenged by the values of the early childhood profession.

As volatile feelings swirled through our discussions, I was energized, seizing student's questions as levers for challenging prior beliefs. I was looking for good arguments. But, for most students, the course was undermining the foundations of their understandings about education—which we might, indeed, see as necessary—yet, leaving them with few resources for returning to their work as teachers or elementary student teachers.

The collection of readings to "share with co-teachers or administrators" and admonitions to "proceed slowly" were meager reassurance for students whose beliefs were shaken and whose knowledge (and support) for rebuilding their view of teaching was limited. Waiting for later course work to address issues of advocacy within their present teaching communities was insufficient from the students' perspective.

More troublesome was the notion that an "us versus them" (Walsh, 1992) mentality had emerged from our class discussions of early childhood education and the public schools. Even with an articulate and thoughtful elementary principal as a member of the class, "unenlightened" teachers and administrators inadvertently became the adversaries in our thinking. The lines of demarcation were drawn boldly and broadly, and the NAEYC document (Bredekamp, 1987) on developmentally appropriate practices added fuel to the fire, polarizing views of teaching in a clearly prescriptive manner. By mid-semester, the divergent camps on educating young children became the central feature of the course. To exacerbate conditions, the required syllabus, (i.e., the wide-ranging content of an introductory course) drove us forward, rather than allowing us to spend time exploring this complicated issue in any satisfying manner.

The semester came to an end with students having experienced tumultuous examinations of topics on the course of study, but given little assistance in using those understandings to impact their teaching. And, most troubling, my background in the comparatively cloistered world of private nursery school made me ill-prepared to address the particular and compelling needs of the students in our program. I needed multiple, extended dialogues both within the university and in the public schools to understand and bring critique to the issues distinctive to this area of our field. As a doctoral student, my continuing course work allowed me to engage these issues, but the work itself was confined to the university classroom, and I continue to search for opportunities to become a competent early childhood teacher educator by linking those theoretical discussions to experiences as they are lived by children, teachers, and parents in the public schools.

ENCOUNTERING THE BOUNDARIES OF THE KNOWLEDGE BASE OF TEACHER EDUCATION

While students brought an urgency for understanding early childhood education in the context of a public school setting, I was dismayed by the absence of the child and the family in our learning. Perhaps because our discussions so often centered on ideology and advocacy, the child and parent seemed only shadowy figures in our talk.

When children did appear, they were often categorized and distanced by the language of adult-views or professional terminology. Children observed in field visits were described by students as "selfish," "tattle-tales," or "bossy." Students with a bit of Piaget explained almost all the actions of children as "egocentric." Other students freely used the vocabulary of "delayed," "at risk," or "not ready."

Parents fared only a bit better, in part because many of the students were parents themselves and could personalize their feelings and frustrations. Unlike the absent child, they could make a case for their full humanity. But, even with the persistent voices of parents in the course, children and parents were one-dimensional strangers in our discussions, and the textbook and journal readings did little to challenge these views of children and parents. Instead, the beliefs of students were often cemented by generalizations, as the textbook language homogenized children and families, draining away their human vitality and variation.

The four field observations traditionally assigned in the course were intended to bring students in touch with the complexity and individuality of children, but often students were stranded in adult-views of incidents. While our textbook assured students that observation would increase empathy and understanding for the child, the progress was slow and discouraging, and students wrestled with breaking with assumptions about children and teaching. Challenged to bring the child and parent into teacher education, I was frustrated by the constraints of creating more complicated views of children and society with a knowledge base grounded in the norms and universalities of developmental psychology.

Again, it was through opportunities to brainstorm with more experienced teacher educators, who, in spite of university expectations for their own research and community involvement, made time to listen, took seriously the questions of a novice, and created the opportunities for experimentation, that I was able to begin an investigation of this new question. Through this collaborative thinking, I was set on the track of Robert Coles's (1989) argument for the use of literature in education, and I began trying out literary portrayals of children and parents as a way to bring human dimensionality to our thinking about teaching.

Struggling to challenge our personal views of children and parents by encountering a diversity of literary families, we read Maxine Hong Kingston's (1975) *The Woman Warrior: A Girlhood Among Ghosts,* Mildred D. Taylor's (1976) *Roll of Thunder, Hear my Cry,* Russell Baker's (1982) *Growing Up,* and Tillie Olsen's (1956) *Tell Me a Riddle.* And, inspired by the impact of personal, narrative accounts of literature, we also read excerpts from Frances Hawkins (1969), Vivian Paley (1986), and Margaret Yonemura (1986), as students searched to hear teachers situate their understandings of childhood and teaching within the lived-experiences of early childhood settings.

Yet, the distance of the university classroom from the lives of children and families—as they are experienced in homes, schools, and neighborhoods of our communities—accentuates the adult/teacher perspective at the expense of children and parents whose lives are shaped by the teacher and school, and protects students from considering the fuller implications of teaching as a social construction (Liston & Zeichner, 1991). And, the isolation of the school of education from the other disciplines that might assist in broadening the resources of the teacher educator—and, here I think we can hear Jonathan Silin's (1988) argument for the inclusion of anthropology, literature, philosophy, and sociology—narrows the possibilities available for challenging the assumptions of students, as well as teacher educators.

Similarly, the traditional separation of early childhood from the other departments in the school of education (Bloch, 1991) discourages the infusion of thinking that currently stimulates other realms of educational thinking, and here I am thinking of the defamiliarizing of teaching brought by critical theorists, or the insights into the larger philosophical, social, and economic issues raised by historical study. It was only through my parallel life as a student that my knowledge and assumptions as an early childhood teacher educator were challenged by widening circles of critique in other departments of the university. While this is not meant to assume early childhood teacher educators do not initiate interdisciplinary encounters, had I been a full-time instructor, faced with a heavier teaching course load and expectations for research, the opportunities for continuing vigorous debate through engaging a multiplicity of disciplinary viewpoints might have been limited by the compartmentalization and constraints of university life.

THE CLOSE-UP VIEW OF "BEING EDUCATED" TO
TEACH YOUNG CHILDREN

As I struggled to broaden the dialogue surrounding teacher education, I also yearned to work intensively—as in my days as a cooperating teacher—with a single student. For I was discovering the powerful force of the student's contributions to teacher education, and I needed to know much more about how a student might live the experience of "being educated" as a teacher. Eager also to investigate my own interests in broadening the knowledge base in educating teachers, I began working with a young undergraduate during the semester of her final practicum—an experience quite different in tone and content, and, I think, necessary as a teacher educator in gathering a more finely grained understanding of a teacher in-the-making.

The student, Joan, was a young undergraduate, living at home and working in the evenings as the manager of a theater. The pace of her life as a self-supporting student gave her little time for stepping back from the activity to reflect on teaching. It was with some hesitation that we added another commitment to her already bursting schedule, but we designed a flexible arrangement, meeting biweekly for several hours of conversation about literature and teaching.

The dual purpose of our work together was to chart the terrain of her thinking about the practicum experience and to explore my interest in creating more dimensional views of children. Joan and I were co-researchers in that effort, recording, reviewing, and evaluating our conversations. It was in the midst of these talks about teaching, when our shared role as researchers erased any hint of evaluation of her learning, that I had new intimations of the process of becoming a teacher and its implications for teacher education.

Rather than using Joan's performance in student teaching as the starting point of our discussions—the traditional focus of practicum supervision—we began by talking about our reading of literary portrayals of children, parents, teachers, and schools. Our discussions of literature took us on varied journeys, through Joan's childhood, back to the text itself, and into her current work with children. It also brought us to consider the questions of differences in class, race, gender, and culture—often uncomfortable territory for groups of students—and the ways in which social institutions provided stepping stones or roadblocks for families.

Through our conversations, I was able to learn more about the thinking of a young teacher, as Joan made connections between the literary and the pedagogical, mobilizing both her personal and professional knowledge. For example, as Joan spoke about the child who wonders about the differences between adults and children in *An American Childhood*, Dillard's (1987) portrayal of a child became, for Joan, the catalyst for her own vividly felt memories of childhood. Retrieving her imaginative capacity as a child through discussion of the literary child, Joan shifted to her teaching, recalling an almost forgotten moment when she observed her children at school hypothesizing about the appearance of the moon in the morning sky. As we spoke, I heard Joan, moved perhaps by the speculative stance of the literary experience to look problematically at her concern as a student teacher in "managing" at the expense of listening to children. And by providing an occasion apart from the very performance-driven and evaluative nature of the student teaching experience, we uncovered the opportunity for an extended exploration of the multiple and sometimes conflicting roles that Joan was discovering in her teaching.

Sometimes these connections between literature, autobiography, and teaching came through leaps of intuition, and other times they were built by slowly embroidered layers of understanding. But, prompted by the stories as well as the aesthetic experience of reading, Joan appeared to be using, as well as challenging, her personal knowledge to create insights into the intentions, feelings, and capacities of children—and to become more thoughtful about her teaching.

This diversion from traditional course and field work into the literary experience as a lens for sharpening reflection on teaching affirmed the challenge raised by contemporary critics (Egan, 1983; Silin, 1988) regarding the immersion of students in psychological and learning theory, at the expense of variant views of children and teaching. If insight into human experience is essential for teaching (Katz & Goffin, 1990; Van Manen, 1991; Yonemura, 1986, 1991), then, how do teacher educators create occasions for deeply experienced dialogues—free from the evaluation inherent in traditional teacher–student relationships—to explore and develop such understanding? If it is, as Margret Buchmann (1991) suggests, important for the teacher, as for the poet, that "sensitivities are keen, vibrant, and refined skills, apposite, ready to hand, and malleable" (p. 294), how do we nourish those skills in our students and in ourselves?

But just as important from Joan's perspective, the research meetings provided the much-needed comfort of a dialogue with someone who would listen, understand her questions, and eventually, challenge her assumptions—a feature I was discovering in my own journey in becoming a teacher educator. If it matters to the student to enter into the world of collegial conversations, how do we carve out time to develop sustained and significant relationships with students?

WHAT IS NECESSARY TO BECOME A COMPETENT TEACHER EDUCATOR?

In describing his first years of teaching, Peter Elbow (1986) writes, "I rocketed off with a kind of pent up animal/intellectual energy. . . . I loved trying to orchestrate a 'well-run discussion.' I think the teaching process helped heighten my excitement with what I was reading and teaching—I suppose by providing me with a constant audience" (p. 67). My experiences as an early childhood teacher educator have much of this same flavor of over-eager naiveté and weakness of pedagogical judgment. At the same time, the first years have added texture, if not dimension, to my early thinking about what might contribute to the inextricable questions of what it takes to become an early childhood teacher and what it takes to become a competent early childhood teacher educator. It will be these hard-won discoveries that I now pose as questions to my more seasoned colleagues.

First, I have come to understand that attending to the *process* of learning is necessary, but not sufficient guidance in the preparation of teachers, or in the development of a teacher educator. The persistent questions of *what* kinds of content are important for *which* students, and *when* that content is most useful intruded continually into our weekly meetings.

In our program, questions of "what" and "when" were complicated by the diversity of student experiences. Many students were not waiting to teach until after a program of study was completed; they were *already* teaching young children. For those students, the course was not one of teacher preparation, but of teacher development. Challenging the traditional path of preparation and entry into teaching, the needs of students in our program reflect the realities of the field of early childhood care and education—a field with great diversity in programmatic features and sponsorship, and without the system of control and certification in elementary and secondary teaching.

Those realities may include greater urgency for addressing issues typically encountered later in a program of teacher preparation, and skew the questions of *what* and *when* in unexpected ways. Furthermore, the course of teacher development often collides against, rather than building on, earlier teacher education. The impact of the collision is potentially laden with strong emotional and social challenges, as the student–teacher attempts to break away or reshape the culture of teaching in her or his school.

Additionally, provocative questions are raised for early childhood teacher educators as we articulate clearly ideological positions of the education of young children (Jones, 1986a). How do we prepare students who must develop knowledge, skills, and dispositions to work in much more ambiguous and complex milieus, where the questions of education, systems, and community values careen into the developmental orientation defining the mainstream of the early childhood profession? How does the teacher educator provide sustained support, and what are the necessary elements of that support? And where is the writing of practitioners on "dilemmas in teaching" (Lampert, 1985) that might assist the early childhood educator navigate the complicated terrain of public school programs? Finally, is it enough to focus our efforts on individual teachers, or is it imperative that as teacher educators, we also work to influence the schools where students will teach (Arnstine, 1990)? If so, how do we create networks among colleagues, both within the university, as well as in the community, for engaging in dialogues, influencing policy, and empowering students to meet the challenge of the worlds in which they will teach?

The second learning to emerge from my early experiences as a teacher educator is the breadth of knowledge necessary to prepare students for the diversity of early childhood programs. My background in the relatively autonomous setting of a private preschool was inadequate to support the challenges of teachers in public school systems. With the umbrella of early childhood extending from birth through 8 years of age, including programs from such disparate realms as home child care and public school education, the early childhood teacher educator must bring expertise about children of multiple ages and distinctive programs. While there are fundamental understandings spanning all ages and programs, a universal approach to teacher preparation overlooks the ways in which early education might be distinctive in particular settings, and how teachers might be differently prepared for those settings.

Is it possible, or even desirable, for one instructor to have this range of knowledge? Or would it provide students with a richer experience to have teaching shared among instructors with varied areas of expertise? If so, how would the team of instructors maintain the sustained involvement and support necessary for relationships with students during the highly disorienting experience of introductory courses? Would mentoring be as critical for students during these first semesters of a program—when closely held beliefs are being challenged—as during the final semester of practicum? Would optimum staffing include a practicing early childhood teacher, who might provide students and teachers with assistance in building collaborative relationships with teachers in their own schools (Cochran-Smith, 1991)?

Third, the strong developmental tradition in early childhood education has been criticized for rubbing away the idiosyncratic features of children, families, and culture, and for obscuring the moral dimensions of teaching (Kessler, 1991; Silin, 1988). Curriculum theorists (Broudy, 1988; Schubert, 1986) have argued that the aesthetic mode presents distinctive ways of creating insights into the complexities of human experience. My very tentative explorations with the literary experience, not only as a means for encountering the lives of children and parents, but also as a distinctive stance toward apprehending and expressing understandings about teaching, suggest the preparation of teachers might be enhanced by alternative frames of knowledge.

If other disciplines or "ways of knowing" (Bruner, 1985) contribute to the process of becoming a teacher, how does the teacher educator become conversant with these domains of thought? Does it occur most effectively through collaboration with instructors from other disciplines? Would other disciplines also challenge the assumptions and rhetoric of our own discipline with a more sensitive ear? Does the homogenized language of much of the writing in our field communicate expectations for practice that unintentionally undermine more profoundly expressed hopes for children and society (Greene, 1988)? If so, how do we, as early childhood teacher educators, read our texts at multiple levels and mediate unintended effects of language? How do we give students the tools and professional language of the field without limiting their visions of the possibilities of teaching?

Finally, if teaching young children requires insights into the intentions and meaning of experiences (Katz & Goffin, 1990), and if the students themselves need recognition of their own lived experiences in learning to become teachers, how do teacher educators attend to these more complicated, time consuming, and less easily "taught" dimensions of becoming a teacher? If students need ample time to work with small groupings of students, practicing teachers, parents, and community members, as well as interdisciplinary viewpoints, how do teacher educators influence their institutions to meet these essential elements of becoming a teacher? And if teachers (and teacher educators) are lifelong learners, how do we continue to provide a collegial community of learners and integrate supports at all levels of learning and teaching—not just the years within the university program?

My own efforts to become a competent teacher educator are sustained and challenged by the close mentorship of more experienced colleagues. But those relationships have been initiated and maintained outside the traditional channels of faculty meetings or university support. How do institutions assure "teacher educators in-the-making" of such mentorship? And, how do we develop colleagues across the diversity of the field and through multiple disciplines, as well as with the community of families who live the experiences set in motion by teacher educators? Who will assist in bringing continuing debate to the purposes and possibilities of our work?

These questions have helped to complicate the process of learning to become a teacher educator. They have arisen from listening and re-visiting conversations with students, parents, teachers, teacher educators, and instructors in other disciplines. They also emerge from the "mentors" I have appropriated from books and journals. Many evenings, when all voices and phones are quiet, I take up imaginary conversations with Margret Buchmann, Robert Coles, Elizabeth Jones, Lilian Katz, Vivian Paley, Jonathan Silin, and Margaret Yonemura, as well as with Maxine Hong Kingston, Tillie Olsen, and Mildred Taylor. Becoming a teacher educator requires networks of intellectual vigor, solace, and rejuvenation, mirroring those we create for children, parents, and the teachers we teach.

REFERENCES

Arnstine, B. (1990). Rational and caring teachers: Reconstructing teacher preparation. *Teachers College Record, 92,* 230–247.

Baker, R. (1982). *Growing up.* New York: New American Library.

Bloch, M. (1991). Critical science and the history of child development's influence on early education research. *Early Education and Development, 2,* 95–108.

Bowman, B. (1989). Self-reflection as an element of professionalization. *Teachers College Record, 90,* 444–451.

Bredekamp, S. (Ed.) (1987). *Developmentally appropriate practice in early childhood programs serving children birth through age 8.* Washington, DC: National Association for the Education of Young Children.

Britzman, D. P. (1986). Cultural myths in the making of a teacher: Biography and social structure in teacher education. *Harvard Educational Review, 56,* 442–472.

Broudy, H. S. (1988). Aesthetics and the curriculum. In W. F. Pinar (Ed.), *Contemporary curriculum discourses* (pp. 332–342). Scottsdale, AR: Gorsuch Scarisbrick.

Bruner, J. (1985). Narrative and paradigmatic modes of thought. In E. Eisner (Ed.), *Learning and teaching the ways of knowing.* Eighty-fourth Yearbook of the National Society for the Study of Education. Part II (pp. 97–115). Chicago: University of Chicago Press.

Buchmann, M. (1991). Making new or making do: An inconclusive argument about teaching. *American Journal of Education, 99* (3), 279–297.

Cochran-Smith, M. (1991). Learning to teach against the grain. *Harvard Educational Review, 61,* 279–309.

Coles, R. (1989). *The call of stories: Teaching and the moral imagination.* Boston: Houghton Mifflin.

Dillard, A. (1987). *An American childhood.* New York: Harper & Row.

Egan, K. (1983). *Education and psychology: Plato, Piaget and scientific psychology.* New York:

Teachers College Press.

Elbow, P. (1986). *Embracing contraries: Explorations in learning and teaching.* New York: Oxford University Press.

Floden, R. E., Buchman, M., & Schwille, J. R. (1987). *Breaking with everyday experience.* Teachers College Record, 88, 485–506.

Greene, M. (1988). Beyond the predictable: Possibilities and purposes. In L.. Williams & D. P. Fromberg (Eds.) *Proceedings of defining the field of early childhood education: An invitational symposium* (pp. 153–179). Charlottesville, VA: W. Alton Jones Foundation.

Hawkins, F. P. (1969). *The logic of action: Young children at work.* New York: Pantheon.

Jones, E. (1986a). Perspectives on teacher education: Some relations between theory and practice. In L. G. Katz (Ed.), *Current topics in early education* (Vol. 6, pp. 123–141). Norwood, NJ: Ablex.

Jones, E. (1986b). *Teaching adults: An active learning approach.* Washington, DC: National Association for the Education of Young Children.

Katz, L. G. (1974). Issues and problems in teacher education. In B. Spodek (Ed.), *Teacher education: Of the teacher, by the teacher, for the teacher* (pp. 55–66). Washington, DC: National Association for the Education of Young Children.

Katz, L. G. (1977). *Challenges to early childhood educators.* Young Children, 32(4), 4–10.

Katz, L. G., & Goffin, S. G. (1990). Issues in the preparation of teachers of young children. In B. Spodek & O. N. Saracho (Eds.), *Early childhood teacher preparation* (Vol. 1, pp. 192–208). New York: Teachers College Press.

Kessler, S. A. (1991). *Early childhood education as development: Critique of the metaphor.* Early Education and Development, 2, 137–152.

Kingston, M. H. (1975). *The woman warrior: Memoirs of a girlhood among ghosts.* New York: Vintage Books.

Lampert, M. (1985). *How do teachers manage to teach? Perspectives on problems in practice.* Harvard Educational Review, 55, 178–194.

Liston, D. P., & Zeichner, K. M. (1991). *Teacher education and the social conditions of schooling.* New York: Routledge.

Mitchell, L. S. (1931). *A cooperative school for student teachers.* Progressive Education, 8, 251–255.

Olsen, T. (1956). *Tell me a riddle.* New York: Delta.

Paley, V. G. (1986). *Molly is three.* Chicago: University of Chicago Press.

Schubert, W. H. (1986). *Curriculum perspective, paradigm, and possibility.* New York: Macmillan.

Silin, J. (1988). On becoming knowledgeable professionals. In B. Spodek, O. N. Saracho, & D. L. Peters (Eds.), *Professionalism and the early childhood practitioner* (pp. 117–134). New York: Teachers College Press.

Taylor, M. D. (1976). *Roll of thunder, hear my cry.* New York: Bantam.

Van Manen, M. (l991). *Reflectivity and the pedagogical moment.* Journal of Curriculum Studies, 23(6), 507–536.

Walsh, D. J. (1992). *Us against them: A few thoughts on separateness.* Early Education and Development 3, 89–91.

Yonemura, M. V. (1986). *A teacher at work: Professional development and the early childhood educator.* New York: Teachers College Press.

Yonemura, M. V. (1991). *Glimpses of becoming an early childhood teacher: A teacher educator's perspective.* Curriculum Inquiry, 21, 397–418.

COMMENTARIES

"Women's Work"

Sally Lubeck

A scene from a university committee, meeting to select recipients of teacher preparation merit scholarships:

> *One award remains, and I make a case for a woman who has been both working and raising three children. "She has dreamed of being a teacher for years," I affirm. "She wasn't able to go to school herself until her children were in school, and she continued to work after she entered a local community college. She has straight As." I struggle to convey the image of a woman whose career trajectory has been mediated by the demands of others. "And she takes other children into her home after school," I conclude meekly. The other committee members smile a bit too kindly. A male colleague makes a case for another candidate, a young man in his twenties. He has studied abroad, traveled extensively, and is fluent in Spanish. "He does not have quite straight As," he acknowledges, with a nod in my direction, "but look at where he's studied!" We all nod at the prestige of the institution. "This is a merit award, after all," mutters another colleague, although he, too, smiles when I look up. "Whose class would you rather be in?" the first asks me pointedly.*

Clearly the ayes have it for the free-wheeling male who ventures out to seek fame and fortune—nay to the milk-toast female who has done little more than take care of children. What is teaching all about anyway?

And, indeed, what is teaching all about? There is little doubt about what counts at many colleges and universities. Until recently, most were dominated and defined by men, but day care centers, preschools, and elementary schools are the domain of women. Madelaine Grumet (1988) has argued that women educators need to acknowledge the "body knowledge" of what we know from our experience of reproduction. As the children of our parents and the parents of our chil-

205

dren, we need to bring our understanding of nurturance, of connection, to public discourse regarding the restructuring of American education.

The fact that early childhood education is a field consisting largely of women, however, is a phenomenon seldom considered worthy of note. Even in the essays in this section, remarkable for their descriptions of new ways to think about and do teacher education, the authors do not attribute their ideas to a gendered understanding. Yet I would argue that it is precisely women's ways of knowing that most inform these essays. The values that animate them—relationship, collaboration, dialoguing, understanding, and intuition—are the concerns of women.

Just as women have maintained that a male bias pervades psychology (Gilligan, 1982), science (Keller, 1985), and the law (MacKinnon, 1989), so is the field of teacher education branded as one oddly out of sync with women's experience. By contrast, the models evoked in these essays seem to rely on "women's ways of knowing." There is, for example, the shift from detached generalization to situated knowledge. Fein describes four characteristics of a transformational model of teacher training: a situated knowledge base, observational fluency, reflection, and interactive routines. Isenberg and Raines also speak of a movement away from teaching as an applied science to a new clinically based view, emphasizing "four overarching programmatic beliefs: (1) a belief in reflective practice, (2) a belief in collaborative programs, (3) a commitment to inquiry-oriented practices, and (4) a commitment to lifelong learning and development as a professional."

Other themes reflected in these essays indicate a move from positivism to interpretivism and from an individual pedagogy to a more social one. Where Fein defines a linear model of teacher education, Fernie and Kantor describe a holistic one, which, from their point of view, integrates and reconciles the often conflicting demands—to teach, conduct research, publish, and fulfill community and campus service requirements—placed on junior faculty at a major research university. The unit they speak of evokes the image of a prism. At the center is the research enterprise and laboratory school; the four "facets" are: (1) collaborative inquiry, (2) social constructionism, (3) ethnography, and (4) a disposition toward educational possibility. Yonemura also draws on a hermeneutic, interpretive perspective to inform her own teaching and to help students to construct their understandings.

Several essays signal a change from didacticism to dialogue. Hutchison bristles at recollections of her orientation to Head Start, at "the experience of being 'talked down to,' of being patronized," and she bemoans the fact that teachers are so frequently "in-serviced," taught what to do through platitudes that fail to draw on their own experience. Wilson and Yonemura elaborate, more specifically, on the kinds of relationships that can help prospective teachers to think about and learn from their experience. Their essays mark a shift from teaching factual knowledge to a concern with values, beliefs, feelings, and intuitions. Yonemura appreciates the tension between students' desire for "technical skills" versus their need for reflection, but she focuses on sharing life stories and draws upon the arts—literature, poetry, film, sculpture and dance—"to bring imaginations and intuitions and feelings, as well as intellects, into our work." Wilson writes as a "teacher educator in-the-making," emphasizing the relational aspects of teaching. She notes that her students often saw labels ("egocentric," "not ready," "at risk") rather than children. To provide history and context and to breathe life into these flattened images, she uses literature in her classes, maintaining with others (Silin, 1988; Egan, 1983) that the field has placed too much emphasis on psychology at the expense of the intuitive, humanistic insights that come from other ways of knowing.

The authors seem to have discovered the lessons Belenky and her colleagues (Belenky, Clinchy, Goldberger, & Tarule, 1986) learned from women they interviewed:

> Educators can help women develop their own authentic voices if they emphasize connection over separation, understanding and acceptance over assessment, and collaboration over debate; if they accord respect to and allow time for the knowledge that emerges from firsthand experience; if instead of imposing their own expectations and arbitrary requirements, they encourage students to evolve their own patterns of work based on the problems they are pursuing. (p. 229)

It is "woman-like" to ground our learning in interaction, or, to use Yonemura's more elegant phrase, in "communities of caring."

What theoretical frame, then, can sustain such insights? LeCompte (in press) has recently highlighted Bateson's notion of "double description" to draw an analogy between binocular vision—"a combination of two versions of an outside universe very slightly different from each other"—and the blurring of "clear boundaries between units such as 'self,' 'other,' 'mind,' 'body,' 'objects,' 'subject,' 'researcher,' and 'researched,'" creating "a picture located in contexts of time, place and belief" (p. 16). This stance entails not only a celebration of diversity but also the development of double consciousness: "Collaboration requires the consciousness, or embrace, of the other" in ways that link people's destinies. Double consciousness also necessitates "links to external context" (LeCompte, in press, pp. 17–18).

Double description is a way of learning about oneself and "the Other." It can be achieved through: (1) learning to describe details (in ways illustrated by Fein, Fernie & Kantor, Yonemura, and Isenberg & Raines), (2) learning the patterns and contexts in which relationships arise (as Wilson and Yonemura describe), and (3) learning how people engage in the process of change, or what Bateson calls "deutero-learning," the ability to change oneself to fit a changing pattern of relationships, as described by Wilson and Yonemura.

LeCompte holds that double description is a good model for feminist research, because women describe their lives in relation to others: "The lives of women always are divided and mediated by the imposition of an Other. Woman has a Self, but it is defined in terms of its negotiation with the Other" (p. 21). I think double description is a good model for a feminist pedagogy as well.

These essays go a very long way in creating new models of teacher education, describing teaching as a process of engagement—of learning to "see" and to reflect on what is seen, of learning to act, of learning about oneself in and through relations. Women's "development of self, voice, and mind" has elsewhere been depicted as a movement from a state of "silence" to one of "voice" and empowerment, from received knowledge, to subjective knowledge, to procedural knowledge, to constructed knowledge (Belenky, Clinchy, Goldberger, & Tarule, 1986).

I would also argue, however, that the authors do not go far enough in linking "double consciousness" to external context. Only Isenberg & Raines and Hutchison mention the importance of advocacy. Yet to address the question of teacher education in the field of early childhood, it is necessary to consider not only relationships but also the contexts in which those relationships arise. And the lives of too many early education teachers are grounded in work that is stressful, unsatisfying and alienating—work that provides little in the way of status or remuneration.

We cannot prepare women to do the work of women without concern for the nature and consequences of such work. The recent statement by the conservative Research and Policy Committee of the Committee for Economic Development (1991) states the problem succinctly: "the low pay, difficult working conditions, and low esteem in which professionals in child care, early childhood education, and human services are held make it difficult to attract and retain well-trained and qualified personnel in these fields" (p. 13). Recent studies (e.g., Whitebrook, Howes, & Phillips, 1989; Kisker, Hofferth, Phillips, & Farquhar, 1990) report similar findings. It is imperative, therefore, that teacher educators take the lead in fostering efforts to change the material conditions of teaching and learning, as well as to effect change in the society more broadly.

These efforts include, but are not limited to, the following:

1. Improved working conditions. How can work be organized so that teachers can collaborate, if they wish to do so? How can time—and space—be organized so that teachers can have periods of time during the day to rejuvenate?
2. Improved pay and benefits. The "trilemma" (Willer, 1987) of affordability, quality, and compensation has proved intractable, and women cannot continue to subsidize programs with their low wages. Changing the situation requires political mobilization and government subsidization.
3. A differentiated career structure. The field explicitly needs to devise ways to increase employment opportunities to women. This entails not only an in-service scheme of credentialing and an in-house career ladder but also career trajectories, so that ways exist to assume other roles within the field. Especially crucial is the need to increase the diversity of the leadership cadre of the field.
4. A rethinking of professionalism. As currently practiced, professionalism has become a thin guise for prejudice and elitism, driving a wedge between parents and professionals and between those within the field with different life experiences and values. How, then, can professionalism be manifested in a way that is more in line with relational values?
5. Reconceptualizing curriculum. Are the guidelines for developmentally appropriate practice (Bredekamp, 1987) universally applicable? Do they

encourage a reflective practice? (Kessler & Swadener, 1992; Swadener & Kessler, 1991; Lubeck, 1993).

6. The organization and availability of child care. While we applaud Head Start and the opportunities it has provided disadvantaged children and parents, we must also remain cognizant of the fact that, by its very structure, it serves to segregate children by race as well as class. How can we develop a universal child care system based on a sliding fee scale?

7. Effecting broad-based social reform. How can we work to promote a national health care system, universal immunization, changes in the AFDC policies and practices, child support enforcement, universal family and medical leave policies, sick leave policies, and changes in the structure of work?

"Stigmatized as 'women's work,'" Grumet (1988) maintains, "teaching rests waiting for us to reclaim it and transform it into the work of women" (p. 58). The essays in this section testify to the fact that women who have entered into and remained in the academy—and the men in early childhood who share the vision— have found their voices there. If these essays reflect general practice, the reclamation effort has begun.

REFERENCES

Belenky, M., Clinchy, B., Goldberger, N., & Tarule, J. (1986). *Women's ways of knowing: The development of self, voice, and mind*. New York: Basic Books.

Egan, K. (l983). *Education and psychology: Plato, Piaget, and scientific psychology*. New York: Teachers College Press.

Gilligan, C. (1982). *In a different voice: Psychological theory and women's development*. Cambridge, MA: Harvard University Press.

Grumet, M. (1988). *Bitter milk: Women and teaching*. Amherst, MA: The University of Massachusetts Press.

Keller, E. (1985). *Reflections on gender and science*. New Haven, CT: Yale University Press.

Kessler, S., & Swadener, B. (1992). *Reconceptualizing the early childhood curriculum: Beginning the dialogue*. New York: Teachers College Press.

Kisker, E., Hofferth, S., Phillips, D., & Farquhar, E. (1990). *A profile of child care settings: Early education and care in 1990*. Washington, DC: U.S. Department of Education.

LeCompte, M. (in press). A framework for hearing silence: What does telling stories mean when we are supposed to be doing science? In D. McLaughlin & W. Tierney (Eds.), *Naming silenced lives*. New York: Routledge.

Lubeck, S. (1993). The politics of developmentally appropriate practice: Exploring issues of culture, class, and curriculum. In B. Mallory and R. New (Eds.), *Diversity and developmentally appropriate practices: Challenges for early childhood education* (pp. 17–43). New York: Teachers College Press.

MacKinnon, C. (1989). *Toward a feminist theory of the state*. Cambridge, MA: Harvard University Press.

Research and Policy Committee of the Committee for Economic Development. (1991). *The unfinished agenda: A new vision for child development and education*. Washington, DC:

Committee for Economic Development.

Silin, J. (1988). On becoming knowledgeable professionals. In B. Spodek, O. N. Saracho, & D. L. Peters (Eds.), *Professionalism and the early childhood practitioner* (pp. 117–134). New York: Teachers College Press.

Swadener, B., & Kessler, S. & (Eds.). (1991). Reconceptualizing early childhood education [special issue], *Early Education and Development, 2*(2).

Whitebrook, M., Howes, C., & Phillips, D. (1989). *Who cares? Child care teachers and the quality of care in America.* Los Angeles, CA: The National Child Care Staffing Study.

Willer, B. (1987). Quality or affordability: Trade-offs for early childhood programs? *Young Children, 42*(8), 41–43.

Thoughts on Educating Teachers

Barbara T. Bowman

As a teacher educator, I expected to find the preceding essays a literal feast of ideas on which to reflect and learn. What I had not expected was the similarities in goals and methods that tie these authors' experiences and their programs to one another and to my own. Recurrent themes I found particularly relevant to my own practice included the importance of basing early childhood pedagogy on developmental principles focused on the "whole child" and resistance to separating care from education, the inclusion of cultural context as a frame for teachers' knowledge, the value of self-reflection and self-knowledge as a way of constructing understanding and informing pedagogy, and the need to widen teachers' responsibilities to embrace advocacy and professional activism.

As much as I enjoyed my colleagues' agreement with many of my own practices, the very similarity made me increasingly uneasy. What are the values that underlie our approaches to teacher education, and why are ours better than others? Is our affinity simply the expression of another orthodoxy, another form of cultural imperialism? Have we merely devised a new rhetoric to validate the historic values and relationships that have traditionally defined the teaching–learning paradigm (Delpit, 1988; Jipson, 1991)?

There are four interconnected aspects of teacher education that I ascribe to and that are described in the preceding papers that touch on my concerns: (1) our emphasis on developmentally appropriate practice, (2) autonomy in thinking, (3) formal reflection, and (4) tolerance of diversity. My contribution to the dialogue is in the form of questions rather than solutions. These questions, which follow, may be included in our next round of discussions about early childhood teacher education.

DEVELOPMENTALLY APPROPRIATE PRACTICE

Obviously, models of what teachers should know and do are drawn from the socioeconomic and philosophical context in which they are created; in other words, they are socially constructed. But once created, like children, the models themselves become protagonists for replicating the past in the future. Thus, the forces that influenced the development of early childhood education as a professional field linger on, shaping its further development and creating ambiguities and conflicts as it strives to adapt to the new and powerful social forces in which it is embedded. Even as the world around changes, the field strives for continuity and consistency with its own past.

One must ask, therefore, are our views of early childhood education, developed in the past, appropriate to a quite different future? An example may make my question clearer. Our present model of early childhood education developed in the first half of this century. It was largely derived from the developmental history and child-rearing beliefs and practices of middle-income America and stressed child-centeredness. Among other beliefs were that children were to be protected from the demands of the adult world, that autonomy and independence were to be encouraged, and that academic achievement should be de-emphasized. Free play, choice of materials and activities, and little interference or direct instruction from teachers became hallmarks of this approach. Groups in society who were outside the mainstream were rarely considered as the traditions of the field were building. And if they were, it was assumed that they would profit from the same type of education defined as appropriate for middle-income America. After World War II, the superiority of western European and American educational, political, and economic institutions was unquestioned, giving impetus to this model of early education.

Today, there is a different reality. Many Americans are less certain that there is a "one best" set of cultural beliefs and practices, and for many, multiculturalism has replaced western superiority as a more fitting orientation for education. The development and achievement of poor and some minority children (groups traditionally outside the orbit of early childhood education) has become increasingly important; yet they do not achieve equally well as middle-income children using traditional methods, leading some to question the appropriateness of this model (Jipson, 1991) lest its class and racial specificity alienate and disadvantage children we now seek to include.

We must question whether the traditional definition of developmentally appropriate practices is facilitating for all children or if this model reinforces the status quo, conferring benefits on the middle class and cheating the poor and powerless. Should the education of children from different cultural groups be different from mainstream groups in order for them to succeed or can the same model benefit all children? Are there alternative pathways to developmental and academic competence that require different educational structures and organizations? And if the answer is that there are multiple satisfactory developmental and achievement trajectories for children, how should we educate teachers to work with so many different students?

AUTONOMY

Yonemura defined the quest for autonomy as a "strategic redefinition" of the teacher–learner relationship in which the student takes the initiative to redefine the discussion, rather than "caving in" or going along—thereby owning what they know. Autonomy in thinking and independence of action are consistent with western European and frontier values and are implicit in developmental theories of Piaget and his followers (Kohlberg & Mayer, 1972). This perspective emphasizes self-constructed knowledge, disparages knowledge derived from autocratic systems and hegemonies, and emphasizes independence of the student from the teacher in the pursuit of knowledge.

My concern is not that autonomy is unimportant but that we have not defined a balance between it and other forms of learning. We know that all change does not come from personal construction, from one's own experience. Other forms of knowing include identification with a valued model in which the learner strives to become the teacher model by incorporating his or her attributes into the self. This is not a thoughtful reconstruction of the ideas of another, but a "gulping down" of the properties of the esteemed model and underlies the synchrony often found between parents and children and some students and their teachers. Is this type of learning to be discarded as unworthy of the autonomous learner? How about co-construction with a more knowledgeable mentor in which teachers scaffold students toward "knowledge" they have that the student does not? At what point is the tutor, by assuming leadership in the learning process, short circuiting the learner's opportunities to arrive at different conclusions? What is the balance between Piaget (1952) and Vygotsky (1978)?

A further complication: all groups in our society do not equally value autonomy in thought and action. Some groups favor consensual, while others prefer more autocratic ways of knowing. Are their points of view inconsistent with our view of teacher education? If so, why?

REFLECTION

Fernie and Kantor defined reflection as the search for and identification of patterns in human behavior, thus helping to demystify and transform knowledge. Implied is that reflection must be formal, logical, intentional, structured, and performance based. Seminars, journals, supervision, and inquiry protocols require students' teachers to articulate for others their own thoughts (Zeichner & Liston, 1987). Students are asked to expose their thoughts and feelings (Bowman, 1989) to people whose relationship with them may be fragmented, conflict ridden, and socially distant.

Even if we agree that this way of organizing knowledge may open doors for understanding, how important is it? Do we discount teachers' knowledge that is intuitive, graphic, or that does not follow conventional rules of logic? I am particularly caught by the practice of requiring students to verbalize their reflections, often in group settings. Is it essential for the student to be able to articulate thought, to exteriorize it, to make it public? Some of my students have complained that sharing personal reflections is difficult. They find it impossible to share their thoughts with other adults in the formal settings of schools and classrooms, or they have difficulty monitoring themselves for inappropriate revelations, or their experiences do not find ready acceptance in the group and to share is to court rejection. Others have contended that group reflection is culturally inappropriate. They distrust those outside their group, or have domains of silence in their communities that preclude easy discussion of what are considered intimate topics.

What weight should we give to individual and cultural differences that inhibit students' abilities to share their thoughts, to engage in "group reflection"? And how about students who excel at verbalizing thought without the concomitant ability to interiorize and act on it? Do we penalize them? I suspect we need to investigate further the different styles by which teachers profitably reflect on their work and help students find forms that work for them rather than requiring all students to think about (and talk about) teaching in the same way.

DIVERSITY AND COMMUNITY

The notion of creating a learning community of supportive relationships to reduce the risk and enhance the quality of learning exemplifies our recognition that teaching and learning are socially referenced activities. Implicit in the idea of community, however, are group norms, codes of action and thought that define that group. Diversity is the opposite: it implies different ways of viewing the world, different codes of conduct and belief. How do we balance these two polar characteristics, particularly in a society torn by class, caste, and national identities? Can we ignore the commonsense observation that there are differences in people's understandings of experience—differences for which they are willing to kill one another? When we endorse a collaborative model of teaching and learning, do we believe that together, students and teachers can arrive at the same or similar conclusions about the nature of experience or the goals of education? Wilson correctly points out that the process approach may leave students committed to their own perspective, characterized by conflict between theoretical and cultural biases and resulting in we–they thinking.

If we accept the legitimacy of the student's personal and cultural thinking and feeling, how do we integrate this with standards of professional practice? Are there unarguable criteria that do not permit dissension? Can we ethically justify certifying student teachers who do not accept (cave in or give in) to such standards of practice? Or is "discourse" between student and teacher no more than a euphemism for a power relationship as old as time? Can we both encourage teachers and children to take risks, to trust in their own ability to think, to accept and respect different representations of reality and at the same time prepare them to fit into a socioeconomic system that requires similar cognitive skills and social behavior?

I applaud the dialogue these essays stimulate. For the next debate, I have suggested that the ambiguities aroused in the dialectic between past traditions and new need to be explored and that we think together about the relationship of professional practice to societal goals. Further, teacher educators should address the relationship between thought, words, and action as we strive to create new and more adaptive ways to educate people. And finally, we need to consider more carefully the balance between the powerful (teachers, schools, and teacher educators) and the less powerful (students, minorities, and the disadvantaged) who must remain at the core of our educational as well as our moral commitments.

REFERENCES

Bowman, B. (1989). Self-reflection as an element of professionalism. *Teachers College Record, 90,* 444–451.

Delpit, L. D. (1988). The silenced dialogue: Power and pedagogy in educating other people's children. *Harvard Educational Review, 58,* 280–298.

Jipson, J. (1991). Extending the discourse on developmental appropriateness: A developmental perspective. *Early Education and Development, 2,* 95 –108.

Kohlberg, L., & Mayer, R. (1972). Development as the aim of education. *Harvard Educational Review, 42,* 449–469.

Piaget, J. (1952). *The origins of intelligence in children.* New York: International Universities Press.

Vygotsky, L. S. (1978). *Mind in society.* Cambridge: Harvard University Press.

Zeichner, K., & Liston, D. (1987). *Teaching student teachers to reflect.* Harvard Education Review, 57, 23–48.

Moving Toward a Vision of Early Childhood Education

Teresa J. Rosegrant

My response to the question "What is needed to become a competent early childhood teacher educator?" reflects my perspective as a kindergarten teacher and teacher educator. In particular, I have focused on three factors consistently identified by these essayists as essential to becoming competent teacher educators:

1. A *vision* that can be conveyed to others about children, classroom practices, schools, and the many roles of teachers.

2. *Ways of understanding* children and their groups, beginning teachers, families, ongoing classroom practices, and diverse communities.
3. A commitment to *building and maintaining relationships* among and between university and school faculties, teacher educators and beginning teachers, teachers and administrators, teachers and parents, and most importantly, children and adults.

In addition, I will address two other factors that, while only explicitly discussed in one or two of the essays, I think are critical to the development of competent early childhood teacher educators. These two elements are:

1. Involvement in *social policy and advocacy* on issues that affect young children and their families.
2. Inclusion in teacher preparation programs of knowledge of children during infancy and through the preschool years, regardless of the grade level at which the teacher intends to teach.

RETHINKING EARLY CHILDHOOD TEACHER PREPARATION

Although each of the teacher educators represented in this section present different theoretical perspectives, each clearly recognizes the need for a vision of early childhood education. I use the term vision to describe a manner in which we see or conceive of something. As educators, it is always important that we "see" what can be, as well as what is.

Even though many of these authors have vast experience in teacher preparation, they share with most of their novice colleagues a sense that our current vision of early childhood education is evolving and that its evolution needs to include collaboration with classroom teachers. I believe that this desire for academics and practitioners to collaborate more closely originates, in part, from a better understanding of the challenges faced by classroom teachers. Poverty, drugs, and violence are touching the lives of increased numbers of young children.

For some teachers, each morning resembles the triage of an emergency room. These problems result from society, not from childhood, and their effect on the well-being of children is so clear that we cannot quibble about whether such work is part of our job descriptions. Unless they can find help in resolving these problems—help that reaches more children—teachers will have to continue selecting the few children each morning who can receive help while too many others wait. Consequently, it is important that academics do more than visit schools the required four times during student teaching. They must become team members in the effort to define and solve the problems that teachers experience each and every day.

Teacher educators such as these authors, who see "sharing stories" as a basis for creating common understanding, show the kind of willingness that can make this teamwork a reality. When I was an academic, I frequently heard faculty members complain about teachers' stories and their wanting to bring specific cases of actual children to class for discussion. My former colleagues viewed these incidents as disruptive; fortunately, these authors view these stories as the basis for sharing their vision with both beginning and experienced teachers, and for modifying that vision through "collaborative inquiry."

These teacher educators realize that a shared vision is more likely to be achieved if participants can see the vision in action in real early childhood classrooms. Yet, new teachers need a very strong vision to succeed. Their first experiences in classrooms should not be contrary to their developing point of view. Early childhood teacher educators, therefore, must work to improve the likelihood of beginning teachers being truly inspired by what they see in their internships and practice teaching.

Although traditional preparation programs for elementary teachers tend to offer a different vision than programs for early childhood educators, the overlap is growing. I believe this commonality has resulted, in part, from the translation of NAEYC'S position paper on developmentally appropriate practice (Bredekamp, 1987) into methodology for improving classrooms and from the whole language movement (Graves, 1983). As mentioned by several of these essayists, neither of these are actually new ideas. These recent interpretations, however, have provided teachers a glimpse of a more interactional definition of their role and an image of a learning environment that can better facilitate children's learning.

Teachers cannot easily implement visionary early childhood classroom environments, however, unless enlightenment toward this vision extends beyond individual classrooms. Social policy and advocacy are therefore essential aspects of teacher education. Advocacy, in particular, becomes the means whereby support for a vision of early childhood education is garnered from parents, building administrators, central office supervisors, and board members.

INCORPORATING NEW UNDERSTANDINGS

Possibly out of a desire to construct, alter, clarify, extend, or simply imagine a better means of focusing on children and their learning, these teacher educators all offer alternative and insightful ways of understanding themselves, children and families, plus beginning and experienced teachers. Their methods, although representing different ways of knowing, suggest the desire for a knowledge base with more sociological and psychological depth, a way of better representing others' perspectives, and the need for co-constructing these interpretations. These suggestions move the definition of our profession's knowledge base beyond traditional education theory to include anthropology, psychology, sociology, literature, and linguistics.

Their focus seems to be on the centrality of meaning. I would agree that we need to focus more on meaning and less on methodology. And I am convinced that understanding that children are "learning how to mean" (Halliday, 1975) will provide teachers with a generative grammar that can lessen the importance of methods classes and provide more opportunity for course work in these important fields.

How can we make this shift in knowing? Hutchison calls on us to become "students of children." Fernie and Kantor offer ethnography as a means for gaining insight into the everyday life of children at school. Isenberg and Raines argue for the development of case studies as a means for developing thick descriptions of children's learning in classroom environments. Yonemura describes how autobiography and insight into one's own childhood can provide us with important understanding of how our own experiences affect our expectations and responses to children. Wilson's use of literature broadens and deepens our feelings about human nature—its strengths and weaknesses—and thereby enables us to share in the experiences of others. And Fein reminds us of the culturally and historically mediated nature of our understandings about children and their care and education.

These six essays also suggest better ways of understanding beginning and experienced teachers through collaborative inquiry, reflective discussions and journals, interpersonal encounters and dialogue, and shared problem solving. And all these ways of understanding involve a commitment to building and maintaining relationships. These authors highlight that to construct authentic relationships (Yonemura) or partnerships (Isenberg and Raines), we need stronger mentorships and more collaboration (Fernie and Kantor; Wilson) that can result, in part, from a cohort model (Fein) that strengthens peer relations and supportive relationships (Hutchison) with teacher educators.

Several of the essayists suggest the importance of laboratory schools as a context for exploring ways of understanding and for building and maintaining relationships. I see some limitations, though, with this endorsement. Although lab schools are wonderful places to begin one's teaching, beginning and experienced teachers also need to learn about the politics and pressures of educational change. This seems particularly important if we are to advance our vision of early childhood education.

A reliance on laboratory schools also may reduce the likelihood of university faculty making strong commitments to improving community schools. Therefore, I strongly agree with the three teacher educators who argued for us to become more action-oriented on issues of policy that affect young children and their families. But I would suggest that we need to be less involved in writing reports and more actively engaged in effecting change. We need to strengthen our understanding of how university faculty can take active roles in fostering change on behalf of young children. We must end our academic debates and begin to do the work that is either yet to be started or in need of more workers in order to go forward.

More time needs to be devoted to enriching the environments in which young children spend their days rather than debating how we might define readiness or quality. We must determine that conditions like homelessness are simply unacceptable for children and join with those who seek to reverse the conditions that have allowed families to lose such a basic right. We must provide teachers with the experiences needed to help them celebrate the diversity found in our schools and protect children from those who have yet to understand that this remains our nation's greatest strength.

Finally, I want to address the importance of beginning teachers gaining knowledge of children during infancy and through the preschool years. The low pay and difficult working conditions make it unlikely that university-trained teachers will choose to teach very young children. But understanding this developmental period will enable university-prepared teachers to better understand how children learn and how early experiences affect development.

Very young children are good teachers. They do not disguise their fears or difficulties. They respond to our efforts at developing relationships and remain engaged when we respect their needs to determine the course of their own learning. They quickly demonstrate their eagerness to learn how to learn. Consequently, teacher preparation programs need to incorporate this developmental phase regardless of future teaching placements.

In conclusion, I hope I have contributed to the answers offered to the question: "What is needed to become a competent early childhood teacher educator?" I feel certain that these essays suggest a new course. Although we will likely be required to cross uncharted waters, I am delighted with the colleagues I find aboard and certain of the results—a better place for teachers and children.

REFERENCES

Bredekamp, S. (1987). *Developmentally appropriate practices for early childhood programs for children birth to age 8*. Washington, DC: National Association for the Education of Young Children.

Graves, D. (1983). *Writing: Teachers and children at work*. Portsmouth, NH: Heinemann.

Halliday, M. A. K. (1975). *Learning how to mean: Explorations in the development of language*. London: Edward Arnold.

Generating New Perspectives in Early Childhood Teacher Education

Stacie G. Goffin and David E. Day

As this project progressed, it became increasingly clear that the essays were not going to succeed in providing entirely new perspectives on early childhood teacher education. Perhaps it was unrealistic for us to have expected this in the first place, but our expectation came from the fact that it isn't often that practitioners are asked to present their thoughts about the essential factors in their education and experiences that have contributed to success in the classroom. We had believed that engaging teachers, teacher educators, and other stakeholders in this task would produce insights useful to continuing dialogue regarding teacher education and development. What we have concluded, however, is that significant new perspectives will not be generated until this dialogue becomes truly interactive and sustained.

The essays written by the classroom teachers revealed a remarkable consistency, even though these teachers taught children of different ages, worked in varied settings, and were asked to respond to developmentally different questions. Six recurring themes were evident in their responses.

1. Knowledge of child development is essential for success at every level of performance.
2. It is essential that teachers view themselves as learners and continue to study children, pedagogy, and the community in which they teach.
3. Teachers need to develop the strength to take risks and accept the possibility of failure.
4. Children's learning is socially driven and contextualized.
5. Teacher educators need to be substantively involved with their students during practica, something the essayists had rarely experienced.
6. Teacher educators should remain engaged with teachers in their classroom settings after they have completed their initial preparation.

The common themes among the teachers' essays is made even more interesting when juxtaposed with the absence of consistent themes in the essays written by the teacher educators. This absence of consistency, however, provides important insights regarding the circumstances in which early childhood teacher education is practiced in our colleges and universities. First, these early childhood teacher educators highlight the influence of the culture of the institutions in which they work. For example, the perspectives of teacher educators were shaped by such factors as expectations for substantial scholarly activity, by the absence of a traditional student body, and by whether initial teacher preparation is an undergraduate or graduate activity. Although the importance of context has become a constant in discussions of school restructuring, it is rarely acknowledged as a factor in teacher education reform, even when it is so implicit in statements like those made by these teacher educators.

Second, the diversity of opinion reflected in the teacher educators' essays reveals the extent to which early childhood teacher educators continue to grapple with the issue of how best to prepare teachers of young children. The approaches reflected by these teacher educators varied in their emphasis on the roles of research, traditional child development knowledge, and the desire to move beyond conventional approaches. In addition, there was variation in the degree to which the types of settings for which the teachers were being prepared influenced the content and design of the teacher education program. Finally, this programmatic diversity led to differing perspectives on the importance and nature of the relationship between teacher educators and their students. These relationships were variously defined by conventional student-teacher interaction, reflective mentoring, and research apprenticeships.

However, notably missing from their array of responses is any mention of the interdependency among initial teacher preparation, ongoing teacher development, and the realities of daily practice. Whereas the classroom teachers' essays consistently spoke about the need for substantive interaction with teacher educators during and after initial preparation, the essays of the practicing teacher educators were notably silent on this topic. This observation takes on special importance in light of this book's search for new perspectives in early childhood teacher education. The issue is not whether there ought to be a single or shared approach to early childhood teacher education, but that teacher educators should not be addressing this issue by themselves.

Throughout the individual essays and commentaries, new possibilities for early childhood teacher education were suggested. But we are convinced that only when a conversation *among* the many stakeholders is initiated and sustained will truly new perspectives on early childhood teacher education finally emerge. It is important, however, that this particular insight would not have surfaced if we had listened to the voices of classroom practitioners, teacher educators, and other public stakeholders in isolation from each other. Our new level of understanding can be directly attributed to the fact that the design of this book provided a forum for these voices to be heard simultaneously. Our hope is that, the next time, their voices will comingle.

INDEX

ABOUT THE EDITORS AND CONTRIBUTORS

DAVID E. DAY is Professor and Chair of the Department of Elementary Education and Reading at the State University College at Buffalo, New York. He received his doctorate in education from Wayne State University in 1963. He is former President of the National Association of Early Childhood Teacher Educators (NAECTE). He is the author of *Early Childhood Education: A Human Ecological Approach* and several articles and monographs on early education.

STACIE G. GOFFIN received her EdD from the University of Houston, Texas, and is currently Senior Specialist, Early Childhood Education and Policy for the Ewing Marion Kauffman Foundation. Much of the work of this book was completed while she was an Associate Professor of Early Childhood Education at the University of Missouri, Kansas City. She has written widely in the areas of early childhood advocacy, early childhood education, and early childhood teacher education. In addition, she has been actively involved in effecting change on behalf of young children in the metropolitan Kansas City community.

JANET ALBARADO has taught first grade for 15 years. She has also served for 1 year as the President of her local NEA Chapter. Presently she is on maternity leave from Claiborne Elementary School in Baton Rouge, Louisiana. She has a BS and an MEd in elementary education from Louisiana State University. For the past 2 years she has been involved in the development of an evaluation program for intern teachers in Louisiana.

DAVID C. BERLINER obtained his doctorate in educational psychology from Stanford University in 1968. He is now Professor of Curriculum and Instruction and Professor of Psychology in Education at the Arizona State University. He is President of the Division of Educational Psychology of the American Psychological Association and former President of the American Educational Research Association. He is co-author of a textbook in educational psychology, co-editor of the *Handbook of Educational Psychology*, and author of over 100 articles and book chapters. His interests are in research on teaching and educational policy.

BARBARA BOWMAN has been Co-Director and Director of Graduate Studies and currently is the Vice-President for Academic Programs at the Erikson Institute. She has a BA from Sarah Lawrence College and an MA from the University of Chicago and a DHL from Bank Street College of Education. Dr. Bowman is a past president of National Association for the Education of Young Children (NAEYC). She is a member of the National Advisory Board, Center on Families, Communities and Children's Learning and of the National Institute for Professional Standards. She has published numerous articles and chapters, most recently (with F. Scott) "Understanding Development in a Cultural Context: The Challenge of Teachers" in *Diversity and Developmentally Appropriate Practices: Challenges for Early Childhood Education.*

SUE BREDEKAMP is Director of Professional Development of the National Association for the Education of Young Children (NAEYC) to which her major contribution has been developing and directing a national, voluntary accreditation system for early childhood centers and schools. She wrote *Accreditation Criteria and Procedures and Guide to Accreditation* and *Developmentally Appropriate Practice in Early Childhood Programs: Serving Children Birth Through Age 8.* Dr. Bredekamp received her doctorate in early childhood education from the University of Maryland. Her professional experience includes teaching college and teaching and directing early childhood programs.

JERLEAN DANIEL is a member of the faculty in the Program in Child Development and Child Care at the University of Pittsburgh, Pennsylvania. She has a BS in political science, an MS in child development, and a PhD in education from the University of Pittsburgh. Dr. Daniel worked for 18 years as a child care center director. She is currently President-Elect of the National Association for the Education of Young Children (NAEYC). Her scholarly interests include public policy and quality programming issues in early care and education.

BARBARA EARLY is an assistant teacher in the toddler room at the University of New Hampshire Child Study and Development Center, where she has worked for 3 years. She was previously head teacher of the toddler room at the Newmarket Child Care Center, a non-profit public agency. She received her undergraduate degree in psychology from the University of New Hampshire, where she is currently enrolled in the master's degree program. This is her first collaboration on an essay for publication.

GRETA G. FEIN is Professor of Education and Psychology at the University of Maryland. She holds a master's degree from Bank Street College of Education and a doctorate in developmental psychology from Yale University. After completing her doctorate, she served as director of child development research at the Merrill Palmer Institute. She has completed research on children's play, especially the forms and functions of symbolic play. Her position at the University of Maryland involves her directly in the preparation of teachers of young children. She is the author of numerous publications (with Clarke-Stewart on *Day Care in Context* and with Fox on an edited volume) on the well-being of daycare infants.

DAVID E. FERNIE is an Associate Professor in Early and Middle Childhood Education at the Ohio State University. He received his EdD in early childhood education from the University of Massachusetts at Amherst and formerly taught at the University of Houston, Texas. His research interests include children's play, peer culture and development, early childhood classroom processes from a socio-cultural perspective, and the influence of various media on children's development.

CLAIRE E. HAMILTON received a BA and MEd from the University of Massachusetts at Amherst and a PhD from UCLA. As the unit coordinator of the toddler program at North Village Children's Center, she became interested in how children develop social relationships with their peers and teachers. She pursued this research as a graduate student and has recently published a number of studies in Child Development. Currently she is Research Fellow in European Child Care at the University of Wales (UK) and is studying child care quality in the European community.

BETTY L. HUTCHISON, Associate Professor, National Louis University in Evanston, Illinois, received her doctorate from the University of Michigan. Early experiences as a kindergarten teacher and district supervisor of Head Start sparked a career-long interest in policies for planning and staffing programs for disadvantaged children. Her professional leadership positions include the 25th Anniversary Panel for Head Start, the Governing Board of NAEYC, the Center for Career Development in Early Care and Education at Wheelock College, and the National Academy of Early Childhood Programs.

JOAN P. ISENBERG is Professor of Education at George Mason University in Fairfax, Virginia, where she coordinates three early childhood programs in the Graduate School of Education. Professor Isenberg has published books, journal articles, and reviews on early childhood education and early childhood teacher education, particularly in the areas of children's play and creative expression and the professional development of teachers. She currently serves on the Governing Board of the NAECTE and is President of the Metro-Washington Branch of the Association for Childhood Education International. She earned her EdD in elementary education from Rutgers University.

REBECCA KANTOR is Associate Professor in Family Relations and Human Development and Director of the A. Sophie Rogers Laboratory for Child and Family Studies at the Ohio State University. She received her EdD in Developmental Psycholinguistics from Boston University. Her research interests include language, literacy, and social processes in early childhood classrooms, young children's friendships and peer culture, and classroom enthnography.

LILIAN KATZ is Professor of Early Childhood Education at the University of Illinois at Urbana, Champaign, where she is also Director of the ERIC Clearinghouse on Elementary and Early Childhood Education. She is currently President of the NAEYC and author of more than one hundred articles, chapters, and books about early childhood, teacher education, and parenting. Her most recent book is *Engaging Children's Minds: The Project Approach* (with S. Chard). Dr. Katz has lectured widely around the world and held visiting appointments at colleges and universities in Canada, Australia, Germany, the West Indies, England, India, and Israel. She has received many awards and honors for her work.

JENNY F. KRAMER is Acting Director, Bennington College Early Childhood Center in Bennington, Vermont. She has held positions as head teacher, Whimpfheimer Nursery School at Vassar College, the Little Red School House in New York City, and at the Corlears School in New York City. She received her BA from Bennington College and an MA in Education from Bank Street College.

DIANE LOUBIER is employed at the Child Study and Development Center at the University of New Hampshire. She is co-head teacher of the infant program, responsible for the care of 10 infants, trains college students, and supervises staff. She has been involved with infant and toddler care for over 12 years, teaching in various child care settings, and has directed her own state-licensed home care program. She is presently studying for a degree in early childhood education at the University of New Hampshire. She lectures often on infant care.

SALLY LUBECK teaches in the School of Education at the University of Michigan. She has been both a Bush Fellow and a Spencer Fellow. Her book, *Sandbox Society: Early Education in Black and White America—A Comparative Ethnography*, received Choice Magazine's Outstanding Academic Book Award in 1987. An edited volume (with B. B. Swadener, *Child and Families "at Promise": Reconstructing the Discourse of Risk*, will be published by SUNY Press in 1995.

ANNE MARTIN has been a classroom teacher for over 25 years, working with children from nursery school through 4th grade. She currently teaches kindergarten at the Lawrence School in the Public Schools of Brookline, Massachusetts. Her major professional concerns are to keep teaching an ever-challenging activity, to write about children in the classroom, and to work collaboratively with other teachers to deepen understanding of children's learning and to improve teaching practice.

GEORGANN OLSON has been a kindergarten and 1st-grade teacher in the Ventura Unified School District, Ventura, California, for the past 19 years. She received BA and MA degrees from the University of Northern Colorado and an MA from California Lutheran University in Thousand Oaks, California. She has been a mentor teacher, was awarded the Teacher of the Month, and was the Ventura County Outstanding Teacher for 1991. Ms. Olson has visited Reggio Emila and continues to study this program through the University of New Hampshire. She has written "Reggio Emila's Approach to Early Education for Take Five, The CKAS Newsletter," Fall 1993.

SHIRLEY RAINES is Professor and Chairperson of the Department of Childhood Education at the University of South Florida in Tampa. She received her doctorate at the University of Tennessee. Her research interests include children's books and case methods. She is a member of the board of ACEI and is active in NAEYC and NAECTE. Her books include *The Whole Language Kindergarten* (Teachers College Press); the S-T-R-E-T-C-H-E-R series (Gryphon House); and *Stories: Children's Literature in Early Education* (Delmar).

TERESA J. ROSEGRANT is Associate Professor of Early Childhood Education at George Mason University, Fairfax, Virginia. She received a PhD from the University of Illinois and was a kindergarten teacher in the Arlington County Public Schools. She has served as a member of the National School Readiness Task Force, Educational Goals in the Year 2000, has been a consulting editor for Young Children, and a member of the board of the National Academy of Early Childhood Programs. She is co-author of the software programs, *Talking Text Writer,* Scholastic, and *Listen to Learn,* IBM Corporation. She co-edited (with S. Bredekamp) *Reaching Potentials,* NAEYC.

DEBORAH J. ROWE received a BA from Colby College, JD from George Washington University, and MEd from the University of New Hampshire. She found life as an attorney unfulfilling and changed careers, working first at a for-profit child care center and ultimately at the University of New Hampshire's Child Study and Development Center as co-head teacher in the infant room. Presently she spends most of her time with her 3-year-old daughter. She consults on parent education and support issues for the Mapletree School and works on the boards of the local toy and book libraries.

THOMAS SCHULTZ is Director of Early Childhood Services at the National Association of State Boards of Education where he directs projects to study and improve child care, preschool, and family support programs, and instructional, assessment, and parent involvement practices in elementary schools. He is consultant to the National Board of Professional Teaching Standards, helping to create standards to assess highly accomplished early childhood teachers. He has also worked for several federal agencies managing national research and school improvement programs, and providing monitoring and training to local Head Start projects. He earned his EdD from Harvard University.

THOMAS SOBOL has been Commissioner of Education for the State of New York since July of 1987. Before that he was Superintendent of Schools, Scarsdale, NY. His accomplishments include the development of A New Compact for Learning, a comprehensive strategy for improving elementary and secondary education in New York State. He received AB and MA degrees from Harvard College and an EdD from Teachers College, Columbia University. Dr. Sobol has published widely on issues in education.

CLAUDIA Q. TULL teaches 2nd grade at Eastbrook Elementary School in Putnam County, West Virginia. She attended Earlham College and graduated from Morris Harvey College in Charleston, West Virginia. She has been an instructor in early childhood education for the University of Charleston and is an adjunct professor for the West Virginia Graduate School. She has been a classroom teacher for 15 years, is active in curriculum committee work, is Chair of the Faculty Senate at her school, a member of the State Mathematics Team, and a representative to the Putnam County Education Association. She frequently presents at inservice and teacher development meetings.

MARION VANARSDELL is an early childhood special education teacher with the public schools in Northampton, Massachusetts. She teaches an integrated preschool serving 3- to 5-year-old children with special needs and their typical peers. She has an MEd in Early Childhood Education from Leslie College and a CAGS in Special Education from Boston University. Previous positions include Director of Head Start for Hampshire County, MA, and teacher–director of a day care center in Northampton. She conducts workshops for teachers and parents on developmental education and the inclusion of children with special learning needs in early childhood programs.

CATHERINE WILSON has been a teacher at Chapel Hill Early Childhood Center and a lecturer at the University of Missouri-Kansas City. Currently she is a doctoral student at UMKC and a children's librarian at the Kansas City Missouri Public Library.

MARGARET YONEMURA taught in and directed two schools for young children before becoming a teacher educator at Queens College, City University, and Teachers College, Columbia University, where she obtained her master's and doctoral degrees. Prior to her present position as Professor of Education, Binghamton University, she was Chairperson of Graduate Studies at Bank Street College of Education. Her research has been reported in articles and books, including *A Teacher at Work: Implications for Professional Development.*